SPRAY

The Ultimate Cruising Boat

SPRAY

The Ultimate Cruising Boat

R Bruce Roberts-Goodson

AM SNAME

ADLARD COLES NAUTICAL
LONDON

ACKNOWLEDGEMENTS

Where to start! So many people have contributed so much; if your name appears in the text, you have helped to make this book possible: so my sincere thanks to you all. Very special thanks are due to the following people: to my wife Gwenda, who has supported me in my work for over thirty years; to Kenneth Slack, author of *In the Wake of the Spray* (without Ken's book many of the Sprays included here, would never have been built): to Andrew Slorach, my long-standing associate and partner; to George Love, my boatbuilding mentor; to the editors of all the boating magazines worldwide who published notices that helped me collect the details of so many Spray replicas; to David Sinnett-Jones, the circumnavigator who encouraged me when I was starting this manuscript; to Philip Sheaf who greatly assisted in collecting the material; and finally, a very special thank you to all the Spray owners who have supplied information and photographs of their boats.

This edition published in 1995 by Adlard Coles Nautical
an imprint of A & C Black (Publishers) Ltd
35 Bedford Row, London WC1R 4JH

Copyright © R Bruce Roberts-Goodson, AM SNAME

ISBN 0-7136-4086-3

A CIP catalogue record of this book is available from
the British Library

Typeset in 11¹/₂pt on 13pt Adobe Garamond
By Christian Brann

Printed and bound in Great Britain by
Butler & Tanner Ltd, Frome and London

Contents

Introduction

In 1962 a Brisbane yachtsman affectionately known locally as 'Shotgun' Spencer presented me with a battered copy of *Sailing Alone Around the World,* Joshua Slocum's story of his circumnavigation in the sloop *Spray.* Mr E H Spencer was a well-respected Brisbane businessman, who took his sailing very seriously. In fact during one important race run by the local yacht club, when another competitor did not obey the starboard rule, he showed his annoyance by firing both barrels across the bows of the offending yacht. 'Shotgun' Spencer had certainly earned his name. Barred from taking part in future races, he was something of a local hero to the younger yachting fraternity.

I would like to recount those early days when I was in my mid twenties and had just learned to sail in one of Australia's skiff classes. The Australian 18ft [5.5m] skiff, is an open boat with a veritable cloud of sail. The 18 footers have a smaller sister, the 12ft [3.6m] skiff. This design is still raced, and is an open boat with an oversized sail plan. The whole arrangement is only kept upright by the weight and tenacity of a crew of four, who are kept busy, especially the bailer person, whose job it is to remove the water that often flows over the gunwhale.

My 12 foot skiff was named *Desire* and had been raced in Sydney and won a national championship, but, as happens with many fine boats, she was in sad shape by the time the hull came into my hands. The rig was unrestricted, so *Desire* was fitted with the complete rig, formerly used on Reg Lipke's race winning, 16ft [4.9m] skiff. Remembering that the hull was 12ft [3.6m] long, the dimensions of the rig make interesting reading; mast 27ft [8.2m], boom 14ft [4.3m] bowsprit 8ft [2.4m] and the spinnaker required a three-piece pole measuring 20ft [6.1m]. There was no ballast, other than that supplied by the live and very active crew.

The next boat I owned was a 28ft [8.5 m] trimaran built by myself; this was the first modern trimaran built in the Southern Hemisphere. When she first appeared on the local yachting scene, Trident caused all types of reactions among the local yachting fraternity.

After a stint of building trimarans, some time was taken out of the boating industry to enable me to study Naval Architecture. Soon after repurchasing my old boatyard in partnership with Andrew Slorach, I became reacquainted with the Spray when Charlie Jupp and John Haskins walked into our office and by coincidence both expressed an interest in having Spray replicas built in glassfibre.

The stories of Joshua Slocum and his sloop Spray are standard reading for any cruising yachtsman. Over the past eighty or so years, *Sailing Alone Around the World* has been the inspiration for many of those who go to sea in small boats.

Early in 1969, John Haskins, a Spray enthusiast, approached our design office and asked if we could prepare plans for building a replica Spray in glassfibre. John had already built a perfectly executed scale model of the boat and had incorporated some small modifications that he felt would update and improve the vessel without losing the concept of the original design.

By some lucky coincidence while we were considering John Haskins's request, another yachtsman, Charlie Jupp approached us with similar requirements. Charlie had just sailed an 8ft draft [2.4m], narrow beam boat out from England to Australia. The experience had convinced him that a shoal draft sailboat was better suited to his needs. Charlie was already familiar with the Spray, and suggested that if our negotiations with John Haskins came to fruition he would also be interested in obtaining a Spray type hull. The possibility of obtaining two orders for similar hulls galvanised our design office into action.

It was a challenge. We researched the project and came up with sufficient information to convince us that the proposition was a practical one and hence work was started on the preliminary plans. At about this time, we were fortunate in securing a copy of Ken Slack's book *In the Wake of the Spray*, which provided a wealth of information for our project. Ken, an Australian, had included details of the original Spray, and had also researched the 20 or so replicas or copies that had been built between 1902 and 1966. For those not already familiar with Joshua Slocum's Spray, perhaps this is a good time to recap some of the exploits of this fine boat, and to lay to rest some misconceptions and half truths that have persisted about her over the past 90 years.

In 1892 at the age of 51, Joshua Slocum was given a decrepit sloop called Spray and spent the next two years rebuilding this vessel. He removed the centreboard and replaced nearly every piece of timber in the hull, deck and superstructure. He sought to improve the seaworthiness by adding some freeboard, so that the boat would be better suited to the deep water sailing he obviously had in mind. All the materials used in the reconstruction were collected around Fairhaven, in Massachusetts, where Spray had lain in a field for several years.

The boat's lineage is clear when one examines photographs of early examples of the North Sea fishing boats that have worked off the coasts of several countries bordering that area; and rumour has it that the Spray was over one hundred years old when she was given to Joshua Slocum. There was a story that she had worked as an oyster dragger off the New England coast. Joshua Slocum, a seaman with vast experience, must have recognised something of the potential of his new acquisition, for otherwise he would not have invested two years of his life in the total rebuilding of her. As it turned out, he could not have made a better choice.

Slocum spent a year commercial fishing in the boat on the Atlantic coast; then, after proving the worth of the vessel to his satisfaction, he decided to make a voyage that, even today, is not undertaken lightly.

Slocum's trip proved a resounding success. Not only did he achieve what he set out to do – that is circumnavigate the world singlehanded – but he proved for all time the many fine features of Spray; features that we have seen proven over and over again in the several hundred replicas that are now in service around the world.

Building replicas of Spray is certainly not new. Although we believe that in 1969 ours were the first ones built of glassfibre, many copies had already been built in timber, following similar construction methods to those used to build and rebuild the original model.

Now is probably a good time to consider just what constitutes a Spray replica. As we know Slocum altered his original boat during the rebuilding; and many replicas, copies and/or Spray types that were built between 1902 and 1968 did vary in one way or another from Slocum's boat as she was when he sailed her around the world. It is our experience, and the evidence of all the hundreds of owners we have made contact with, that – without exception – Spray replicas and near copies have retained all the fine features attributed to the original boat. It is the underwater shape that counts and replicas or copies do retain the same characteristics of the original. As far as we have been able to discover, the first replica was built in England by Gill of Rochester in 1902, and the fascinating history of this early copy will be covered later in the book.

As mentioned earlier, Ken Slack's book *In The Wake of the Spray*, covered the subject up until 1966. Our design office prepared our first Spray replica design in 1969, and since that time we have sold over 5000 sets of plans for various sized Spray replicas. To our knowledge over 800 boats have been completed from those plans. Several hundred additional Spray replicas are currently being built in all parts of the world. The interest in the Spray continues to the extent that we have recently completed plans for 45ft [13.7m], 50ft [15.2m], 55ft [16.8m] and 75ft [22.9m] versions.

The interest in the Spray is stronger now than it has ever been. Circumstances including the advent of the 100th anniversary of the start of Slocum's voyage can only enhance the popularity of the remarkable Spray design.

As a person who has had an abiding interest in the Spray for almost thirty years, I am deeply indebted to all of those who have chronicled the original history of the boat. Starting with Slocum himself, followed by Ken Slack, I am also indebted to early owners and builders of Spray replicas, including Pete Culler, Gilbert Klingel and the prolific writer on Joshua Slocum and the Spray, Mr Walter Teller. These and many others, have all contributed to our knowledge of this fine boat.

I would like to appeal to all of you who have knowledge of Spray replicas, copies and Spray types, please send details, photographs and any other material you feel will be useful for future editions of this book. It is my intention to make regular updates and your help will be most appreciated. Please feel free to contact me:

R. Bruce Roberts-Goodson AM SNAME
13 Preston Grove, Faversham, Kent ME13 8JZ
England UK.
Telephone or fax 44 (01) 795 534 204

CHAPTER 1
Sailing Alone Around the World

If you have not read *Sailing Alone Around the World*, you may regard this chapter as a primer to help you understand why the Spray is such a successful boat, perhaps even the ultimate cruising boat. In any case we strongly recommend that you read the entire text of Slocum's book.

April 1995 marks the centenary of the start of Slocum's singlehanded circumnavigation, and there will be many new books – and maybe even a film or two – about the man. This book is essentially about Slocum's Spray and the many copies and near replicas that have followed. The condensed extracts of *Sailing Alone Around the World* given here are intended to give you an idea of the qualities of the original boat.

Slocum faithfully records the experiences encountered during his great voyage; although he does not go into much detail about Spray's performance, there are a few exceptions such as

Joshua Slocum aboard Spray in 1907.
Photo courtesy of New Bedford Whaling Museum.

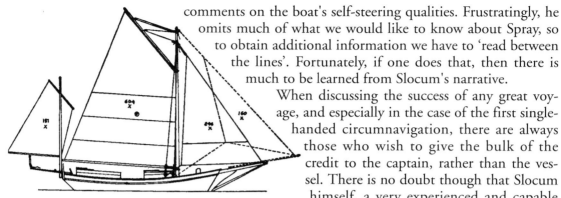

The yawl sail plan that Slocum used for most of his singlehanded voyage around the world in Spray.

comments on the boat's self-steering qualities. Frustratingly, he omits much of what we would like to know about Spray, so to obtain additional information we have to 'read between the lines'. Fortunately, if one does that, then there is much to be learned from Slocum's narrative.

When discussing the success of any great voyage, and especially in the case of the first single-handed circumnavigation, there are always those who wish to give the bulk of the credit to the captain, rather than the vessel. There is no doubt though that Slocum himself, a very experienced and capable seaman, would have been aware that he would have to rely on Spray to look after herself while he rested.

Today we expect that any vessel intended for singlehanded long distance sailing must be capable of looking after herself; no sailor can consistently go without sleep for more than a couple of days at a time. Slocum had the opportunity to test his rebuilt boat during the season spent fishing off the New England coast and there is no doubt that he would have assessed her various capabilities before making the decision to circumnavigate.

Slocum sailed Spray out of Boston on 24 April 1895. One wonders whether he knew or anticipated all the adventures he would encounter during the next three years and two months. Only after reading the entire text of *Sailing Alone Around the World*, can one appreciate the enormity of the task that Slocum had set himself and his sloop.

The first stage of the voyage was to sail from Boston to Nova Scotia which Slocum considered to be a shake-down cruise; a preparation for the transatlantic crossing that lay ahead. After loading up with adequate provisions he set sail and covered the first 1200 miles [1 931km] in eight days. It was during this period that Slocum first reports the boat's self-steering qualities. Eventually he would be able to adjust the sails so that Spray would steer herself for days on end – and, amazingly, sometimes even for weeks on end. Later you will see that many of the owners of Spray replicas have reported exactly the same phenomenon.

The first port after leaving Nova Scotia was Fayal in the Azores, and here Spray was topped up with provisions including fresh plums and cheese. This combination seems to have had a very bad effect on Captain Slocum, and the resulting cramps were such as to force him to reef the boat and leave her to her own devices while he retired to the cabin sole in great pain. It was during this experience that the pilot of the *Pinta* appeared as an apparition and, according to Slocum, guided Spray through the gale-driven heavy seas:

'When I came to, as I thought, from my swoon, I realized that the sloop was plunging into a heavy sea, and looking out the companionway, to my amazement I saw a tall man at the helm. His right hand, grasping the spokes of the wheel, held them as in a vice. One may imagine my astonishment. His rig was that of a foreign sailor, and the large red cap he wore was cock-billed over his left ear, and all was set off with shaggy black whiskers. He would have been taken for a pirate in any part of the world. "Senor," said he, doffing his cap, "I have come to do you no harm, I am to aid you. I am one of Columbus's crew. I am the pilot of the Pinta come to aid you. Lie quiet Senor Captain, and I will guide your ship tonight."

Slocum goes on to recount how the pilot helmed the boat through the gale, and by the time the captain recovered all was well with his sloop; it was still on course. Needless to say the remaining plums were thrown overboard!

On reaching Gibraltar Slocum was feted by the British Navy; and during his three-week stay he was treated as a hero. This was not surprising – Slocum and Spray were already making history. His original plan was to sail through the Mediterranean and on into the Red Sea via the Suez Canal, and then east-about around the world. However at Gibraltar the British warned him of pirates operating along that route, so a change of plan was called for. Slocum decided to sail west-about, and so leaving Gibraltar he sailed south westward down the African coast. Off the coast of Morocco he was chased by a pirate felucca, and just when all seemed lost and it appeared that he would be overtaken and captured, chance took a hand. The felucca broached on a great wave and was dismasted, leaving Slocum to sail on after making some repairs to his vessel's main boom.

Just before reaching the Equator, Spray sailed into the doldrums. For ten days she was held up in turns, by the calms, squalls and thunderstorms that are common in that area. After clawing her way out of these notorious conditions, Spray reached Pernambuco and then sailed on to Rio de Janeiro where Slocum enjoyed some respite. Next stop was Montevideo, where he spent Christmas after sailing up the River Plate to Buenos Aires; and there he spent New Year's Day of 1896. During this stopover, as with many other ports of call, Slocum was able to renew acquaintances and meet up with friends from his earlier voyaging days.

Sailing down the coast of Patagonia and making for the Straits of Magellan, Spray was almost overwhelmed by a huge tidal wave that roared over her during a storm. Slocum had the presence of mind to drop the sails and climb into the rigging, whereafter Spray shook herself free of the green water and bobbed to the surface. However yet another gale had to be weathered before Slocum could sail on to the Chilean coaling station at Punta Arenas.

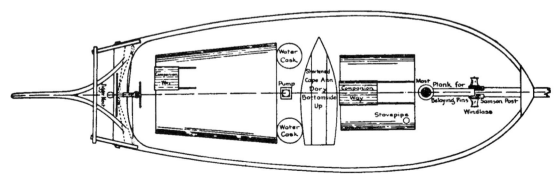

Deck plan of Slocum's Spray, as shown in Sailing Alone Around the World.

The locals warned of savage Indians further on, and Slocum was advised to ship additional crew to fight off these savages. No one seemed willing to form part of this additional crew, so the captain loaded his guns and purchased a bag of carpet tacks. He was later to remark that these tacks were 'worth more than all the fighting men and dogs of Tierra del Fuego'.

The Straits of Magellan are famous, or infamous, for winds known as willawaws. These terrible squalls are compressed gales of wind, and although many yachtsmen will have encountered similar gales at one time or another, one is assured that the willawaws are the worst example of this type of 'bullet' experienced in many areas of the world.

After various encounters with the local Indians, Slocum always kept his gun handy. Spray sailed on into the Pacific, encountering another great storm, and was forced to back-track through the Straits of Magellan. On his second trip through the Straits, Slocum had another brush with Indians, and this is where the carpet tacks came in handy. When he needed to get some rest he sprinkled the decks with the tacks, making sure that many of them stood business end up. That did the trick; the Indians sneaking on board soon discovered that 'there was something afoot', and left Spray in a great hurry! According to Slocum, 'they howled like a pack of dogs', mostly diving straight into the sea to escape the agony by the tacks doing their job.

Cabin of Spray, looking for'd (above) and looking aft (right) drawn by Robbert Das. Slocum used two berths, the starboard one when at anchor in calm water, the port one, his sea berth, allowed him to see the wheel and mainsail. The picture shows his depth sounding lead on the port side and his chart table opposite with his compass above, visible also from the cockpit. Slocum's clock/chronometer, his mug, pipe and tobacco are on his chest. As a trained seaman he would have rigged his lee cloth with a slip knot so that he could get out in a hurry.

This rare photograph shows Spray off Sydney with Slocum and Mark Foy. The are trying out the new set of sails that Foy presented to Slocum.Photo courtesy of Dr Kenneth E Slack.

Spray passed Cape Pillar for the second time, and then sailed on into the Pacific. Most single-handed circum-navigators by contrast have taken a different route around the Cape Horn, giving Tierra del Fuego a wide berth. By now, Slocum had the worst part of the voyage behind him. Although he would encounter a few gales and storms during the remainder of the trip, nothing compared in ferocity to the conditions he had encountered off Tierra del Fuego.

What a relief for Slocum, to experience the easy rolling motion of the relatively gentle Pacific. He now set course for Juan Fernandez, a remote island where the Robinson Crusoe prototype, Alexander Selkirk, had lived alone for over four years. Slocum was able to visit the cave where Selkirk lived for some time, and also paid a visit to the home Selkirk had occupied during his stay on the island. Next Slocum set course for Samoa, and Spray simply flew along under the South East trades, so that for a whole month the vessel held her course while he caught up on the chores, and was able to relax and eat his meals in peace. He records that he had a near collision with a great whale, a not uncommon occurrence in today's oceans and yet another argument for a strong boat. Slocum was a great reader and during this part of the voyage he indulged in this hobby while Spray sailed on unaided. He reported, 'Nothing could be more restful than my voyage in the trade winds.' After 43 days out, the Marquesas were sighted and Slocum was able to confirm his longitude. Pressing on to Samoa, Spray came to anchor after another 29 days, making a total of 72 days at sea without making port.

During his stay on the island Slocum paid a visit to Mrs Robert Louis Stevenson at Vailima, and was shown the desk where the great writer had worked. Mrs Stevenson presented Slocum with four beautiful volumes of sailing directions for the Mediterranean and wrote on the fly leaf: 'To Captain Slocum. These volumes have been read and re-read many times by my husband, and I am very sure that he would be pleased that they should be passed on to the sort of seafaring man that he liked above all others.' The inscription was signed Fanny V De G Stevenson.

After a most enjoyable six week stay in Samoa where he met many local dignitaries, Slocum again headed Spray out to sea, setting sail for Australia while passing to the north of Fiji. The first Australian port of call was Newcastle. Here he was greeted by the US consul where, in Slocum's words, nothing was too good for Spray. After a few days' respite, he sailed on to Sydney. Then, as now, Sydney was a great centre for yachting and the magnificent harbour was 'blooming' with yachts. It was still early in the summer season, but it seemed to Slocum as if everybody owned a boat.

Spray rested in Sydney for several months while her skipper was entertained by the locals. Slocum gives a good description of the local yachting fraternity and their charges, including this description of the boats he saw sailing in the magnificent harbour: 'The typical Sydney boat is a handy sloop of great beam and enormous sail-carrying power; but a capsize is not uncommon, for they carry sail like Vikings.' Slocum was of course referring to the ancestors of the famous 18ft [5.4m] skiffs, which boasted a spread of sail of up to 70ft [21.3m] from boom end to outboard tip of the spinnaker pole. He goes on to say, 'In Sydney I saw all manner of craft, from the smart steam launch and sailing cutter, to the smaller sloop and canoe pleasuring on the bay.' He was presented with a new suit of sails for the boat, the donor being Commodore Foy, a renowned yachtsman of the day.

On 6 December 1896, Slocum sailed out of Sydney harbour and headed south. After a few days spent sheltering in Waterloo Bay, he sailed through the 'Heads' at the mouth of Port Philip Bay and made his way up to the port of Melbourne. After an enjoyable stay here, Slocum sailed across Bass Straight and visited Tasmania, where he spent a considerable time visiting the inland forests of the island. Slocum was very impressed with the beauty of Tasmania, and enjoyed the great hospitality of the locals.

Reprovisioned and with a fresh coat of antifouling, Spray was headed northward, retracing her steps past Sydney and up through the Barrier Reef to Thursday Island off the coast of Queensland. Next she sailed on through tropical waters to the Arafura Sea. As Slocum sailed across the Indian Ocean he again remarked on Spray's self-steering qualities. Next stop was the Cocos Keeling Islands, where hundreds of children of all ages and sizes greeted Slocum as his vessel was secured to the local jetty.

By now Slocum had passed nearly all of the dangers of the Coral Sea and Torres Straight and, as he remarked, 'The dangers were not a few.' The many yachtsmen who have lost their vessels in this very place will certainly testify to the hazards of the area.

The trade wind was blowing fresh, and could be safely counted on down to the coast of Madagascar if not beyond for it was still early in the season. Slocum wrote, 'I had no wish to arrive off the Cape of Good Hope before midsummer, and it was now early winter. I had been off the Cape once in July, which of course was midwinter there. The stout ship I then commanded encountered only fierce hurricanes and she bore them ill. It was not that I feared them more, being in Spray instead of a large ship, but I preferred fine weather in any case.'

Two things are very noticeable here. Slocum by now had absolute confidence in his sloop; and yet, as a prudent sailor, he did not go looking for trouble. He decided to make something of a detour and visit the Cocos Keeling Islands, passing Timor and the Christmas Islands, and reaching Cocos Keeling 23 days out from Thursday Island. Slocum wrote, 'During those 23 days I had not spent all-together more than three hours at the helm, including the time occupied in beating into Keeling Harbour. I just lashed the helm and let her go; whether the wind was abeam or dead aft, it was all the same: she always sailed her course.' The Cocos Keeling Islands have been in the news over the past few years. After being 'ruled' by the Clunies Ross family as a fiefdom for many years, democracy, for better or worse, has at last been established on the islands. There is the story of the Clunies Ross family taking possession of the islands, and their experiences with one Alexander Hare, who was already in occupation. Hare had established his idea of Eden, being accompanied by 40 Malay women he had imported from the coast of Africa. All the details are related by Slocum in *Sailing Alone Around the World*. In view of the more recent history of the islands, it all makes fascinating reading.

Leaving Cocos Keeling, Slocum sailed on to Rodriguez Island; here he provisioned Spray, taking on fresh vegetables, sweet potatoes, pomegranates and beef. Next he set course for Mauritius, where he was again given every courtesy; Spray was berthed at the military dock free of charge while a considerable amount of refitting to the boat was undertaken by the port authorities. Slocum does not say, but one assumes that refitting was also carried out free of charge.

It is a great tribute to Slocum that wherever he went he was received and farewelled with the greatest courtesy. The times in between his arrival and departure at a port were filled with great hospitality both given and received.

As the favourable season had now arrived Slocum set sail for South Africa; and after a brief conversation with the pilot off Reunion, Spray's course was set for Madagascar and on to Port Natal, which is the port for Durban, South Africa. The boat weathered several gales in the 22 day passage from Mauritius to Port Natal. During his stay in Durban, Slocum was asked to back up President Kruger's assertion that the world was flat; and Slocum's writing on this experience makes fine reading.

The next part of the voyage was to round the Cape of Good Hope, which turned out to be a stormy 800 mile passage. On arriving in Cape Town, Slocum was offered a free berth in the Alfred dry docks where he left the boat while he travelled around South Africa on a free rail pass provided by the government; everywhere he went he was entertained and feted.

On 26 March 1898, Spray sailed from South Africa and set course for St Helena. Slocum wrote:

'31 March, the fresh southeast wind had come to stay. Spray was running under single reefed mainsail, a whole jib, and a flying jib besides, set on Vailima bamboo, while I was reading Stevenson's delightful Inland Voyage. The sloop was again doing her work smoothly, hardly rolling at all, just leaping along among the white horses, a thousand gambolling porpoises keeping her company on all sides.'

Slocum put in to St Helena, the island made famous as Napoleon's place of exile, and he was presented with a goat as he was leaving. This animal chewed everything in sight and should have considered itself lucky that it was deposited on Ascension Island, instead of meeting a much stickier end.

Two weeks after leaving Ascension, Spray crossed her own outward bound track. She had now circled the world, and made history along with her captain. When Slocum reached the West Indies he had to rely on memory; the goat had eaten the chart of this area!

On 5 June 1898 Slocum set sail on the final leg of his voyage, heading at first direct for Cape Hatteras and on to Newport Harbour, arriving on 27 June 1898. Slocum and Spray went into the record books with a singlehanded voyage of over 46 000 miles, a voyage that is as memorable today as it was almost one hundred years ago.

CHAPTER 2
Books, Models and Background

When Joshua Slocum returned home to the USA after his epic and record-setting voyage, he was immediately recognised for his great achievement. He was helped in the writing of *Sailing Alone Around the World* by 24-year-old Mabel Wagnalls, the unmarried daughter of publisher Adam Wagnalls. We are indebted to this young lady for inspiring Slocum, and helping him to express his experiences. Slocum's book was published in 1900, and the fact that it is still in print today speaks for itself.

There have been many books written about Joshua Slocum and Spray, but one of the most beautiful is a presentation edition of *Sailing Alone Around the World,* published by Volvo Penta, the Swedish automobile and marine engine manufacturer. This book features the magnificent illustrations of James E Mitchell. The question that has often been asked is –When is a Spray not a Spray? The original lines as published in Slocum's book are often referred to as the ultimate yardstick when discussing copies and replicas of the boat. However I prefer to think of any of them as a 'Spray type' or, as we advertise in our own catalogue, 'the Spray series'. Before the purists throw up their hands in horror, consider the following.

Almost from the date of first publication, there has been controversy about the authenticity of Spray's lines as shown in Slocum's book. Slocum

This beautiful Spray model is manufactured by Blue Jacket Ship Crafters of Stockton Springs, USA.

himself wrote, 'I gladly produce the lines of the Spray. No pains have been spared to give them accurately. The Spray was taken from New York to Bridgeport, Connecticut, and, under supervision of the Park City Yacht Club, was hauled out of the water and very carefully measured in every way to secure a satisfactory result. Captain Robins produced a model.' Well, that seems clear enough one would think. But not so.

All things being equal, we would take Slocum's statement to imply that the lines published in his book were a direct result of the measurements taken at Bridgeport. However, when one researches a little further and reads the letters that passed between Slocum and his publisher, it appears that the lines were actually taken from a model of Spray constructed by Captain Robins. Ken Slack in *In the Wake of the Spray* goes into great detail on the events surrounding the recreating of the boat's lines; that is the lines that appeared in Slocum's book. Luminaries such as Howard Chapelle, who was an apprentice to the naval architect Charles Mower, are quoted, and from all the information available it would appear that exact lines of the Spray may never be known.

Does it matter? No, I don't think so, and in any case there is not much that can be done to establish the facts at this late stage. Suffice to say that the original boat as presented to Slocum, was altered as he rebuilt her. The rebuilt version was measured in several ways, and the results of those measurements have been the starting point for the many replicas that have been built over the last 90 years. Generally, I classify Sprays as follows:

SPRAY REPLICA A Spray built of timber and built exactly from the lines in Captain Slocum's book.

NEAR COPY A boat built of timber using Spray's original lines as a guide, but modified either in size or some other way.

SPRAY TYPE A boat built of any material other than timber, and boats that have been scaled up or down and where the hull has been modified, but not so modified as to make the vessel unrecognisable. Most of such boats retain the best of Spray's features. It has been proved that it is the 'balance' of the design and the parameters that go to make up the Spray underwater shape, that produce the results that are so highly regarded by all who have owned and sailed a Spray replica or a Spray type. Additional information on this subject is given in later chapters.

SPRAY MODELS

Naturally, many Spray models have been constructed during the past 90 odd years. Slocum's younger son, Benjamin Aymar Slocum, made one excellent model, which he presented to the Peabody Museum of Salem Massachusetts, where it can still be seen today. This model is of the complete boat, fully rigged, and is so accurate, that set in the right background you could imagine that you are looking at the real thing.

Frank Shaw of Massachusetts made several models of famous boats, including two known models of Spray. One of these was presented to Philip Shea, a descendant of Joshua Slocum on his mother's side. Philip, who is now one of the driving forces of the Slocum Society, told me about the two Spray models, which are each about 18in [457mm] long and very good representations of the original boat.

While Ken Slack was researching his book and was on the trail of the *St Kilda Spray*, he unearthed a model made by a professional ship modeller, John B Walker, and was able to purchase it from him. Ken's book also details what his research reveals on several other models that have been made over the years.

The first example of a Spray model that I ever saw was the one made by John Haskins of Brisbane. This faithfully followed the lines of the Spray up to the waterline. The topsides were also those of Spray with the exception that the bow above the waterline was faired into the cutwater, so as not to present a bluff bow when ploughing into a head sea. We decided that this somewhat minor change above the waterline would not detract from the reputed performance and self-steering qualities of the boat, and we were right because the many Sprays that have been built following the lines of John Haskins' model have all proved to be excellent sea boats, retaining all the attributes of the original vessel.

Many intending builders of replicas of Spray have built models either as an aid to laying out the interior, or in many cases 'to get the feel of' the boat before making the total commitment to build the full scale vessel. Building a model often eases the pain of waiting to get started on a project that has for one reason or another had to be delayed. Edisom do Nasimento of Brazil wrote, 'Here in Brazil the economic situation is not good and boat construction is stopped for a while. Two years ago a very hard storm destroyed my temporary shed. I saved the frames and rebuilt the shed. I am trying to sell my power boat and meantime I build this model. As you know, all Spray builders are dreamers, and as dreamers we never give up.'

Another model of a Spray sits on my desk, and was made by Philip Sheaf of Easton, in Suffolk. Phil decided to order a hull and deck moulding for one of the glassfibre Spray 28s being built in the UK, and built the fully rigged model prior to committing himself to the full-scale boat. Once he obtained the real thing, Phil presented me with his beautiful model.

SPRAY BOOKS

There is so much continuing interest in Spray that for some time now I have thought it was time someone updated the information available on this wonderful boat and her descendants. As mentioned earlier, Ken Slack's *In the Wake of the Spray* covered the subject up until 1966. Our design office prepared our first Spray replica design in 1969 and since that time we have sold over five thousand sets of plans for various sizes of replica. To our knowledge, over eight hundred additional replicas are currently being built in all parts of the world. The interest in Spray continues, to the extent that we have recently completed plans for 45ft, 50ft, 55ft and 75ft [13.7, 15.2, 16.7, 22.6m] versions of the boat.

The interest in the Spray is stronger now than it has ever been; and events such as the centenary of the start of Slocum's voyage can only enhance the popularity of the boat's remarkable design.

CHAPTER 3

The Rebuilding of Spray

It was 1891 that Joshua Slocum was given Spray by his friend Captain Eben Pierce during a period when he was 'between commands'. Slocum had no idea what type of vessel his gift consisted of so he eagerly travelled from Boston to Fairhaven to inspect his new acquisition. Captain Pierce had warned Slocum that the boat needed some repairs, a warning that turned out to be something of an understatement.

One can only imagine Slocum's dismay when he first laid eyes on the tired and decrepid Spray as she lay propped up in the field in Fairhaven in Massachusetts. We do not know who had brought her to what was obviously intended to be her last resting place, but at least Slocum must have been grateful that the vessel was properly blocked for the hull itself had not yet deteriorated into a useless mass of rotting timbers.' It didn't take Slocum long, though, to realise that the vessel was far from being the 'ship' referred to by Captain Pierce.

On a more positive note, Slocum would have noted the fine lines of Spray, and he may well have been familiar with her type; and having nothing better to do at the time he decided to undertake a complete rebuilding of the sloop.

One of Slocum's first decisions was to modify the hull to suit his intended use. Spray was a centre boarder and as such would have been subject to leaks around the case. The hull only had modest freeboard, so it was decided to remove the board and case and replace this with a solid keel; the freeboard was increased by adding 14in [356mm] bulwarks.

Captain Slocum rebuilding the sloop Spray. Sketch by Robbert Das.

Like all boatbuilding projects, the rebuilding of the Spray attracted many experts to offer advice. One of the most often heard comments was 'Will she pay?' I feel sure that this was one question answered very much in the affirmative by Slocum himself. Rebuilding a wooden boat such as the Spray is very labour intensive, and great care must be taken to preserve the shape of the original while replacing the whole or a large part of the structure. In some ways, the rebuilding of any boat is more difficult and often more expensive than constructing a new one from scratch. There are many reasons for rebuilding a boat, the most obvious one being that the intending builder thinks there will be cost saving which in most cases does not materialise. However if the reason for deciding to build is to preserve a particular type of hull, then the many disadvantages of rebuilding may well be justified.

Slocum removed the original keel and centre board trunk by carefully sawing through the floor timbers without disturbing the garboard planks, the stem or the sternpost, and deadwood.

The new keel was made of one piece of 'pasture oak' which Slocum had cut down himself in a nearby field. This particular type of oak had long been used by New England boatbuilders, who appreciated its fine qualities as a boatbuilding timber. The timber was given its name by the fact that it referred to an oak that had naturally seeded in the middle of a field rather than in a forest. The tree had grown from seed, and all its life it had to withstand the ravages of the many gales that are common to the area. Naturally grown, without the protection of other trees as in a forest, the pasture oak produced hardy and long-lasting timber that was ideal for boatbuilding. Unfortunately, this particular timber is very hard to come by today.

The new keel was trimmed with a broad axe and carefully inserted in place of the old one. A whole new set of steam-bent pasture oak floor timbers were installed, and the garboards were then temporarily attached to the new floor timbers. Next, frames were steam-bent and placed in position for about one-third the length of the vessel; these frames were held against the original planking with temporary fastenings.

During the process of removing and replacing the keel and floor timbers, Slocum did not disturb the deck and upper works; they were required as bracing, and served to hold the boat together while the lower sections of the hull were renewed.

The new stem was shaped from a fine butt of a pasture oak, the quality of this piece of timber being severely tested when, as the stem of Spray, it split a coral head in two when Slocum visited the Cocos Keeling Islands. The stem structure consisted of the stem piece, the stem knee and the apron, all assembled and through-bolted before being installed in the hull.

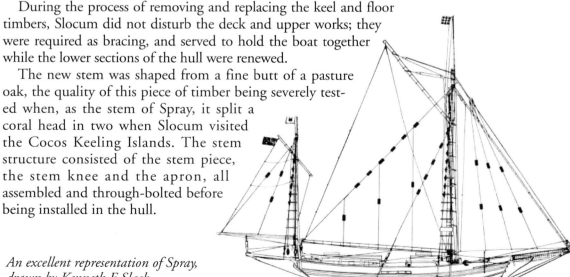

An excellent representation of Spray, drawn by Kenneth E Slack.

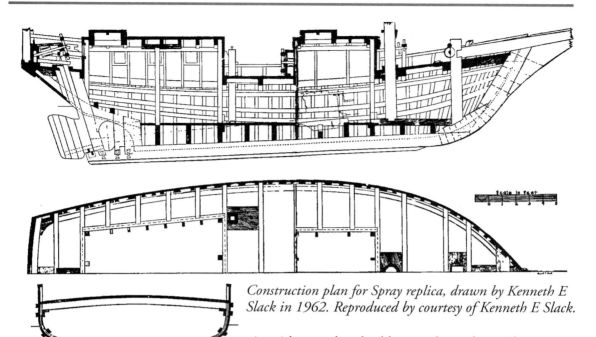

Construction plan for Spray replica, drawn by Kenneth E Slack in 1962. Reproduced by courtesy of Kenneth E Slack.

As with most boatbuilders working alone, Slocum was always willing to down tools to discuss the project with the frequent callers who came to inspect his progress. There were always many whaling captains and other knowledgeable seafaring types on hand to offer advice and provide an excuse for a break stoppage, allowing Slocum to rest on his adze in the time honoured boatbuilding tradition.

Next, the deadwood, sternpost and transom were removed and rebuilt from new oak in a similar manner to the methods used to build the stem structure. Now that Spray had a new backbone formed by the bow, keel and stern timbers, attention could be turned to the installation of the remainder of the frame timbers, so they were ready to receive the planking.

Spray's hull features an 'apple bow', so it was necessary to steam-bend the forward part of each plank to assist in securing it to the frames without breaking the timber. To do this, and to steam-bend many of the other parts of the boat, it was necessary to rig a steam box. The various timber parts were put in this box and treated to a bath of scalding steam until they were supple enough to be positioned in place without breaking. Once the timber had cooled, it set up hard and retained its new shape without straining the fastenings used to secure it in position. In the case of pasture oak, it was reputed to be so flexible when properly steamed that you could tie it in a knot.

The new planking was 1.5in [38mm] thick Georgia pine and Slocum reported that installing these planks was somewhat tedious. The thicker 3in [76mm] bilge planks, which doubled as stringers, were particularly difficult to place correctly, and large screw clamps were used to help pull them into position. The planking was copper nailed and roved to the frames. The butts were through-fastened to the skin and frames, with bolts backed up with nuts and generous-sized washers. Over 1000 bolts were used in the entire construction.

The bulwarks were built up on 14in [356mm] high white oak stanchions and planked with $^7/_8$ in [21mm] white pine. The stanchions were morticed through a 2in [50mm] covering board and were caulked with thin cedar wedges to ensure that they remained tight. The deck was planked with 1.5in x 3in [38mm x 75mm] white pine over Georgia pine deck beams located 3ft [914mm] apart.

Once the deck was completed Slocum turned his attention to building the cabin structures; these consisted of one 6ft by 6ft [1.8m x 1.8m] for a galley and another 10ft x 6ft [3m x 1.8m] for the main cabin, which was situated aft of amidships. The sides of the trunk cabins rose 3ft [914mm] above the deck; and this, combined with a reasonable width of sole, was sufficient to allow full standing headroom.

The fitting out of Spray allowed for creature comforts; and although simplicity was maintained, the interior proved very comfortable for the crew of one. Slocum did install additional bunks and one can assume that he intended to ship some crew mates at some stage during the voyage. In fact he mentions on more than one occasion that he asked others to accompany him; however for various reasons these offers were declined. From our point of view, the fact that the spare bunks were only used for stowage is fortunate, for had Slocum been accompanied by one or more crew during his round-the-world epic, then his achievements would probably have long since been forgotten and perhaps gone unrecorded altogether.

After the fitting of the cabins and the installation of the basic interior joinery, Slocum turned his attention to caulking Spray. The seams were caulked with cotton with a thread of oakum (caulking cotton) driven on top of it; they were then payed with filling cement and the underwater surface was given two coats of copper paint. Two coats of white lead were then applied to the topsides and bulwarks. Next the rudder having previously been rebuilt was painted and hung in position. On the very next day, the Spray was relaunched. This was a great moment for Slocum, who wrote, 'As she rode at her ancient anchor, she sat on the water like a swan.' Spray was taken down to the harbour where a fine New Hampshire spruce mast was stepped and rigged. It was fitted with a square doubling with crosstree cap and topmast. The boom and gaff were rigged in the traditional manner using boom and gaff jaws and mast hoops to secure the sails to the mast.

Initially, the sail plan was a double-headed rigged sloop, and the bowsprit was almost as long as the vessel. There was also adequate provision for setting enough sail area to take advantage of the lightest breeze. As we know, Slocum later modified the rig to more modest proportions, more in keeping with the requirements for long-distance, offshore voyaging.

Much has been made of the tin alarm clock Slocum used as a chronometer, and there have been many comments about some of the other rather basic equipment he used during his record-setting voyage. However, careful study of the equipment and gear that was fitted to Spray reveals that she was a well-found sailboat and, as proved by subsequent events, well suited for the purpose for which she was employed.

CHAPTER 4
Technical Aspects of Spray and True Replicas

As many of the replicas are faithful copies of the original Spray, now is a good time for a detailed analysis of this vessel. There have been several studies of the lines, hull balance, sail plan and other aspects affecting the performance characteristics of the original Spray and the exact replicas that followed.

One of the most informed technical studies was undertaken by C Andrade Jr, and considering no one has been able to challenge the technical correctness of the following treatise on the subject, we include it here. His analysis of the lines of Spray were undertaken in 1909 and the resulting article appeared in the June issue of *Rudder* magazine. These calculations have been rechecked, dissected and worked over many times and have been proven accurate in all respects.

CRITICAL ANALYSIS OF THE YAWL SPRAY *by C Andrade Jr*

' "I did not know the centre of effort in her sails, except as it hit me in practice at sea, nor did I care a rope yarn about it. Mathematical calculations, however, are all right in a good boat, and Spray could have stood them. She was easily balanced and easily kept in trim."

With these words, Captain Joshua Slocum dismisses the technique of Spray's design. Considering the unparalleled performances of this little boat, it is remarkable that no one has ever attempted an analysis of her lines and sail plan.

Spray was built about the year 1800, and was used as an oysterman on the coast of Delaware. Her original lines were those of a North Sea fisherman. For almost a century she ranged up and down the Atlantic coasts, and at length found her way to Fairhaven, at the head of Buzzard's Bay. There she was finally hauled out, as everyone supposed, for her last rest.

In the year 1892, however, Captain Eben Pierce, her then owner, presented her to Captain Slocum. Slocum set to work with his own hands and rebuilt her from the keel up, so that not a particle of the original fabric remained, except the windlass, and the 'fiddle head' or carving on the end of the cut-water. In rebuilding her, Slocum added to her freeboard 12in [305mm] amidships, 18in [457mm] forward and 14in [355mm] aft. The lines published herewith show her as thus rebuilt.

Under a sloop rig, Slocum sailed Spray from New Bedford, Massachusetts, to Gibraltar, thence back again across the Atlantic, down the South American coast and through the Strait of Magellan. Then he changed her rig to a yawl, and completed his circumnavigation of the globe by way of the Southern Pacific and Cape of Good Hope, and back across the Atlantic to New England, a gross of some 46 000 sea miles – all single-handed.

One of the most remarkable things about Spray is her ability to hold her course for hours or days at a time with no one at the helm. Had she not possessed this quality, Slocum's performance would have been a physical impossibility. For example, she ran from Thursday Island to the Cocos Keeling islands, 2 700 miles in 23 days. Slocum stood at the helm for one hour during that

ELEMENTS OF THE YAWL SPRAY
CALCULATED BY C ANDRADE JR, DEC. 1908
SCALE $\frac{1}{2}$" = 1'

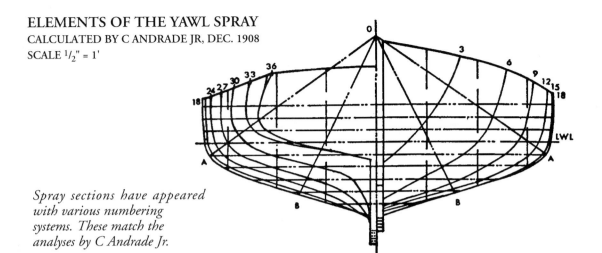

Spray sections have appeared with various numbering systems. These match the analyses by C Andrade Jr.

LOA	36ft 9in [11.20m]
LOA (including cutwater)	41ft $\frac{3}{4}$ in [12.52m]
LWL	32ft 1in [9.78m]
Beam	14ft 1in [4.29m]
WL Beam	13ft 10in [4.22m]
Draft	4ft 1in [1.24m]
Freeboard (excluding rail) Bow	4ft 1in [1.24m]
Waist	1ft 9 $\frac{3}{4}$ in [0.55m]
Stern	2ft 9 $\frac{3}{4}$ in [0.86m]
Rail	1ft 2in [0.36m]
Area Mid section immersed	26.32sq ft [2.44sq m]
Area Lateral plane immersed	111.88sq ft [10.39sq m]
Area LWL plane	349.04sq ft [32.43sq m]
Area wetted surface	443.18sq ft [41.17sq m]
Area rudder	7.52sq ft [0.70sq m]
Sail area actual	1161sq ft [107.86sq m]
Jib	246sq ft [22.85sq m]
Mainsail	604sq ft [56.11sq m]
Mizzen	151sq ft [14.03sq m]
Flying jib	160sq ft [14.86sq m]
Displacement	556.72cu ft [51.72sq m]
Displacement	35 658lb [16 174.47kg]
Pounds per inch immersion at LWL	1863lb
Kg per 25mm immersion at LWL	831kg

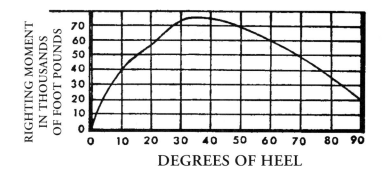

time. Her average distance made good for the run was over 117 miles a day, or about 5 miles an hour. This was a fair cruising speed for Spray and she maintained that speed of 5 knots for 23 consecutive days, or 552 consecutive hours. The impossibility of steering a boat for that time, or for any considerable portion of that time, is of course obvious. There are well-known men right here in New York City who have seen boats do the same thing for comparatively short distances. Thus, Mr Day records that after he had converted *Sea-Bird* into a keel boat and had lengthened her keel, he laid her on a course and she held that course for an hour and a half, at the end of which time there came a change in the wind. Now if a boat will hold her course along for an hour and a half, she will hold it for a year and a half, provided always that the wind and sea remain unchanged.

Examine an ocean chart of Spray's voyage, and you will see that Slocum systematically ran down the trades, not only for hundreds of miles but for thousands of miles, and his wind and sea conditions for whole days and weeks must have been practically constant. This is one of the reasons for Spray's phenomenal runs. Perfect balance is the other reason.

After a thorough analysis of Spray's lines, I found her to have a theoretically perfect balance. Her balance is marvellous, almost uncanny. Try as I would, one element after the other, they all swung into the same identical line. I attacked her with proportional dividers, planimeter, rota meter, Simpson's rule, Froude's coefficients, Dixon Kemp's formulae, series, curves, differentials, and all the appliances of modern yacht designing, and she emerged from the ordeal a theoretically perfect boat. For when she is under way, every element of resistance, stability, weight, heeling effort and propulsive force is in one transverse plane, and that plane is the boat's midship section. I know of no similar case in the whole field of naval architecture, ancient or modern. There may be similar cases in existence, but it has not been my good fortune to know of them.

Before passing to a critical analysis of the figures, I shall take up a few general questions concerning this unusual boat.

GENERAL APPEARANCE

Spray's lines appear, in much reduced size, at the end of Slocum's book, *Sailing Alone Around the World*. When I first looked at them, and read Slocum's statement that this hull had been driven at a speed of 8 knots, I thought he must be mistaken. Slocum, however, is an accurate historian, and I therefore set to work with proportional dividers, and laid Spray out to a scale of $^1/_2$ inch to the foot [1=24], in order to acquire an intimate personal knowledge of her lines, for merely looking at them in a book will not always suffice. I next swept in two diagonals (A and B in the half breadth plan), which are omitted from the lines as published in Slocum's book, and then I realised that he was justified in his claim of 8 knots.

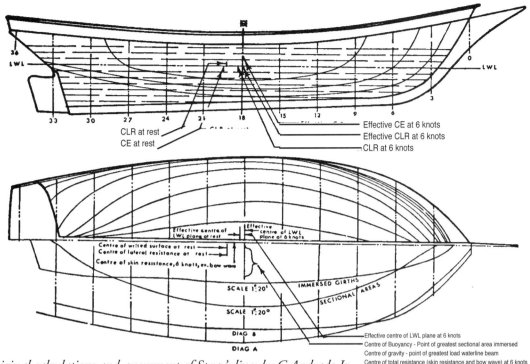

CLR at rest
CE at rest

Effective CE at 6 knots
Effective CLR at 6 knots
CLR at 6 knots

Effective centre of LWL plane at rest
Effective centre of LWL plane at 6 knots
Centre of wetted surface at rest
Centre of lateral resistance at rest
Centre of skin resistance, 6 knots, ex. bow wave

SCALE 1:20'

SCALE 1:20°

IMMERSED GIRTHS
SECTIONAL AREAS

DIAG B
DIAG A

Effective centre of LWL plane at 6 knots
Centre of Buoyancy - Point of greatest sectional area immersed
Centre of gravity - point of greatest load waterline beam
Centre of total resistance (skin resistance and bow wave) at 6 knots
Centre of effective lateral resistance at 6 knots
Centre of effective effort of sails at 6 knots
Midship section - point of greatest depth of bilge
Point of greatest overall beam - middle displacement curve

Original calculations and assesssment of Spray's lines by C Andrade Jr in 1909 and re-checked by Kenneth E Slack in 1966. Note how all relevant centres are at or about the centre section of the Spray hull.

DIAGONALS

If you will look at the drawings, you will see that Spray's real working line is the diagonal B, which is a normal practically the whole length of the boat. On the half breadth plan, you will see that diagonal B is marked by a little cross between stations 3 and 6. At this point she takes the water. From the cross to station 6, there is a very coarse angle of entrance, of which I shall have more to say in a moment. From station 6 to the transom, a run of over 27ft [8.2m], diagonal B is as clean a line, as fine drawn, easy running and fair as you will find in any racer of the Larchmont fleet and that is the line that bears her; it is the line she runs on, and it is the measure of her speed.

Now let us take up that coarse entrance angle of diagonal B from the cross to station 6, a matter of some 2ft [610mm]. Twenty years ago, Mr Herreshoff announced that hollow bow lines were not essential to speed. The Whitehead torpedo, which travels at about 30 knots, has a nose as round as a cannon ball.

Some of the little scow boats on the Western lakes develop great speed, and they hold this speed through rough water (that is, rough for their size and length), and their bows show hard curves, and in some cases even flat transoms.

Viewing all these things with impartial eyes, I should say that the 2ft [610mm] of diagonal B in Spray from the cross to section 6 would be no detriment whatever to her speed.

BOW

Let us now consider that portion of diagonal B which lies forward of the cross. This portion of the diagonal runs up to the stem-head at an angle somewhere in the neighbourhood of 45 degrees. The water-lines do the same and the buttock lines do the same. The result is a bow of terrific power. With her 35 000lb [15 876kg] of dead weight and a few more thousand sail pressure on top of that, Spray can go coasting down the side of a roller, and then when she turns from the long down-grade up-hill again, instead of running under, or carrying a ton or so of water aft along her decks, that bow will lift her. And it is the only bow that would lift her.

STERN

Spray's stern is the best that my limited experience could suggest. There is just enough rake in her transom to lift her handsomely over any following sea. Her transom is broad enough and deep enough to hold her water-lines and buttocks easy to the very last moment. And the practice of dropping the bottom of her transom below the waterline finds support in such examples as Mr Crane's *Dixie II* and Mr Herreshoff's *Sea Shell*, and many other master-designed craft. It does ease up the buttock lines so; and contrary to popular superstition, it does not create any material draft of dead water. The Crosbys have been building catboats this way for years. By dropping the transom below the waterline, the water lifts the boat to the very end of the run, and one of the resultants of that lift on the buttock lines is a forward thrust. On the other hand, where the knuckle of the transom is above the waterline, the exact opposite takes place, and the water, instead of lifting the boat and thrusting her forward, is lifted by the boat and holds her back.

MIDSHIP SECTION

Spray's midsection at first glance would seem much wider and shallower than a seagoing model would require. But, like everything else about her, there is a very good reason for Spray's form of midsection; in fact, there are several good reasons.

First: I have heard it said that her immunity from loss is due to the fact that when she is hove-to, she yields and gives to the sea, constantly easing away to leeward; whereas a deeper, more ardent model, holding in uncompromising fashion to the wind, would be battered and strained into destruction.

Second: Spray's great breadth gives her no end of deck room. Now when you are living on a boat weeks and months and years, deck room becomes not only important, but essential. Without adequate deck room for walking and exercise, a man could not exist for that length of time. He would fall ill of some sickness and die.

Third: The form of Spray's midship section insures that she will never heel to an uncomfortable angle. She would rarely go down much below 10 degrees of heel, and in good sailing breezes she would probably not exceed 5 degrees. Now equally with deck room, this matter of heel is most essential to the comfort and, in the long run, the health of the crew. The strain of living on a boat at 25 degrees or 30 degrees of heel may be borne for the brief period of a race, maybe a race as far as Bermuda, but when it comes to living on a boat thus for weeks at a time, no human being could stand it.

Fourth: Spray is a much better boat to windward than her form of midsection would at first glance indicate. To the casual observer, it would seem almost impossible to drive her to windward at all without a centreboard (and she has no centreboard). But on careful analysis it will appear that there are three reasons why Spray should be a fairly good boat to windward.

In the first place, she has an unusually hard bilge and an unusually flat vertical side, and the result is that even at a small angle of heel, her lee side acts as an efficient leeboard of very considerable area.

In the second place, she has a long, fairly deep keel, and as this keel rakes downward from the forefoot to the rudder, it is constantly entering solid water at every portion of its length, and is very much more efficient than if the keel were horizontal. In the third place, Spray has a large lateral plane in proportion to her sail spread.

Therefore, like everything else about her, I should say that her form of midsection was fully justified.

DISPLACEMENT

For a boat of 32ft [9.7m] waterline, Spray's displacement is enormous, 35 658lb [16 174kg]. Of course, this is an essential in her design. Being an oceangoing cruiser, her construction is heavy, 1.5in [38mm] yellow pine planking. Her great breadth requires heavy deck beams, 6in x 6in [152mm x 152mm] yellow pine; and her construction in other particulars is equally massive. All this means displacement. Then her crew, even one man, consumes a good deal of water, food and fuel in the course of several months. She must carry a large supply of spare gear and stores. Her large displacement then is necessary, unavoidable; and, besides, it gives her power to carry on through a sea.

By reason of her large waterline plane, her displacement per inch immersion at the load waterline is very large, 1863lb [845kg]. This is a good feature, as it makes little difference in her trim whether she has a ton or so more or less of stores on board. This feature is still another advantage accruing from her wide, shallow form of midship section.

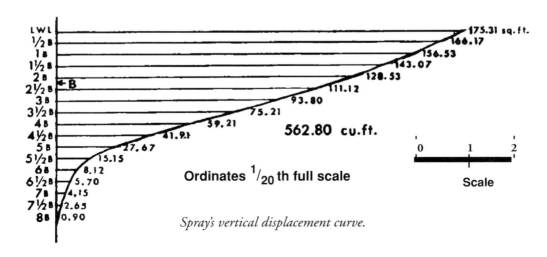

Spray's vertical displacement curve.

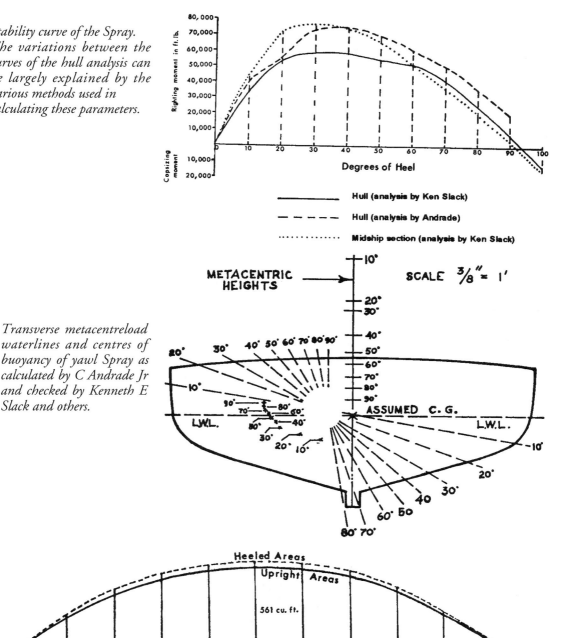

Stability curve of the Spray. The variations between the curves of the hull analysis can be largely explained by the various methods used in calculating these parameters.

Hull (analysis by Ken Slack)

Hull (analysis by Andrade)

Midship section (analysis by Ken Slack)

Transverse metacentreload waterlines and centres of buoyancy of yawl Spray as calculated by C Andrade Jr and checked by Kenneth E Slack and others.

Curve of upright and heeled areas. Note the even distribution of the curves and compare these with those of some modern designs.

CENTRES OF RESISTANCE, WEIGHTS ETC

We now come to the inner mystery of Spray's design. I suppose that the extraordinary focusing of her centres is the result of chance. Spray was laid down about the year 1800. Analytic boat designing, as we understand it, was unknown at that time. Spray's perfection of balance, then, must be purely empirical, but it is none the less marvellous for that.

To begin with, Spray's centre of buoyancy is located exactly at the boat's midship section. This is unusual. In fact, at the moment I do not recall any other design that has even this peculiarity. Axiomatically, the centre of gravity and the centre of buoyancy must lie in the same vertical line; and thus at the very outset of our investigations we find that the centre of gravity, the centre of buoyancy, the greatest breadth, the greatest depth of bilge, and the maximum point in the boat's curve of displacement, all fall exactly on the same line, which happens to be station 18.

And what is still more unusual, it will be observed that station 18, containing within itself all these elements, falls at exactly the effective middle point of the boat's curve of displacement. A glance at the curve of displacement will show that for all practical purposes the portion lying forward of station 3, and aft of station 33, can be disregarded. In other words, for all practical purposes, the curve begins at station 3 and ends at station 33, and exactly midway between station 3 and station 33 lies station 18, at which are focused all the points above mentioned.

Let us now examine station 18 with reference to its position on the load waterline. The old school of designers who pinned their faith to the wave line theory held that the maximum point in the curve of displacement (station 18 in Spray) should be 0.60 of the LW aft from the forward point of immersion. Modern practice has discarded the coefficient 0.60 and says that it should be 0.55; and the measurement rule now in force adopts this coefficient of 0.55. Spray's coefficient, however, instead of being 0.60, or 0.55, is only 0.506; which means that her midsection is somewhat forward of the position that has been decreed by modern practice.

Hull values at rest and heeled

Now, all displacement curves under the wave line rule and under the modern practice show a marked hollow at the bow. Obviously, where the bow portion of the displacement curve is hollow, it is essential that the boat's centre of gravity should be thrown as far aft as possible, in order to keep her head from burying when running under a press of sail; and this entails putting the midship section as far aft as possible; all of which doubtless had much to do with the adoption of the coefficients 0.60 and 0.55 above mentioned.

But in the case of Spray, it will be noted that the displacement curve of the boat's entrance is not hollow at all, but convex. Therefore, there is no reason for throwing her centre of gravity very far aft, because her bow is powerful enough to lift her at all times and under all circumstances. On the other hand, in Spray there is a very good reason for not throwing the centre of gravity very far aft of the middle of the LWL, and the reason is this:

to throw the centre of gravity aft is to throw the midship section aft, and as the boat of necessity has great displacement, the placing of the midship section very far aft would result in hard lines (either buttocks, waterlines or diagonals), and would produce a form of run that would inevitably create a heavy stern wave and make a slow boat.

The next element to be considered is the centre of lateral resistance. This centre lies 0.044 of the LWL aft of station 18 when the boat is at rest, and here it is well to remember that the position of the CLR is not always thoroughly appreciated in all its aspects. The CLR as laid out on the drawings represents the point on which the boat (rudder and all) would balance if pushed sideways through the water. Take the case now under discussion. Suppose you were to make a working model of Spray and put her in a tank of still water. Then suppose you took the point of a knife, and pressed it against the side of the model at the exact point marked 'CLR at rest' in the drawing. Now, if you pushed the model sideways at right angles to her keel, she would just balance on the knife point, the boat moving bodily sideways, without turning either the stern or the bow, and that is all that is meant by the CLR as shown on the plans.

The instant, however, that the boat starts to move forward, the CLR starts to move forward toward the bow of the boat. This is in obedience to a well-known law. As the bow works in solid water, and the stern dead wood in broken water, the bow holds on better than the stern, and a square foot of lateral plane at the bow holds better than a square foot of lateral plane at the stern. The net result is that the effective CLR moves forward. The question of just how far the CLR moves forward when the boat begins to move ahead is a question involving some rather tedious calculation. Froude compiled a set of figures, showing the change of resistance per square foot at various portions of a surface located at various distances aft from the leading edge. They relate specifically to skin resistance, but I assume that the lateral resistance would vary in the same ratio. A table of these coefficients is given at page 135 of Mackrow's Pocket Book. Froude gives the figures for 2, 8, 20 and 50ft [0.6, 2.4, 6 and 15m]. By interpolation, using a variable differential to satisfy the points established by Froude, it is possible to get the correct coefficient for any intermediate point. Then by applying the appropriate coefficients to the various stations of the immersed lateral plane, and applying Simpson's formula, it is possible to find how far the CLR will move forward for any predetermined speed. 'In the specific case of Spray moving at a speed of 6 knots, the CLR moves, from a point 1.45ft [442mm] aft of station 18, to 0.4 of 1ft [11mm] aft of station 18, a forward movement of 1.05ft [320mm]. This gives us the actual working location of Spray's CLR at 6 knots, disregarding the bow wave. In order to make our calculation complete, we must further reckon with the bow wave. The question of stern wave may be disregarded, because from the pictures and photographs of Spray under way, it clearly appears that the boat creates no sensible stern wave, she has too clean a run for that. She does raise a moderate bow wave, and the effect of that bow wave is of course to bring her effective CLR a little bit forward.

The question of just exactly how far forward the bow wave will carry the CLR is a matter beyond the ken of precise calculation. Judging from the height of the bow wave as shown on Spray, I should say it would amount to a little over one per cent of the LWL, and if that assumption is correct, it would bring Spray's effective working CLR exactly on station 18. Of course, every heave of the sea, every slant of wind, every touch on the helm throws this centre a little bit forward or aft; it is no more fixed and stable than her angle of heel is fixed and stable. Constantly it plays forward and aft, but the central average point of its play must be station 18 or within a fraction of an inch of it.

In order to make my analysis of Spray's hull quite complete, I also calculated a centre that is seldom considered at all in yacht design, and yet that must have some significance, that is, the centre of wetted surface. In other words, I determined the effective centre of curve of immersed girths by Simpson's formula. To my surprise, this centre worked out to a hair on identically the same line as the CLR at rest, viz 1.45ft [442mm] aft of station 18, another of the extraordinary coincidences in Spray's design.

Now exactly the same considerations which apply to the CLR apply also to this centre of wetted surface. In other words, when the boat begins to move forward, the focal point of her skin resistance begins to move forward from the place occupied by the centre of wetted surface at rest. Thus, by applying Froude and Simpson, as in the case of the lateral plane, we find that at a speed of 6 knots, Spray's centre of skin resistance moves forward from a point 1.45ft [442mm] aft of station 18, to a point 0.6 of a foot [182mm] aft of station 18, a forward movement of 0.85ft [259mm]; that is, leaving the bow wave out of account. To complete our calculation, we must again reckon with the bow wave.

Now the bow wave will have a more potent effect in carrying forward the centre of skin resistance, than in carrying forward the centre of lateral resistance. And for this reason, the boat throws off two bow waves, one from the weather bow and one from the lee bow. Both of these waves affect the wetted surface, whereas only the lee wave affects the lateral plane. Of course, the wave on the lee bow is heavier than the wave on the weather bow, and therefore we may safely say that the two bow waves will not move the centre of skin resistance forward twice as far as the lee bow wave moves the CLR forward. We thus reach the conclusion that the boat's wave action will throw the centre of skin resistance forward further than the CLR is thrown forward, and yet not so much as twice that distance. We have already seen that the wave action throws her CLR forward 0.4 of a foot [121mm]. Therefore the wave action will throw her centre of skin resistance forward between 0.4 and 0.8 of a foot [121 and 244mm], say 0.6 of a foot [183mm] as a mean, and when we do move her centre of skin resistance forward 0.6 of a foot, we land again exactly to a hair on station 18. Another in the series of coincidences.

Even the effective centre of the LWL plane falls only 0.4 of a foot [121mm] aft of station 18 when the boat is at rest; and the piling up of the bow waves under the bow, when she is under way, must bring this centre also just about on station 18. (Unlike the CLR and the centre of skin resistance, the effective centre of the LWL plane is not affected by the forward motion of the boat; it is affected only by the bow wave.)

From an inspection of the LWL plane, the almost perfect symmetry of the curve of displacement with reference to station 18 as an axis, and the symmetry of the boat's ends, it is quite evident that the longitudinal metacentre for a given angle of pitch forward will be at practically the same height as for an equal angle of pitch aft.

I know of no other conceivable factor of weight, displacement, buoyancy or resistance that can be calculated for a hull, so far as longitudinal balance is concerned, and I shall leave discussion of Spray's hull with the statement that every one of these factors, when she is under way, is concentrated exactly at her midship section (station 18). So much for Spray's hull.

SAIL PLAN

Let us now examine Spray's sail plan. At the outset, it should be remarked that the flying jib will be eliminated from the discussion of sail balance, as it is a light weather sail, set standing on a light bamboo jib boom, which is merely lashed to the bowsprit when the flying jib is set, and is stowed when the flying jib is stowed, and is never used on the wind.

When Spray is on the wind, she carries three sails only, the jib, mainsail and mizzen. The combined centre of effort of these three sails at rest falls about 0.17 of a foot forward of the CLR at rest. This 0.7 of a foot [214mm] is only a little over 0.5 of 1% of the LWL. Modern practice calls for from 1 per cent to 3 per cent of the LWL, but it must be remembered that the 1 per cent to 3 per cent coefficient is used for sloops with large mainsails and small jibs, whereas Spray is a yawl with an unusually large jib and a comparatively small mainsail. (Author's note: modern yacht hulls require a greater lead – that is CLP related to CLR, so these calculations refer to the Spray type hulls only.)

On this state of facts no less an authority than Dixon Kemp uses the following language (*Yacht Architecture* – Third Edition, Page 100); "In the case of yawls it is generally found that the calculated centre of effort requires (relatively to the centre of lateral resistance) to be a little further aft than in either cutters or schooners, as the mizzen is not a very effective sail on a wind, the eddy wind of the mainsail causing it to lift; also a yawl's mainmast is usually further forward than a cutter's, and it should be noted that the position of the centre of effort of the largest driving sail influences the position of the general CE more than the calculation shows."

Spray's centre of effort is therefore amply justified by authority, and the authority, in turn, is justified by Spray's actual performance under the sail plan shown. For Slocum says of her, "Briefly I have to say that when close hauled in a light wind under all sail she required little or no weather helm. As the wind increased I would go on deck, if below, and turn the wheel up a spoke more or less, re-lash it or, as sailors say, put it in a becket, and then leave it as before."

Of course, in order to attain this balance, Spray's efficient centre of effort must be over her effective CLR and, as we have already seen that the effective CLR at 6 knots falls exactly on station 18, so her efficient centre of effort also at that speed must fall exactly on station 18.

It is obvious that, just as effective CLR moves forward, as the boat moves forward so the efficient centre of effort moves forward on the sail plan when the boat sails forward. This has long been known by naval architects; and the recent activity in aeroplane flight has led to much experiment on the subject. The CE seems to move forward more slowly than the CLR as the boat's speed increases, and the result is that although the CE at rest is forward of the CLR, yet when the boat is at her normal speed, these two centres, advancing at unequal rates, come into exact balance; and when the boat's speed is increased still more by a harder wind, the CLR continuing to work forward faster than the CE makes the boat carry a harder and harder weather helm as the wind increases. This is a matter of common observation.

CURVE OF STABILITY AND TRANSVERSE METACENTRE

The curve of stability shows that Spray is theoretically uncapsizable. Because of 90 degrees of heel she still has left a righting moment of over 20 000 foot-pounds. This is most remarkable for a boat of her shallow draft; doubly remarkable in view of the fact that she carries no outside

Righting Moments on Heeling

Heel	*Righting Lever	Righting Moment	
		ft lb	ft tons
10°	0-11- 0	33,186	14.82
20°	1- 5-10	53,026	23.67
30°	1- 7-11	59,158	26.41
40°	1- 7 - 5	58,076	25.84
50°	1- 6 - 4	54,829	24.48
60°	1- 4 -15	50,862	22.71
70°	1 -1 - 6	40,040	17.87
80°	0 -8 - 6	25,250	11.27
90°	0 -2 - 9	7,575	3.38
100°	-(0 -3 - 6)	-10,100	-4.51

* Measurement in feet, inches, sixteenths

Curve of Heeled Areas (Hull Rise $1^1/_2$")

Station	Heeled Immersed Areas (sq ft)	Ordinates
Fore end LWL	0	0
1	1.46	0.29
2	11.17	2.23
3	18.40	3.68
4	23.03	4.61
5	25.60	5.12
6	26.62	5.32
7	25.33	5.07
8	22.50	4.50
9	18.08	3.62
10	12.21	2.44
11	*Ψ 1.49	0.30
Aft end LWL	Ψ 0.73	0.15

*including rudder   ΨRudder thickness 3in assumed

Area curve heeled areas:	112.19 sq ft
Correction for scale (x 5) ➔ Displacement:	560.95 cu ft
Displacement:	36,069 lb

This compares favourably with the upright displacement of 36,072

Weight per inch Immersion/Demersion at LWL

Weight added	Distance LWL raised /Boat lowered	Weight subtracted	Distance LWL lowered /Boat raised
1,800	1 inch	1,800	1 inch
3,700	2 inches	3,670	2 inches
5,650	3 inches	5,370	3 inches
7,500	4 inches	7,200	4 inches
9,480	5 inches	9,000	5 inches
11,440	6 inches		

ballast whatever, and even her inside ballast consists merely of cement blocks. All boatmen of experience say that stone or cement ballast makes a livelier, "corkier" boat than the same weight of lead or iron. Her maximum stability is at about 35 degrees of heel, where she has a righting moment of 75 000 foot-pounds.

As she should never be sailed much lower than 10 degrees of heel, it will be seen that she has an ample margin of safety at all times.

In plotting the curve of stability, I assumed the centre of gravity to lie exactly at the LWL, which I think is conservative.

I have also plotted the transverse LWL transverse centre of buoyancy, and metacentric height for each 10 degrees of heel up to 90 degrees.

CONCLUSION

I conclude my analysis of Spray's lines with a feeling of profound admiration and respect. She is not only an able boat, but a beautiful boat; using the term "beautiful" as defined by Charles Elliott Norton, "that form most perfectly adapted to perform its allotted work", beautiful in the same sense that Sandow, or the Farnese Hercules, is beautiful. From the man who loves boats and the sea, and in some measure understands them (for it has been given to no one yet to know all their ways), Spray will receive the recognition that is her due.

She is the perfection of her type, a perfection demonstrated not only on paper, but by the ordeal of actual achievement. She is an oceangoing cruiser, in the largest sense of that term. After sailing 46 000 miles, and weathering a hundred gales, some of which foundered great ships in his near vicinity, Slocum says of her, "I have given in the plans of Spray the dimensions of such a ship as I should call seaworthy in all conditions of weather and on all seas." These words, coming from such a source, are not lightly to be disregarded.

The question is one of such interest that *Rudder* invites the opinions of all amateur and professional designers and practical boatmen to see if they would suggest any departures whatever from Spray's lines in a boat intended to circumnavigate the globe singlehanded.

Of course, if the question were to design the best possible boat to race on Long Island Sound or to Block Island, or even to Bermuda, there is no question but what other characteristics than those of Spray would be adopted. But let the question be clearly apprehended: what would be the best boat with which to circumnavigate the globe singlehanded? Would the ideal boat for that purpose depart in any measure from Spray's lines; and if so, why?

On this question, a full discussion will be of the utmost interest. We trust that all who are interested will contribute their views, and not only their views, but their reasons for their views.'

So ends Andrade Jr's most informative article in the June 1909 issue of *Rudder*. In many aspects, it could have been written only last week!

CHAPTER 5
Traditional Spray Replicas

As Joshua Slocum was a Canadian by birth and an American by choice, and as the Spray was rebuilt and sailed from the USA, one would imagine that the first copies of the boat would originate from that country. Yet this is not the case. The first known copy was built in 1902 by Gill of Rochester in England.

ROCHESTER SPRAY

This copy, as with many replicas of Spray, was not exactly the same size as the original, but measured 54ft [16.4m] overall. Subsequent information about this vessel seems to indicate that the overall length included the bowsprit. A letter by Frank Gilliland, which appeared in the 1918 issue of *Yachting Monthly*, reported, 'I always thought a Spray had been built ten to fifteen years ago either in Medway or Burnham districts, identical as far as the hull is concerned, with Captain Slocum's vessel.' In the next issue a letter to the editor confirmed this. Shortly afterwards, this boat was advertised for sale in the *Yachtsman*, where an illustration accompanying the advertisement showed that the Spray had been given a much more contemporary appearance, especially above the waterline.

In a 1928 issue of *Yachting Monthly*, additional correspondence appeared in the letters column when Norman Deakin wrote to take the editor to task for stating that no replica of the Spray had been built in England up to that time. Deakin went on to quote Lloyd's Register and listed the principal dimensions of the copy of the Spray built by Gill: LBP 42.6ft [12.9m], Beam 14.1ft [4.3m], Depth 5.6ft [1.7m], aux engine Kelvin 4 cyl. The *Rochester Spray* was reputed to have varnished topsides and was rigged as a cutter; she was built for A E Mason. The design was credited to the builder, E A Gill, but all sources agree that the lines were taken from those already published of the original Spray.

The history of this first known copy becomes more interesting. In 1912 she was sold to Gustav Kruger of Hamburg, and in 1914 was converted to a yawl. She next appears on the yacht register in 1926 under the name of *Drei Rosen*, and her owner was Fritz Leisegang of Stettin. In the 1929 issue of *Yachting Monthly* a letter by Otto A Erdmannn of Berlin gave further information on the vessel:

'I have read with interest the comment Mr Norman Deakin made about the Spray which was built by Gill of Rochester 1902 on the lines of the original boat built by Slocum. Spray is very well known to me, having been owned successively by Dr A Haltermann of Hamburg, Herr F Behnche and Herr Leisegang of Berlin, who owns her still and renamed her *Heimat*. I inspected this boat a couple of years ago and found her absolutely sound.'

When Herr Leisegang bought the vessel in 1925 she was called *Drei Rosen* and, not being aware of Spray's fame, he renamed her *Heimat*. Later, Herr Leisegang was to report that there was a bell with the word Spray on it on board the now renamed *Heimat*. Herr Leisegang sold the boat in 1930 to a Dr Sharnowski of Poland and lost touch with her.

Another letter appeared in *Yachting World* in 1959 referring to the Gill *Rochester Spray*. Wlodzimierz Glowacki, president of the Polish Yacht Association, wrote about copies of Slocum's Spray:

'One of those copies, built in 1902 by Gill of Rochester, was owned by Herr Leisegang of Berlin, and called *Heimat*. She is probably the same *Heimat* which had been bought in June 1930 in Stettin by Polish yachtsmen Dr Cz Czarnowski and J Fischer, who changed her name to *Jurand*. Under her new name, this Rochester copy of Spray had been bought in 1935 by Akademicki Zwiazek Morski (Students Sea Association in Poland) and was in use up to the beginning of the Second World War. In September 1939, *Jurand* was taken out on the shore, and from this time we haven't any information about her further fate, because during the last war the Nazi Germans expelled Polish people from Gdynia. After the war we couldn't find any trace of *Jurand,* and presumed that she had been wrecked. *Jurand* had a bell, with her first name Spray and, according to verbal tradition, she had been built in England for some scientific expedition into the polar waters before the First World War. She has about 180 square metre sails, yawl rigging.'

From now on the history of the Gill *Rochester Spray* becomes a little clouded. However, it had been suggested that a boat called *Heimat* was used by the Luftwaffe as a training vessel at their sailing school located in Lobbe on the Rugen. The Germans did take many of the boats captured in Poland back to Germany, where they were put to use in their war effort. It is reasonable to assume that a boat in excellent condition, such as the Gill *Rochester Spray,* would be put to good use! Towards the end of the war this vessel was also used for transporting refugees to Denmark. From here she went to Schleswig, where she came under the care of the RAF and may have been towed back to England as were several other boats that were captured during that period. One can only speculate as to her present whereabouts or whether she still exists.

ULULA

Another early English copy, named *Ulula*, was built in 1934 by GJ Allanson & Son of Freckleton, Lancashire, England, for a Blackpool chemist who had won the Irish sweep and wanted a yacht like Spray. According to various reports, the hull was beautifully built, but the rigging was somewhat light; and the sails and rigging generally were not up to the standard of the hull. Does this suggest that the original owner ran short of cash as the boat neared completion? A common occurrence, no doubt. Evidently, the chemist only kept the boat a few months; he may have found he did not like sailing, and the rig she carried at that time was reputedly hard to handle. She was sold twice in 1934, once to a Mr Alston. My appeal for information from current and former Spray owners in *Yachting World* produced the following response from H F Alston of Scarborough:

'In the early thirties I gave my brother-in-law, William Cooke, a copy of Captain Slocum's book. Some time after he asked me to go with him to Freckleton, where there was a local boatyard by the name of Allanson. Here he showed me his new boat *Ulula,* a copy of Spray. I think, but am not sure, that he had a Kelvin sleeve motor installed. He was a small man, with little experience in sailing. I think he found he had bought something beyond his ability to control. He got it to the River Wyne at Fleetwood, and I do not think he used it again, but sold it to a man who wished to have a "two masted boat" to display illuminated advertisements off the beach at Blackpool. The last I heard of her was when I was passing along the Gloucester and Berkeley Canal, where she had preceded me and trapped herself with the mainmast stuck in the works of an overhead railway bridge.'

Another letter from Alston revealed, 'It is a long time ago, but I seem to recall my brother-in-law showing me a half model of *Ulula* at Allanson's. If it were still in existence, I thought it might be of interest to you. He said that the firm used this for their offsets.' Subsequent enquiries revealed that the model from G J Allanson's has long since disappeared, but of the *Ulula* we have more information.

After *Ulula* was used for displaying illuminated signs at Blackpool, she was purchased by Charles Hinman, who reported that when he bought her she had a lighting set aboard that was subsequently used to light a 12 room house. The next owner was Mostyn Williams, who took her down to Bristol. It appears that Charles Hinman bought back *Ulula* from Mostyn Williams for £3000 less than he sold her for, and proceeded to totally rerig her and generally tidy her up. Hinman reports that she sailed well. It seems that this may have been the first chance the boat had to show her good form. During the Second World War, Mr Hinman used *Ulula* as a liveaboard while away from home, serving in a wartime job. After the war she was fitted with a new suit of sails and wheel steering, and was eventually sold to an officer serving in the Irish navy.

PANDORA

The first of many Spray replicas to be built in Australia was *Pandora*. This boat was built in Perth, in Western Australia, and is credited as being the first small boat to sail around Cape Horn; remember that Slocum took his boat through the Straits of Magellan. One Perth newspaper reported, 'George McCarter is now engaged on an interesting vessel for Mr F B Blythe. She is being built to sail around the world and her owner has adopted the design of the famous yacht Spray as being most suitable. She is 37ft LOA [11.2m] with a beam of no less than 14ft [4.2m]. She is planked with jarrah laid on a jarrah keel, and the ribs are bent timbers of blackwood and stringybark built in three pieces each. As may be judged, she is unusually roomy and her career will be watched with interest.'

Locals reported that *Pandora* was in fact an exact replica of Slocum's Spray, and the measurements quoted in the Perth newspaper article would seem to bear this out. *Pandora* sailed from Bunbury, Western Australia, on 3 May 1910, and arrived in Melbourne on 29 May. Fortunately, one Melbourne newspaper featured the arrival of *Pandora* with the following article:

'Recollections of the adventurous round the world voyages accomplished some years ago by the small sailing vessels *Spray* and *Tilikum,* both of which visited Melbourne, are revived by the similar expedition on which *Pandora,* a 9 ton yawl, is about to embark. *Pandora* is slightly smaller than Captain Slocum's Spray (this seems in conflict with other contemporary reports, which state that *Pandora* was exactly the same size as Spray, and in fact measurements quoted later in the article are exactly those of the original Spray) is constructed on the same principle as that vessel, which, naturally, she closely resembles.'

The article then went on to give a long account of the proposed round the world voyage of *Pandora.* After a six-week stay in Melbourne, *Pandora* sailed on 10 July headed for Sydney. On 16 August she arrived in Sydney and after staying only one day, she sailed for Auckland in New Zealand.

Knowing the conditions that prevail off the Australian coast, and considering the usually stormy crossing to New Zealand, crew of *Pandora* must have established a good deal of trust in their vessel. A one-day stopover suggests a very successful passage up to this point. In fact, *Pandora* did have a very rough time crossing the Tasman, and spent a month in Auckland, and then headed for Pitcairn and on to Easter Island. The crew of *Pandora* spent a week ashore on Easter Island inspecting the giant statues for which that Island is famous.

From Easter Island *Pandora* set sail for Cape Horn, passing it on 16 January 1911. Just one week later, *Pandora* was struck by a huge wave that completely rolled her over. The Falkland Islands were nearby so *Pandora* called there to allow repairs to be made to her rigging. Later, *Pandora* crossed to St Helena, and then on to Ascension Island. When she finally arrived safely in New York, the *Pandora* had covered 22 000 miles in just under 14 months.

St Kilda Spray

The fact that there should be an early replica of the Spray built in Melbourne, Australia, is not surprising. Slocum stayed in Melbourne for nearly a month and Spray was moored at St Kilda, which was then (as now) a sizeable yachting centre on the shores of Port Phillip Bay. Victor Slocum, Joshua's son, records in the biography of his father that a Mr Shaw obtained the lines of Spray and was building a copy. Evidently the builder was JB Jones, who built the boat for Mr Shaw in about 1926 or 1927. Mr Savage, a well known and respected boatbuilder, reported that the *St Kilda Spray* lay in his boatyard for several years. Savage is a member of a long-established boatbuilding family, and said that his father had met Slocum when he was in Melbourne, and he always believed that the *St Kilda Spray* was indeed an exact replica of the original vessel.

Recently, additional information about this replica appeared in the *Slocum Society Newsletter* through a letter from Bob and Betty Dack of Metung Victoria, Australia who wrote:

'My wife and I bought the *St Kilda Spray* in November 1986, having known the three previous owners and fallen in love with the boat. Our biggest adventure on *St Kilda Spray* was to sail her to Sydney in 1988 for Australia's Bicentenary celebrations. Although not officially part of the fleet, we were in fact one of the oldest boats there. There followed a magnificent sail home, averaging 9 knots and surfing down the front of big waves, with the needle running off the end of

St Kilda Spray: *this famous replica is now owned by R & E Dack of Metung, Victoria, Australia.*

the clock! Last month Betty and I took in partners Julie and Ian Farmer to our business, and Ian is working hard with me to build up the cruise business.'

A letter from Bob and Betty Dack confirms that the Dacks' charter business is now thriving and that the old *St Kilda Spray* is earning her keep in style. It is very noticeable that most of the letters received from Spray owners are written from a couple rather than just the male or female partner. Does this mean that Spray-owning couples are more happily and demonstratively together than members of the general populace? Could we even say that a couple that 'Sprays together, stays together'?

LITTLE SPRAY

The first known of the Sprays to be built in the USA was in fact a two-thirds replica, designed and built by Cipriano Andrade Jr. This was the author of the analysis of the original Spray, which appeared in the 1909 *Rudder* magazine and which appears in Chapter 4. Cipriano Andrade Jr wrote in a contemporary issue of *Fore and Aft* magazine:

'In the winter of 1908 I made as complete a technical analysis of Spray as I could devise. A few years after that, my old friend Nutting asked me to build my next boat as a duplicate of Spray. In the fall of 1918 I began a design of the Spray exactly like the original, but with all dimensions just 2/3 of the original Spray, and with auxiliary power and an iron keel. By the summer of 1920 this little duplicate Spray was finished and in the water. She amply justified my faith in the original.' (See *Susan Constant* later in this chapter; there may be some connection.)

FAITH

John G Hanna, a well-known yacht designer in the first half of this century, also designed replicas and near replicas of Spray. Hanna is perhaps better known for his Tahiti Ketch sailboats, and *Fore and Aft* magazine has run an article by him:

'Published herewith are lines of a modified Spray I drew for a large vessel. Her outside proportions are conventional for her size. As nearly everyone knows, large craft must have relatively less beam than small ones. The formulae of modification were very complex, and to be sure of results I checked measurements of principal centres, finding that they came out on the midship section line for this hull just exactly as they do on the original Spray. She should be well balanced, as easy to handle, as capable of handling herself, as was Slocum's boat. Moreover, she should also sail at a small angle of heel, for this is a characteristic that depends on balance between the upsetting and righting forces, and while she has relatively less righting force than the beamy Spray, she still has the characteristically powerful Spray section and a sail plan that has a relatively lower centre of pressure, and so less upsetting force. Like Spray, her sailing angle should be about ten degrees.'

It would appear from the above description and other factors that the lines shown and described were those of the 87ft [26.5m] ketch called *Faith*. This vessel was certainly the largest copy of Spray ever built.

FOAM

According to the article in *Fore and Aft*, John Hanna had designed another modification of Spray. This design was called *Foam*, and Hanna wrote about it in *Motor Boat*:

'For many years I have stood second only to Mr Cipriano Andrade Jr as a student of Spray. Could Spray be altered so as to bring her within limits a yachtsman would consider, and yet keep strictly to her characteristic form and preserve as far as possible her marvellously perfect balance, as proved by Andrade's analysis of all her centres? This question was so alluring that I dusted off the old drawing board at once, grabbed a pencil, and was unable to let go for 22 hours. I ask that it be especially noted that I made no attempt to "improve" the lines anywhere by altering their character, nor their dimensions a hair's breadth otherwise as imposed by the requisite narrowing of the hull, all of which was done in strict proportionality.'

The vessel that Hanna refers to in the *Fore and Aft* article was built in Tonawanda on Lake Ontario, Canada by George Reid Richardson in 1926 for Dr Harvey Slocum, a physician who lived in New York and believed to be a distant relative of Joshua Slocum. Dr Slocum subsequently sold the boat to Matthew H Knapp of New York. During this period the well-connected Mr Knapp entertained several dignitaries aboard, including the late John Foster Dulles, the first Secretary of State under President Eisenhower. After a succession of owners this vessel was subsequently sold to Horace W Schmahl of New York, who renamed the boat *Island Trader;* later she was sailed around the world.

SAGAMORE OR FOAM II

John Hanna finally seemed to see the light when he was asked to prepare yet another Spray design. This time he was requested to follow the lines of the original as closely as possible. The person commissioning the new design was a neighbour of Matthew Knapp and knew just what he wanted; and in fact Hanna turned out plans for a vessel that closely resembled the original Spray. When built and sailed, this boat proved to be superior to the original Hanna-designed *Foam.* Hanna then sold many sets of *Foam II* plans, and a number of vessels were built from those plans. He wrote in 1944 that eight boats had already been built from the *Foam II* plans, and since then it can be assumed that several others have been completed. Included in the number of *Foam* II Spray replicas is the *Sagamore,* which was built in 1939 at Balboa in the Canal Zone, by Captain Elmer B Small, a retired Panama Canal pilot. Unfortunately for Captain Small, the boat was completed and launched in 1940, just in time for the military to requisition her for coastal patrol duty. After the war, Captain Small repurchased her, and after a refit was able to enjoy at last the boat that he and his son had built. *Sagamore* then cruised the South American coast, as well as the West Indies and up the inland waterway to New York.

OXFORD SPRAY

This Spray replica is one of the best known examples in the USA. In 1929 Captain R D (Pete) Culler decided that he wanted to have a boat built that would be within his means and within the abilities of a yard that was used to building fishing boats and the like. As he said himself when referring to his reasons for choosing the Spray, 'The model was not a type suited to or needing the skills of such as Lawley or Nevins.' For those unfamiliar with American boatbuilding traditions, Lawley and Nevins were the finest of boatbuilders, and when it came to fine yacht construction they set the standards of their time.

Pete Culler chose a yard at Oxford, Maryland, USA, where the master boatbuilder was Alonzo R Conley. This yard was experienced at building fishing vessels and ideally suited to building a Spray replica.The plans were prepared by Victor Slocum, who reputedly scaled up the lines from those outlined in *Sailing Alone Around the World.* Pete Culler had a high regard for the master boatbuilder Conley, and worked out an arrangement that he, Culler, could serve as a 'learning apprentice', working under the master boatbuilder on his own and other boats. This was done because Culler was keen to learn all he could about boatbuilding, as well as save costs on his own Spray replica. Evidently the system worked well, as Culler reports that the total cost of his Spray was less than that originally estimated. Try to achieve that in today's world !

One interesting facet of this Spray's construction was that in the area between the planking and the ceiling (a light inner planking inside the frames), she carried a ton of salt.This treatment was often employed in the old coasters, and is intended to pickle and preserve the timber from inside as well as absorb moisture, thus keeping the interior of the boat dry. The auxiliary engine was 40 hp, and the original Spray sail plan was used with the addition of a topsail. The topsail came in handy in the Chesapeake Bay area where the summer winds can be exceedingly light, and sometimes in my experience, exceedingly strong.

Pete and Toni Culler's Oxford Spray – *one of the finest and best known Spray replicas ever built.*

Captain Culler owned his Spray for 23 years, and he and his wife used her as a home, for their charter business, and occasionally to carry freight. On many occasions Captain Culler remarked on the excellent self-steering qualities of the Spray. Mrs Culler wrote in *Rudder* magazine about the boat that her husband had built, and that they shared for so many years:

'Pete, my husband, was and is a Slocum enthusiast. At the age of 16 he brought a pair of brass Navy bow chocks from an old Scotsman on the west coast. He knew that some day his Spray would be built around these. Pete's enthusiasm went one step further than most. He recognised in Slocum's exploits not only his amazing seamanship, but also his wisdom in choosing a model of a boat that would be seaworthy, comfortable and workable for extended cruising anywhere. Ten years ago, after 18 months of the hardest and most satisfying work in the world, he completed his ship and she slid down the slipway into the water, the chocks in place on the Spray's bow.'

After Captain Culler and Mrs Culler sold their Spray, she changed hands several times; and one owner reputedly fitted out the boat with all the latest gear, including Edson steering, an electric windlass, speedo, foam mattresses, fire control system and many other luxuries.

Another owner of this vessel, Dr Charles Johnson and his wife, undertook an 8 000-mile cruise and sailed it from Boston to the Azores, Madeira and the Canaries, and back across the Atlantic to the West Indies.

According to recent reports, this same Spray was owned by Rocky Harris, and some years ago a client of mine sent me a photograph of this fine vessel. Another good photograph of this Spray was given to Pete Greenfield, publisher of *The Boatman* (see appendix) and it was while trying to contact Mrs Culler for permission to reproduce the photograph that I learned she had died about three years ago.

BASILISK

This Spray replica was built at the same yard in Oxford, Maryland, USA, that accomplished such a fine job of building Pete Culler's Spray. It is not surprising that this second Spray copy was built, and that she was built from the same set of lines used to build the first Spray built at the Oxford yard. Quite often one order for a particular type of vessel brings forth another when it is apparent that a fine boat is under construction. The name *Basilisk* is the name of a West Indian lizard, and the appropriateness of the name becomes apparent when one learns that the boat was sponsored by the American Museum of Natural History, who intended to use her for a scientific expedition to the West Indies. The museum's magazine, *Natural History,* revealed some details: 'A boat was needed that would be seaworthy, comfortable to live in, staunch, yet small enough for one or two men to handle in any weather. It must be able to carry water for a period of several months, and provisions for at least half a year, and yet allow space to work and live.'

The requirements are similar, with some modifications, to those requested by clients today seeking a long-distance cruising vessel. With the advent of reasonably priced desalinators, it is not necessary to carry great quantities of water, but the remainder of the requirements seem reasonable for any long-distance cruising boat. The Spray can easily fulfil all of these needs and more.

Unfortunately, this second Spray copy built by the Oxford yard did not have a very long history as she was wrecked on Great Inagua Island in the Bahamas. However, the actual owner of the vessel, Gilbert C Klingel, remained on Great Inagua Island and later wrote a book entitled *Inagua,* which gave details of the voyage and the shipwreck as well as detailing the wildlife on the island and surrounding sea. Of his Spray replica, Klingel wrote:

'We had chosen a famous model. In fact, we had chosen one of the most famous models of all time. Our ship was to be an exact replica, except for the cabin and fittings, of the famous Spray of Captain Slocum who, it will be remembered, sailed the original around the world single-handed in the late 1890s. He set a precedent in maritime history and proved beyond all question that open ocean sailing in small boats was both practical and safe. All honour to him. As time proved, if we had searched the world over we could not have selected a better model.'

JOSHUA-S

The following letter is typical of the correspondence we have received from Spray owners all over the world:

'My name is Philip Bromley and I am replying to your article in *Amateur Boatbuilder* referring to the Spray. I have a Slocum Spray replica called *Joshua-S,* which I bought in 1988 at Southport (near Brisbane in Queensland, Australia). On chasing the history of my boat, I found out it was built in New Zealand in the Bay of Islands and launched in 1962. *Joshua-S* is built of New Zealand kauri, strip planked, and glued and tre-nailed on kauri frames, has a kauri mast, and is gaff rigged.

In 1989, on a return trip from the Whitsunday Islands off the Australian Queensland coast, we met at Coffs Harbour a retired Lt Commander in the Canadian Navy who built his Spray over eight years and was on a world trip. He was a member of the Slocum Society in Canada, and he had a number of items from the Society including a wall plate.'

SUSAN CONSTANT
Another respondent to my request for Spray information was J O'Donnell of Oriental, North Carolina. Mr O'Donnell wrote:

'Around 1967 when we lived in the White Hall Creek, Annapolis, Maryland, I owned *Susan Constant,* the first registered boat in Maryland with a number of 1000AA. She was a two-thirds copy of Spray, built, I was told, on Long Island in the early to mid 1930s. I put a new stem in her and replaced her gaff sail, which was made in England in 1966. The stem was most interesting in that it was installed by a very old man using a beautiful, curved lip-sided adze; he whittled it out of a section of red 12in by 12in [305mm x 305mm] yellow pine. This piece of timber was a joist liberated from the tearing down of the Southern Hotel in Baltimore. The work was done in a boatyard on Back Creek in Annapolis in 1966. She had an Atomic four in her. I have one or two photos if you would like to see them. You might see if she is still alive through the Maryland boat registry. If you find her please let me know.'

At the time of writing I am still trying to find out more about *Susan Constant.* I wonder if she might be *Little Spray* built by Cipriano Andrade Jr, for the timing is not that far out. Andrade's Spray was launched in 1920, and the information received by O'Donnell was that his boat was built in the early to mid 1930s. Perhaps the salesman wanted to make the boat appear younger, not an unusual occurrence when describing a wooden boat. One has to remember that as Spray enthusiasts, we tend to forget that not everyone appreciates the value of an *old* wooden boat!

Another letter from O'Donnell enclosed copies of some old photographs and some additional information. *Susan Constant* had been the supply ship to the *Ark* and *Dove* in Jamestown which I assume were much larger vessels. So there we have it. Could this boat be *Little Spray?* Perhaps someone will come up with the answer.

IGDRASIL
This Spray replica is very well known because of the extensive cruises made by the first owner. Roger S Strout built *Igdrasil* in Savannah, Georgia, in about 1933, and he and his wife sailed it around the world, starting in 1934 and completing the cruise in 1937.

This voyage included stopovers in the West Indies, and on through the Panama Canal, calling at Galapagos, the Marquesas, Tahiti, Samoa, Fiji and on to New Zealand. After leaving New Zealand, the Strouts sailed across the Tasman to Brisbane and then up northwards inside the Great Barrier Reef, through the Torres Straight and across the Indian Ocean to Durban. You may notice some similarity between parts of the route of *Igdrasil* and that taken by Joshua Slocum. The Strouts called at Christmas Island, the Cocos Keeling Islands and Rodriguez. After reaching Durban, the next part of the voyage was to sail around the Cape of Good Hope and on to St Helena and the Ascension Islands and then across the Atlantic to the US east coast, thus completing the circumnavigation.

After this the Strouts did not stay on for long, for in 1938 they sailed to Alaska and back, a cruise of 14 000 miles. This trip is a memorable voyage in itself, and they accomplished the 14 000 miles in only ten months. The trip to Alaska included stops in the West Indies, again through the Panama Canal across the Pacific to Hawaii, and on to Alaska. The return trip was mostly along the west coast and back through the Panama Canal.

Igdrasil was slightly wider than the original Spray, being 14ft 6in [4.42m] beam. Her draft was 5ft [1.52m], which is also a little deeper than the original. As we will see with some of the more recently built copies/replicas, small changes to the original seem to offer some improvements without adversely affecting the performance. Minor changes are especially beneficial in the draft; a small amount of extra keel area on the Spray offers a great improvement in the performance, especially in the windward ability. The following comments by Roger Strout appeared in an article in *Yachting*:

'When I determined to try the glare of the sun on dancing waves, instead of on chromium plate along our dusty highways, I was totally devoid of those rabid prejudices one usually encounters among yachtsmen in favour of their local designs, for I had never owned or sailed anything larger than a canoe. This does not imply ignorance of boats, for I had spent much of my life on the coast of Maine, and seen boats, talked boats, and felt on intimate terms with the smaller working types up to the six-masted schooners they once turned out in the nearby city of Bath, USA. With this background, I naturally approached ocean cruising with the idea of shrinking down a work-boat model to meet requirements, rather than strengthening up a yacht design. I began my plans about the time the present spurt of ocean racing was getting into full swing. I admired the costly flyers and respected their records, but I did not envy their owners. Crossing the Atlantic in two and a half weeks is nice, if you can move ashore for a rest afterwards, but that isn't cruising. I felt then, and three years' continuous cruising has strengthened my conviction, that although they are both great sports, ocean racing and ocean cruising have nothing in common except the ocean. Seaworthiness, comfort and carrying capacity are the standards by which an ocean cruiser must be judged. So the cruising man wants a small cargo boat design, polished up to look respectable under the yacht ensign. When considering such designs one cannot avoid the broad, round-nosed, comparatively shallow type that was the ancestor of Captain Slocum's Spray. It has great carrying capacity, may be beached almost anywhere, is comfortable in the extreme. Spray proved that her ability is not confined to Dutch canals. A study of the record shows that Spray was faster on long passages than any of the more modern boats. The general form is that of an eminently satisfactory craft and that is all that is wanted.'

In 1939 the *Igdrasil* was sold to D Grant and L Smith, who changed her name to *Tane*. Later she was resold and renamed *Faith,* and Newport Beach in California was her home.

In response to one of my notices in the boating press, I received a most interesting letter from a former yacht broker, C Rutherford of Kealakekua, Hawaii, who wrote:

'Perhaps one of the many Sprays wound up in my clutches at Berkeley Yacht Harbour, California, in 1939. I was a yacht salesman for broker Morris Dratt, and Mr and Mrs Roger Strout, owners of *Igdrasil* (the original owners I think), were aboard, and while we discussed some of their extensive cruises, I don't recall them all. I listed and sold the boat for their figure of $3500, then proceeded to outfit her for the new buyers for their projected world cruise. New sails, rigging, supplies ad finitum were added, not least of which was a series of Bon Voyage cocktail parties at the exclusive St Francis Yacht Club. Finally, the saga began and they sailed out of the Golden Gate, only to return because a turnbuckle had unwound. Again they sailed out, and the next report was from Newport Beach Harbour, California (only a few hundred miles down the coast), where *Igdrasil* was sold for a La Salle convertible and $600.

As an avid Star class sailor in 1937 I read most sea stories, including Slocum's "tacks on the deck at Tierra del Fuego". In April 1994 I will be 80, I have made the Los Angeles to Tahiti race, sailed a 27ft [8.2m] boat from LA to Honolulu in 35 days. Roger Strout wound up in the Naval Net Department at Tibu-son California as did I, WW2 anti sub warfare Pacific region.

THANE

Recently, Len Pearson of Victoria, British Columbia, in Canada informed me about his Spray replica called *Thane*. Len's boat is 39ft 6in [12m] on deck and 57ft [17.3m] overall, beam is 15ft 3in [4.6m] and the draft is 6ft 4in [1.9m]. She is planked with 2in [50mm] yellow cedar and the keel is 20in by 6in [508mm x 152mm] Douglas fir.

As far as Len can tell, *Thane* was built from the lines given in *Sailing Alone Around the World* and, as Len puts it, 'She was just prodded here and there. A bit wider in the beam, a little deeper in the hull, and the bow pulled out above the waterline, similar to the Roberts Sprays. The keel is extended down 1ft 6in [457mm], so she tracks well and does not slide sideways like some other shallow draft types I have seen.'

In 1975 Len found his Spray under an apple tree in 1975 at Saanwich near Victoria, British Columbia, where she had apparently lain for about ten years. The boat consisted of the hull, most of the deck, and part of the forward cabin. The hull was in a poor condition and

Len Pearson found his Spray replica, a neglected and abandoned project, near Victoria, BC. He painstakingly completed Thane *using quality materials retrieved from demolished houses. He now uses her for charter work around British Columbia.*

open to the elements, but worth saving. Len traded in a 1968 Chevy, and hauled his Spray off to Sidney, British Columbia. A succession of owners of this unfinished hull had left Len with considerable work in undoing much of the construction, and this needed to be done before work could proceed in earnest. Len recounts:

'I was 31, newly retired from my teaching job, and completely broke. I hoped I had not made a mistake. Fortunately, the building boom was resulting in beautiful old houses being demolished, so there was no shortage of cheap timber and scrap metal to be had. These were recycled into my boat. Some of the timber I recovered included fir, Australian jarrah, teak, Californian redwood, cedar, and even some yew. One can not even buy some of these beautiful species of timber now at any price, and to think that some of them ended up in landfills. Even my lignum vitae cleats and deadeyes are made from scrounged material.

The rudder that I designed has some balance, and was built from 1/2 in [12mm] steel plate. The boat will turn in its own length even when laid over at full speed. *Thane* will turn in a full circle in her own length, round and round; either way, she is wonderfully manoeuvrable, which is a great asset in crowded harbours. Under sail, she balances well under full rig, but needs some headsail for good control, mainly tacking. The squaresail yard is set from the deck using a single halyard, and the tack clews snap to bulls-eyes on the forward braces and slide up and down, takes a bit of practice, but works well. The sail shows well and pulls well and is used for running or on a quartering breeze. The main course is over 700sq ft [65sq m] and furls to the centre, vertically. *Thane* is a real picture with everything flying, including main, mizzen, staysail, a 600sq ft [55.7sq m] genoa plus the topsail and squaresail.'

Len is particularly pleased with the design of his davits. He says it has transformed the social aspect of the boat, and is a great place to put everything: crab traps, fenders and spare lines; it is also a very useful location for mounting Loran and GPS antennas. He keeps the propane bottle in the dinghy; this seems to keep the charter and insurance people happy. The boat is well equipped with radar, Wagner autopilot, VHF, cellular Loran, VCR, two television sets, and a great sound system. His home comforts also include a hot and cold pressure water system. Len continued:

'Somehow my ideas for KISS (Keep It Simple Stupid), the hemp and oil lamp mentality got misplaced. I like my toys, but still have the oil lamps etc, as a back-up. The layout is centre cockpit, with a double berth forward, two berths under the side decks, a large washroom and shower, and an amidship dinette and well-equipped galley. The galley equipment includes a primus stove, electric oven, and a microwave. Heating is supplied by a wood burner backed by an oil burning stove.

The aft cabin contains a double berth, plus there is adequate room for a freezer and a ton of storage. The engine room houses the 60 hp Ford diesel, two fuel tanks totalling 190 gal [863 lit] plus a 4 kw Yanmar generating set, a 2500 watt inverter and 120 amp charger. There is adequate room to store tools, table saw and diving gear.

The cockpit covers are like a convertible, vinyl side and back curtains make it comfortable in any weather, and we are still able to handle the sheets without stepping outside the cockpit.

We sail all year round here, but we are not dumb! In the winters I have flown to various locations looking for other Sprays, and have met Bob Carr of *Sirius* fame, found the *Oxford Spray* in San Francisco, and was aboard the *St Kilda Spray* in Australia in 1985.

Twenty years on, I am still sort of retired, and *Thane* enables me to make a comfortable living and provides me with a wonderful home. I use *Thane* for charter during the summer months; there is plenty of business with the beautiful Gulf Islands around Victoria providing ideal cruising grounds.'

STARBOUND

The plans that were drawn up by Victor Slocum and used to build the *Oxford Spray* were also utilised as the basis for another Spray copy. *Starbound* was an enlarged version measuring 62ft [18.9m] by 18ft 6in [5.6m] beam. Based on scaled-up lines from Victor Slocum's plans, *Starbound* was rigged as a ketch. In about 1957 this boat was sold to well-known folk singer Burl Ives and renamed *Black Spoonbill*. It seems from later writings in the 1981 Slocum Society journal, *The Spray*, that this boat may be again called *Starbound*.

MINNEAPOLIS SPRAY

This Spray was built in 1949 in Minneapolis, USA. It was reputably an exact replica of Slocum's boat and probably was built from the lines given in *Sailing Alone Around the World*. It seems as if this Spray was never finished off properly, but was sailed on the east coast of the USA down to Florida. The last report was that she was used as a fishing boat; not too ignominious an end for a descendant of the original Spray which served as a fishing boat before Slocum rebuilt her and sailed her into history.

MONK SPRAY

The late Edwin Monk, well-known naval architect of Seattle in Washington, designed a Spray replica and details of this design appeared in *Rudder*. The boat was designed for Karl A Shearer who wanted a family cruising vessel, and suggested to Monk that a modernised version of Spray might be suitable for his needs. This boat carried no outside ballast and the overall dimensions, including the draft, were similar to the original vessel.

Monk designed another version from the same plans but this time increased the draft to 5ft 4in [1.6m]; he believed that the second version would be superior because of the additional draft. This accords with our experience and, as stated elsewhere, we usually add a small amount of extra draft to any Spray design emanating from our office.

SIRIUS

This is another Spray replica inspired by reading Slocum's book. Bob W Carr built his Spray *Sirius* between 1950 and 1956, having read *Sailing Alone Around the World* in 1936 when he was on leave in the Panama Canal Zone. Like most people who pick up that book, he read it from cover to cover and right there and then decided to build a little ship of his own. The following was written by Gordon P Manning and appeared in *Motor Boating* magazine:

'The fabulous story of the original Spray enchanted this boy who had been born in Massachusetts, but brought up on the shores of the blue Pacific. It was rather appealing, and particularly to a young man who loved the sea, and who loved old fashioned sail the way Bob Carr did. "The idea came to me about a week later that I would like to build myself an exact copy of the Spray. I suppose it had been in the back of my mind ever since I had read about Joshua Slocum and his voyage. My dad was a good carpenter, and I knew a little about tools, as I'd been brought up on a farm, and you learn a little about everything there. Captain Slocum told about going into the woods for young oak saplings for his frames, and I wanted to do the same thing when I built my boat. We had plenty of oak trees on the place, so I knew that would be no problem."

Bob Carr touches up the paintwork on Sirius. *Inspired by reading* Sailing Alone Around the World *in 1936, he built his Spray replica in four years, crafting every part by hand. Photo courtesy of Peter Fromm.*

Because of the intervention of the Second World War, it was the summer of 1950 before the big project got under way. The difference between the construction of the Spray built by Bob Carr and the original, was that Bob worked alone and built his vessel by hand. I remember reading about Bob Carr going into the woods and literally felling the timber to build his boat, and then shaping all of the planks in the old-fashioned way. Hence it took four years to build *Sirius.* Bob made his own spars and hand-sewed two complete sets of sails out of heavy canvas. What a wonderful experience for someone willing to undertake all that work, and all by hand. Bob also hand-forged all of the ironwork for the rigging fittings; he then sailed the east coast of the USA, and the first two cruises down to South Carolina and back to Nova Scotia were solo voyages.

Not long ago, a letter arrived from Peter Fromm, a professional photographer currently living on Lopez Island, Washington State, USA: 'Enclosed is a copy of the cover of *Northwest Yachting Magazine,* which features a photograph I took of Bob Carr's *Sirius,* a hand-built wooden Spray replica. Bob Carr and *Sirius* are currently in Costa Rica and you may be able to get in touch with him through Stephanie and Keith Sternberg.' After a further exchange of letters with the Sternbergs and Peter Fromm, there arrived a set of photographs and the information that *Sirius* had been run down by a freighter. Although the boat suffered some damage, Bob Carr and *Sirius* are still around to sail another day.

Peter Kittel of *Tehani* wrote to the Slocum Society on behalf of Bob Carr:

'On 20 September 1993 at 6.30 am in bright daylight, *Sirius* was in international waters off Punta Burica, Costa Rica/Panama. The engineless *Sirius* was in a trough when she was hit by a freighter. Fortunately, it was more or less a glancing blow. Unfortunately, *Sirius* was dismasted, losing both the main and mizzen and her bulwarks were stove in. The ship took off after the collision, turning this incident into a hit and run.'

Bob, in all the excitement, managed to read the name *Ocean Gold* and what seemed to be part of the home port, even though it was on the bow: *Bougai...* possibly *Bougainville*. Bob, 78, was alone on the boat and it took him 14 days to be found and given a tow into Puntarenas where he notified the Canadian Embassy. At this time, he is pursuing the matter through international sea law; meanwhile, *Sirius* is being repaired and made ready for her next cruise.

SUCCESS II
The hull for this Spray was built in Cowes, Isle of Wight, UK, by David Cheverton and Partners for Captain J Cappelen Jr of Williamsberg, Virginia. The construction was started in 1958 and included 1in [25mm] mahogany planking. The completed hull was shipped to Williamsberg, where the owner fitted out the boat himself.

SOJOURNER
This Spray replica was built using the Victor Slocum plans by master shipwright John E Gamage of Rockland, Maine. *The Maine Coast Fisherman* carried the following information on the construction of this boat:

'John E Gamage of this seacoast town has probably built more wooden ship tonnage than any other man living today (well over 100 000 tons by his own estimate), but the chances are that the 44ft [13.4m] vessel now being framed in the Snow Boat Yard here will bring this master builder more satisfaction, foot for foot, than anything he's tackled in his long career. Sixty-five years ago, when Captain Joshua Slocum made his famous solo sailing trip around the world, he started something. More accurately, his little wooden vessel did. When the Captain stated in his book, *Sailing Alone Around the World,* that in the course of a 23-day 2 700-mile journey he found it necessary to stay at the wheel but one hour, it was inevitable that sailing men all over the globe would look to the lines of his yawl, Spray. That is, if what they wanted was a seaworthy little craft that needed little tending.'

John Gamage had quit the boatbuilding trade and was selling insurance when a man approached him requesting a copy of Spray. He figured I was the man who could build the way he wanted her built. Apparently the client was planning to retire from the army and he and his wife wanted to see the world, so he wanted a vessel built in the old-fashioned way, solid strong, and with no skimping on time and materials.

Sadly John Gamage's client, Captain Brunn, died of leukaemia before he could realise his dream of sailing round the world. Hence *Soujourner* was purchased by Richard Nakashian, who completed the fitting out and ran charter parties around Boston. This Spray replica was licensed to carry 49 passengers and a crew of four, another indication of the Spray's carrying power.

BANGKOK SPRAY
In the book *Macpherson's Voyages* the author A G H Macpherson mentions meeting a copy of the Spray near the Spice Islands in 1938. It is believed that a Swiss national commissioned the building of this vessel and that the lines from *Sailing Alone Around the World* were used to build it.

HARAMBEE

One of the many responses I received from notices that appeared in the boating magazines worldwide came from Carol Munro of the Troon Marina, who wrote:

'In the winter of 1992-93, a Danish couple came to our marina and stayed for nearly a year aboard their Spray replica. Peter Jensen is a boatbuilder by trade, and built the vessel around his piano! They still live aboard, but are now back in Denmark with their new daughter Fiona. While they were here, Peter did some beautiful restoration work on a neighbouring vessel, and they made many friends in Scotland.'

Unfortunately, Carol Munro was not able to give me a current address for Peter Jensen; however, as in many instances, luck took a hand and I received the following communication accompanied by a set of photographs:

'With great interest I read of your search for Spray replica owners in the Danish Yachting magazine *Bad Nyt*. I enclose my contribution. My intentions were to build a boat comfort-

Outwardly, Harambee *is a traditional Spray replica, but below decks it is spaciously designed as a family liveaboard. Built and sailed by Danish boatbuilder Peter Bauder Jensen.*

able enough to live on as a home, and with reasonable sailing abilities. When I started looking around for a boat to suit my needs, I accidentally discovered that a replica of the original Spray, *Spray II,* had been built in the small village of Arosund in southern Denmark. I contacted the owner, Bjarne Baagoe Beck, and after spending a few weekends and a summer holiday sailing on this beautiful vessel, I was certain that the Spray would suit my demands for room, comfort and nostalgia.'

Peter started construction in January 1983, and used the following timber to build the hull. Planking is oak on sawn frames, the deck beams are oak, the bulwarks are larch on oak stanchions, and the deck is teak laid over plywood. The cabin sides and framing, as well as the rudder post and rudder, are oak, and the cabin tops are larch; the spars are spruce.

Peter's deck layout was different from the original Spray, and it has been altered even more since his boat was launched. When first built, *Harambee* had a small trunk cabin aft that served as an engine room, navigation area and a workshop. This was a very cosy and functional little cabin. As Peter said, 'Due to all the technical installations, it provided a considerable number of excuses when the skipper needed some peace and quiet.' A 100 gal [454 lit] fuel tank was placed under the deck between the aft and main cabin.

The aft and main cabins were separated by a watertight bulkhead, and on deck there was a 3ft [914mm] passage between the two structures. The boat is so big that there was room for a large horseshoe shaped galley, and Peter was lucky enough to find a large paraffin stove with a sizeable oven. When living aboard on the longer passages, Peter says that he finds the galley functions of great importance. He said 'also in the main cabin are two single bunks and a double bunk, and a big table, and as it is our home I included a piano!'

The steering is the same as Spray, a simple and very functional system with the advantage of always being able to see the rudder position. Peter rigged *Harambee* in the same way as Spray, with the addition of a topmast; the topsail is very useful and he uses it whenever conditions permit. The launching took place in the port of Skovshoved north of Copenhagen, on 20 June 1987. During the spring of 1988, Peter made and fitted the rigging, and in June of the same year the sails were set for the first time and Peter made a maiden voyage around Danish waters. Peter said:

'Almost every part of the boat has been altered since I first launched her, nothing can change things like a woman! So after I married, the alterations began. During the building I had short-sightedly only thought about the interior from the bachelor point of view. The alterations started when I built a small fore cabin in which was installed a double bunk and a large skylight to give the cosy cabin a feeling of spaciousness.'

After a few seasons of sailing, Peter decided to make some alterations to the rigging. Having the mizzen so far aft (as per the original Spray) he found very inconvenient so he moved this sail forward enough to convert the vessel to a ketch; this moved the centre of effort forward, and improved the balance as well as the sail handling. Now the mizzen is much more accessible and is used in much stronger wind conditions; and, as with most ketch-rigged boats, Peter has found that the mizzen and jib are a good combination when it really blows up. Another change is the addition of a spar on the masts on which to set a square sail. These small square sails are quite common on traditional boats in Denmark. Peter continued:

'The self-steering qualities are great. In the beginning I could only make her steer herself when going to windward, but now after having gained some experience I find she can steer herself on any course. This is a wonderful ability, and one of our typical self-steering passages was from Orkney to the Shetland Islands in the summer of 1992 when we covered 70 miles in 11 hours, averaging 6.36 knots and holding her course all the way with a fresh south-easterly breeze. When sailing the boat single-handed I would sit on the main cabin hatch, keeping an eye on the kettle as well as lookout, and simply steer by adjusting the mizzen sheet.

The addition of a wife brings children, so now the crew has increased to four and we still live on board. Our youngest, Fiona, will soon require more space, so the "bachelor suite" (the aft cabin) has been replaced by a wheelhouse. The aft deck was lifted 16in [406mm] in order to gain extra space, and between the dinghy davits I have built a small platform which, in all modesty, I call the "helicopter deck". Sitting here, I have a good view over the wheelhouse.

During the past few seasons we have cruised extensively around Europe, visiting Scotland, Ireland and nearby areas. During this fall and winter, the galley will be moved to the wheelhouse and additional toilet and showering facilities will be added.'

EHU KAI

Judging from the photograph shown in the 1990 Slocum Society magazine, *The Spray*, it is evident that *Ehu Kai* is a traditional Spray replica. The photograph reveals that the builders, Lee and Derrick Griffin, did a fine construction job; the vessel is pictured under sail on Bellingham Bay, Washington State, USA.

JOANNA

This Spray was built in Australia on the lines of Pete Culler's *Oxford Spray*, which in turn are the lines prepared by Victor Slocum from *Sailing Alone Around the World*. Rick and Gaynor Stillman commented:

'I gather you are writing about the captain. We have owned *Joanna* for seven years, and she is currently moored outside our home on Karragarra Island opposite Lamb Island (these islands are in Morton Bay, near Brisbane, Queensland). She has a carvel planked hull built over many years, and may be of interest to you. The lines are those of the *Oxford Spray*'s which of course is the boat built by Pete Culler from the lines prepared by Joshua Slocum's son, Victor.'

Joanna was launched in Brisbane at Gilbert's slip in Doboy Creek, Brisbane, in 1984. She was built by John Brown, who dedicated 17 years of his life to building his dream ship. He enlisted the help of the late Les 'Tiny' Thomas, who is a legend in the local history of building heavy-timbered workboats. No expense was spared in her construction. She is massively built of 1¹/₂in [38mm] spotted gum above and below the waterline, the frames are also spotted gum triple laminates 4in [100mm] wide and 3in [75mm] thick at 9in [228mm] centres, copper clenched and silicon bronze screw fastenings throughout.

The deck beams are 6in x 6in [150mm x 150mm], and the deck planking is 1¹/₂in [38mm] Queensland beech over bituminastic on ³/₄in [20mm] marine plywood over internal deck head in tongue and groove. The floor timbers are massive and grown timbers have been used, as are the knees which are also from grown timbers. The engine is a three-cylinder Lister JP3, approximately 1948 vintage; and apparently she runs as sweet as the day she was made. The cooling is by raw sea water and requires only minimal maintenance. The engine turns a 24 inch three-bladed prop with a two to one reduction giving a shaft speed of 600 rpm and an average cruising speed of 5 knots in all but the heaviest of weather.

Joanna is rigged as a topsail yawl, mainmast is laminated oregon 44ft [13.41m] and 16in [400mm] diameter at the base. The topmast stands from the crosstrees and is 18ft [5.49m] overall. The jigger mast is also gaff rigged and the Stillmans use wooden hoops on both masts, which they find quite satisfactory. The sails are heavy and dark tan in colour. They have tried to keep her as traditional as possible, the only plastic aboard is the toilet seat! They said:

'She sails well and is stiff and has a soft easy motion; she will self-steer providing the wind is

This beautiful Spray replica Joanna *was built on the lines of* Peter Culler's *Oxford Spray.* Joanna *is now owned by Rick and Gaynor Stillman who lived aboard her for four years.*

reasonably constant in strength. We came by *Joanna* in 1987, when we spotted her in a marina and immediately fell in love with her. As we had just bought another boat and were in the middle of a major refit, the timing could not have been worse.

So enchanted were we with *Joanna* that we sold our house and were soon living aboard the other 40ft [12.2m] boat alongside. Much energy went into finishing this other boat, which we subsequently sold, and in refitting *Joanna.* Gaynor and I lived aboard for four years and had some very enjoyable cruising up this coastline. As mentioned earlier, she is now moored in front of our home.'

On reading the various accounts of the building, cruising and joy of owning a Spray replica, one is struck by the warmth of feeling that all of these people have for their boats. As a designer, and after having contact with all types of boats and boating people for over thirty years, I know of no other design that has given so much pleasure to so many people.

Joshua, *this 1975 ferro-cement Spray replica has been cruised extensively by her owner Gene Zace.*

JOSHUA
Mr Gene Zace reports:

'I am a Spray replica owner. My vessel was built in Hilo, Hawaii, and launched in 1975. She is constructed of ferro-cement and sailed to the west coast of the USA, then down through the Panama Canal, and then to the west coast of Florida. I purchased her in February 1984, moved on board in June 1985 and have lived on board continuously until the present. I have cruised the Caribbean, mostly the Bahamas, but have also cruised Jamaica, the Caymans and Mexico's Yucatan.

The vessel was called *La Roche* when I purchased her from the owner and builder Charles Bullard. I changed her name to *Joshua*, what else? *Joshua* is traditionally rigged with gaff, block and tackle. I have to admire old Joshua Slocum for sailing Spray around the world with that rig. When I get under way I call it my "Jane Fonda" workout. I have seen many replicas of Sprays constructed on your plans. The hulls all looked like Spray, but it all seems to stop there. Everyone goes modern design after that, not that I blame them. *Joshua* has been my home, job and hobby for almost ten years. I have countless tons of tools, spare parts and junk on board, and it seems that the more weight I add, the better she sails.'

LA BRUJA

This Spray replica was built by Ron Attwater, and from all reports looks like the true workboat that the original Spray once was. Built using very traditional methods, the only information we have of this vessel is as mentioned by George Maynard, owner/builder of the Spray replica *Scud*.

SCUD

In 1976, when our design office was situated in Newport Beach, California, a customer sent us two photographs of a Spray replica that has the appearance of the original Spray, though a bit of detective work has established that this was a photo of *Scud*. *South African Yachting* editor Neil Rusch has said that of all of the replicas he's seen, *Scud* is the most authentic. This is an extract from an article that he wrote:

'Joshua Slocum and his 9 ton yawl, *Spray*, sailed into the Royal Cape Yacht Basin late one afternoon last month...convincingly assured that this was for real, even though it was Tuesday, 24 January 1978, and 81 years had drifted by since the worthy sea captain from Boston performed the first solo circumnavigation. I simply had to check the truth of this statement. So late in the evening, midnight to be exact, I found myself tentatively walking in the late night fog that enshrouded *Spray*, very much alive and tugging at her mooring lines. Reluctant to shatter the dream I hesitated, savouring this late night vision before just reaching out to...touch her. Substantiating what logic discredits, but the senses force one to believe, were the oaken water casks, kerosene navigation lights, the old chimney stack hinting at the antique wood-burning stove below and anchor capstan which surely had to be the old crab as Slocum calls it. Visually probing everything aboard, I expected to see Slocum appear in the companionway and, in some strange way, I felt like the Feugian Indians secretively, cautiously picking my way closer to plunder the sanctity of the old ship. By some preconceived notion brought about by this time muddle, or could it very possibly just have been the time of night, I kept looking for carpet tacks on the deck...reality suddenly came when a yellow and white Azorian cattle dog, just as fierce as the sound of his credentials, stuck his head out above the cockpit coaming and barked in my face. Just as effective as any carpet tacks at repelling boarders. The skipper was roused from the stern cabin, and finally showed in the wane light that it was not Joshua Slocum. The name on the beaming bow was *Scud* not *Spray*.'

Rusch goes on to outline the conversation he had the following night in the paraffin light of *Scud*'s cabin, when skipper George Maynard related the story of *Scud*:

"We laid the keel in May 1971 and progressed to framing up in native white oak, which was planked over with pine from the eastern shore of Maryland USA. Fittings I forged myself because we were working on a total cost of $3500." The narrative by George Maynard describes how he made his decision to build a Spray replica and then he goes on to say, "in 1965 I started a wood carving business, but before that I worked in boatyards absorbing the generations of local maritime knowledge that abounds in the little village of Noank. Then in 1970 I discovered that Slocum's Spray had once been owned in Noank." [George proceeded

George Maynard's Scud *coasting among the South Pacific islands. Neil Rusch, editor of* South African Yachting, *who provided me with the photograph, has said that of all the Spray replicas he has seen,* Scud *is one of the most authentic with fascinating detail, such as oak water casks, kerosene navigation lights and an antique wood-burning stove. Photo by by Victoria Carkhuff.*

to convince Rusch by reading from a well-worn paperback of *Sailing Alone Around the World*:] "The Spray as I sailed her was entirely a new boat built over from a sloop that had the same name, and that, tradition said, had first served as an oysterman, about one hundred years ago, on the coast of Delaware. There was no record in the custom house of where she was built. She was once owned at Noank, Connecticut, afterwards at New Bedford, and when Captain Eben Pierce presented her to me at the end of her natural life, she stood as I have already described, propped up in a field at Fairhaven. Her lines were supposed to be those of a North Sea Fisherman. In rebuilding timber by timber and plank by plank." George closed the book reverently, trying to preserve the thumbed pages and the tattered cover that was on the verge of falling apart.

"So that's how it was," George continued, "we were right there where Spray once sailed. Actually, in their hey-day there were sixty of these craft sailing out from the east coast to fish the Grand Banks. Soon after the discovery (of Spray having sailed in the area), I met Ron Atwater and *La Bruja.* She is a Spray, but rough, real rough. Her manner of construction imported this ruggedness to her lines. She was not ugly, in fact, it gave her a character of her own. After all, these were workboats.The thing about building in wood is that it's a living material. Take *La Bruja* and *Scud,* both are built to the Spray design, yet the two boats could not be more different. Wooden boatbuilding is an art, and it's a craft, and if you stretch a point, you can say it's a science, what with seasoning and forestry theory.

So with the discovery that Slocum rebuilt Spray just 50 miles from Noank, and the inspiration of *La Bruja,* which in Spanish means the witch, Mary and I swopped roles. She worked as a day reporter on the *New London Day* while I went full at it for the next two years working on building *Scud.* The first obstacle was to overcome the unavailability of suitable plans. I had to translate and expand on the lines given in Slocum's book. Other details I gleaned from photographs I was fortunate to get from the Maritime Museum at Mystic. Board widths, size of blocks, the way the railings were secured, and innumerable other important details like the curve of the stern loop, for instance, all of this was found in the photographs. I also relied on the opinion of other builders: Major William Smyth, Captain Jack Wilbur and Fred Cousins. All this accumulated knowledge and information came together in *Scud* as she is today. Originally, as I mentioned, we planned on a total figure of $3500. So to keep the cost down, we bought the timber 'in the log' at a North Stongington sawmill. I worked with George Miner, the mill owner, choosing curved logs to use for the curved deck beams, and enough straight timber for frames, stem, sternpost, rudder post and other structural members. We cut the logs to required thickness at the mill, and these we then carted to our yard as flitch boards, that is, with the bark on. Although it was time-consuming to lay out, saw and plane each board and plank, the process allowed me to use every scrap of timber."'

George saw that Rusch was taking particular notice of the stove, so proceeded to enlighten him.

'You'll go a long way to find one of them. They are particularly handy in keeping the cabin warm when it's cold and wet up top. These you will find in just about any Nova Scotia fisherman. Ours we got from Canada. In fact, much of our stuff was contributed by other vessels, a large portlight from the Latvian refugee ship *Grundel,* the bilge pump from the 106-year-old Noank sloop *Emma C Berry,* the wheel from Captain Ellery Thompson's dragger *Eleanor,* a spar from the old Noank catboat *Sweetheart,* a lugsail from the lifeboat of the steamer *Exemplar,* a flag from the South African ketch *Sandefjord.'*

The cost, even with these contributions, ended up at around $7000, which was twice as much as George had originally bargained for, but much cheaper than most boats around today. Many people have criticised the Spray design, and even accused Slocum of exaggeration. But George had this to say:

'Slocum tells us so much implicitly, and one can glean so much from what he said. Take, for instance, his description of her self-steering ability. It's exactly as he says. But you have to have the boat under you to really understand. Hey...she just may be around still when other boats have long gone to rest. In his book, Slocum wrote the dedication: "To the one who said: The Spray will come back." She's done just that.'

A letter from Harry Sherman of Newport, Rhode Island, USA reveals that a Spray replica which he believes to be *Scud* was sold to his friend Guy Beradin and his wife Mitzi and that the boat is now in France.

KOKKEN

All we know about this Spray is that it was built in Norway and visited the port of Dover in the UK in 1991. Looking at the photographs of it, it is apparent that this round bilge hull is probably built of timber or perhaps glassfibre. The photographs also reveal a very traditional interior, with that warm look that can only be achieved in a real 'live-aboard' boat. The registered number carved into the main beam is LK3395.

The Norwegian-built Spray Kokken *visited Dover in 1991.*

SPRAY II

Bjarne Baagoe Beck and his wife Haderslev now sail this beautiful Spray replica, which was built by Bjarne's father in 1976. Bjarne gave me the following details:

'I write to you because I am the proud owner of a copy of Spray. My boat was built in Arosund in Denmark in 1976 by my parents. The hull was set up by ship's carpenter Johannes Heeboll, and the rest of the work was undertaken by my parents, mostly by my father, Kai Baagoe Beck, an electrician.

Spray II was built as far as possible as an exact copy of the original Spray. The hull is made of Danish oak, on grown oak timbers. My Spray is equipped with a 22 hp diesel engine, placed in the hull between the two deckhouses.

We obtained the drawings from Kenneth Slack; he was living on Hawaii in the early 1970s. We used copies of the original drawings, which were taken in 1904 after Joshua Slocum's first voyage around the world. My wife and I, and now our two children, took over the boat in 1988 and we are still sailing her as a pleasure boat.

I know about some other Spray copies, one built in Denmark in 1987 by a friend of mine, Peter Bauder; and another also built here in the late 1970s by another friend of mine, this one built in ferro-cement. Another Spray built of steel, called *Lu Lu,* is now sailing around somewhere in the world. I am 31 years old, a qualified ship master, now sailing as Mate in a Danish rescue and fisheries control vessel. I also have been sailing as Chief Mate on the training ship *Danamark,* which is a full-rigged sailing ship.'

BISHOP SPRAY

This replica of Slocum's Spray is being built using traditional timber boatbuilding techniques by the students at the International Boat Building Training College at Oulton Broad, Lowestoft, in England, and work is well under way on the replica. This vessel was commissioned by Andrew Bishop of Epic Ventures in

A Spray replica being built by students at the International Boat Building Training College at Lowestoft, England. This Spray was commissioned by Andrew Bishop, Secretary of the Slocum Spray Society. Photo courtesy of the Eastern Daily Press.

Wimbledon. Many of the techniques being used to build this modern counterpart would be familiar to an eighteenth-century sailor. Modern design dictates an engine and some ballast in the keel, but the skill with which the students are fashioning the iroko, oak and mahogany into shape would make Slocum feel at home.

The above information appeared in the *Eastern Daily Press.* I have since been in touch with Andrew, who told me that he intends to fit out the interior in a functional manner but with modern equipment.

As we know, Slocum's Spray relied on internal ballast that sometimes was cargo, and at other times was various items that Slocum picked up along the way. In the case of this Spray, $1^1/_2$ tons of lead external ballast will be fitted into the keel. The keel has been deepened by 6in [150mm].

Andrew is interested in meeting up with other Sprays and, as not everyone will have the time and opportunity to circumnavigate the world hopes that rallies can be arranged at one or more ports where Slocum called during his voyage, maybe Gibraltar or the Azores. Andrew Bishop has now accepted the post of Secretary of the newly formed Slocum Society (Europe).

NICHOLYAVICH SPRAY

Another timber Spray replica is being built with the same plans as were once used in Pete Culler's *Oxford Spray,* by Nicolas Nicholyavich of Olympia, Washington State, USA. Nicolas wrote to say that he was building a copy from Pete Culler's plans and the vessel will draw 5ft [1.5m]. He goes on to list the exact construction of his Spray and mentions that outside ballast will be bolted to the keel. The hull is planked using the strip plank method, incorporating the convex/concave method we have often recommended for builders of this type of vessel.

The boat's name is carved right into the apron of the stem. Nicolas said:
'For the time being I must concentrate on making a living and finishing the project. Some call

it a dream, but they are in error; it is only a dream until you start to loft; from then on it becomes a project. Dreams are just an idea waiting to happen. A project is a job waiting to be finished.'

HENDRIKJE VISSER

When the information about *Scud* arrived from *South African Yachting,* details of another Spray-type-yacht were also included. John Van der Linden reported:

'Like so many readers of yachting magazines all over the world, I too curled myself up in my favourite chair and stared glassy-eyed at pictures of bow-spritted gaffers sailing into the sunset from palm-fronded shores. As I read more and more, and eventually met several people who had built their own yachts, it dawned on me that there were two ways in which to make the dream come true. It was either get rich and buy a yacht or knuckle down and build one myself.

Steel would be the medium and a shallow keel would allow us to cruise the inland waterways and get to out-of-the-way places. Our choice of the gaff rig was met with the experts saying, "A gaffer, you need your head read! No way. Gaff won't get you to windward and it will take ages to cross an ocean." The first expenditure of the partnership to build the steel gaff ketch *Hendrikje Visser* was for drawing up a valid partnership contract, something that in my opinion is a must if a partnership is to last and to weather the inevitable trivial squabbles that have sunk many a boating venture.'

Their first material purchase was the entire stock of single and double blocks, held in the bins of a local chandler, which today, after nine years, has proved to be an excellent investment. Not being able to afford yacht shop prices, they set out to scrounge whatever there was available as long as the quality was good. Stainless steel fittings, brass screws, teak, epoxy glues, marine ply, oregon pine for masts and polycarbonate windows were only some of the materials for which they would accept no inferior substitute.

With this in mind, they made a list of all materials and items they were likely to need and put the word out to family and friends to be on the alert for bargains. Old floor-boards being removed at John's work-place, to accommodate computer lines, were donated to him, providing he dug them out from under the pile of rubble in the basement. His colleagues thought him mad, until he later explained that the boards were white English oak, with which the yacht's interior has now been panelled. Although a request to buy an old railway carriage for its teak content did not come off, John heard that Irvin and Johnson were to scuttle some old trawlers and this resulted in him purchasing several sheets of marine ply.

Despite the old adage that the wind is free, John felt that an engine was a must. John's brother-in-law told him of a 70 hp Ford diesel and a Capitol gearbox which had been traded in and, after talking to his brother-in-law's manager, John picked them up for the proverbial song. They got the company's outdated professional marinising kit for next to nothing, and several spare parts such as clutch plates and oil coolers were thrown in free of charge.

Their objective was to pre-blast and prime all the metal before welding. They had repaired an old scrapped compressor, and by using a small hand-blasting apparatus they would be able to blast the welded areas. The way in which they did this with relative ease was to allow all welds to rust for a week before sandblasting them centimetre by centimetre. With the frames in position, the shape of the hull soon took shape and plating was the next step.

John and his colleagues had read widely on the subject of building in steel but found themselves being forced to use the cutting torch to cut the plates to the correct shapes. However once again, lady luck, in the form of a family friend, came to the rescue. Looking over their impoverished boatyard, the friend asked why they did not use a nibbler or guillotine to cut the plates, which would not shrink the edges. When told that they did not have the money to hire one, he offered to loan them a guillotine that was just standing idle in his workshop. Once the plate was ready, it was tacked into place until the whole hull was covered. After marking the plates, they took them all down; and using a borrowed truck they drove them to Frits's workshop where they had them all sandblasted and covered with a vinyl primer.

After this, it was back to the boat again where the whole process of tacking was done again before welding, using the back step method to eliminate distortion.The plating still distorted slightly, but a colleague of Frits, Jo Hakemuller, a retired boilermaker with wrists like thighs, did wonders with a cutting torch, small hammer, a pail of cold water and a dirty rag. He also devised a special press with which they were finally able to set right the stainless steel capping on the sheerline before they covered it with afrormosia. The afrormosia, or Afro-teak, in itself has a nice story behind it, as Frits managed to purchase a whole stack of planks from a veneer manufacturer who sold the wood (the section left in the clamps after veneer was cut from both sides) for a nominal fee.

All the time, their friends came up with suggestions of bargains. One of these was a marine toilet that was inside a derelict ski boat. The owner wanted R80 for it, but when they discovered that the local watchman and his buddies had used it until it was to the brim, they offered him R45 for the loo as well as a fuel lift pump and two bronze cleats, an offer that he immediately accepted as long as they cleaned the bowl themselves.

At John's work-place, several old desks had been offered for sale, and although they were rather worn and bulky he managed to buy two very reasonably. Being over 40 years old, they were solid teak, and one of the tops, slightly smaller and well sanded with several cigarette-burn marks and the odd word or two still showing, for character's sake, became their saloon table. Sails were also needed, and their finances soon allowed them to purchase them from Lam sail-makers in Hong Kong.

Agenda Yacht Services in Durban arranged the sale for them, and five sails, yankee, staysail, main, mizzen and storm sail (tan to keep the traditional look), a repair kit and set of signal flags spirited another chunk out of their kitty. An almost 4ft 11in [1.5m] tall stainless steel tank, destined for the rubbish heap, was spotted by John as it was wheeled out of a doorway and a promise to take the 'bloody rust heap' off the owner's hands made him the new owner. The rust turned out to be photographic chemicals that came off with elbow grease, Vim and Brillo pad. It now serves as a rather spacious deepfreeze cabinet. A former school friend of John's, in charge of an Argon arc welding plant, cut and welded it to the right size for old times' sake.

John and his colleagues decided to create a stunning taffrail and pin-rail in turned wood.

For this, they used the afrormosia, and made use of John's father's life-long desire to own his own lathe. The lathe was bought from the Brackenfell Hyperama, and after designing and turning a few examples of deadeyes, belaying pins, teak rings for portholes and dorado vents, as well as taffrail and pin-rail stanchions and parrel beads, they presented the lathe to Van Der Linden senior, who took to wood turning like a duck to water.

With the hull the right way up and with only the top chine to be welded in place, their master-piece was inspected by an engineer friend of Frits, who wanted to know what they would be using for ballast. 'Steel because it is cheaper,' they said. 'Oh,' he said, 'would it be a lot?' 'No, only 4 tons [4064kg] or so,' they replied, and before we could continue he offered them some of the punchings from chasses that his company were manufacturing, as long as they picked them up.

Cheap it certainly was, for the owner of the truck even declined the petrol money they offered. The thick mild steel discs they welded into cylinders of equal weight, and after carefully weighing them they were placed into the keel where John and his friends poured half a ton of lead between them for good measure. The bottom of the keel was of solid $^3/_4$in [18mm] steel plate, which meant that the heat would not even blister the paint-work, saving yet another bit of labour.

Throughout the building years John and his friends were supported by their wives, who were often on board to approve any new ideas or changes. The galley was theirs and both Annette and Henke were often on board standing against mock-ups of galley and stove to get the heights and reaches just right. Henke also fed John and his friends each weekend, keeping everybody's strength and spirits up.The wives were also involved in all the uphol-stery choices, and, after getting their hands on a special offer of expensive but limited imported pure wool material, John's worries were over.

DAVIS SPRAY

I learned of this Spray replica built by Edwin Davis through Donn Slocum. After my initial contact with Edwin, the following information was supplied, with photographs of the boat:

'Here is a brief summary of the building and sailing of *Spray,* my replica of Slocum's boat. Her home port is on the Maine coast, although she covers most of New England for that purpose. I launched *Spray* on the Maine coast in 1982 after four years of construction. The hull was built exactly to the lines given in *Sailing Alone Around the World.* I built the entire vessel of wood, using the same traditional plank on frame type of construction as was used in the original. Almost all of the timber used in the construction came from my own woodlot. I shaped the keel with the ancient broad axe and adze. With the help of a chain saw, I made parts of the vessel in the forest where the trees were cut down. This is not only very economical, but also gave me the personal experience of knowing my future boat as living trees. Each piece of wood was chosen for certain characteristics that would make a strong and long-lasting vessel. The spars were from black and red spruce, the knightheads and rudder of locust, the decks were made of white cedar. Nearly all the planking is hackmatack (larch).'

Edwin Davis used a coal forge to make the hardware and other fittings. Like Slocum's original ves-

A faithful Spray copy, built entirely of wood using the traditional plank on frame construction by Edwin Davis of Massachusetts, USA. Edwin used timber from his own woodlot and a coal forge to make authentic fittings.

sel, very few parts came from the marine supply store, which means that replacements can also be made anywhere in the world. As completion drew near and it was obvious that Edwin was going to complete the project, many old timers appeared on the scene with bits of nineteenth-century hardware and beautiful wooden blocks to donate to his Spray. After caulking the boat with cotton and oakum and a final painting, Edwin launched his vessel from the field where he built her and used a handmade log railway that was greased for the occasion.

The Spray has been a very successful vessel for Edwin. He has braved the North Atlantic in the winter and put her to the test; and in the thousands of ocean miles that he has sailed since the launching, he has found his Spray to be the most comfortable vessel he has ever sailed.

Edwin lived on her for seven years as his only home. Sometimes he lived in the tropics, and at other times he faced a few New England winters, with ice around the hull. In every case, his Spray's thick wooden hull provided him with a comfortable home. He can carry enough water and supplies for a three-month voyage, including a half-ton of coal, and have it barely show on the boat's waterline. This is quite remarkable for a boat of this size.

When he launched her, Edwin rigged the vessel with the sail plan that Slocum had drawn. However, after several years of using this rig, he found it to be heavy and not entirely handy. Edwin noted that Slocum had changed Spray's rig three times: first to a sloop, then a gaff yawl, and finally to a marconi with a Bahamian-type sail. In that spirit Edwin decided to make a major change and convert my Spray to a schooner. He was very concerned that he might lose her magical self-steering that he had come to enjoy, so he saved the old rig. However, Edwin says that he will never go back to it. His Spray makes not only a very handy schooner, but a schooner that self-steers on all points of sail.

Edwin's Spray is now 12 years old, and he recently finished a six-month voyage from Maine to the Caribbean by way of Bermuda. On the way back he took advantage of his boat's shoal draft to explore the Bahamian islands. As to the future? Just more of the same fun cruising on his Spray, he says.

DULCINEA

Another Spray replica that came to light through the Slocum Society journal is *Dulcinea,* which was built by Slocum Society member Peter da Silva; he launched his 42ft [12.8m] hull in 1990. Peter, who is a railway engine driver by profession, fell in love with the lines of the Spray when he read Kenneth Slack's book, and decided to build his own Spray in his spare time. From the photographs of his vessel, it appears that this is either a glassfibre or ferro-cement version of the Bruce Roberts-designed Spray *Variant.* The yacht was built in the back-yard of Peter's house on the banks of the George's River, which runs through suburban Sydney. The fitting out was made easier for him as he had access to some beautiful old cedar timber from railway carriages. Needless to say, his ballast is made up of old railway line.

DOUBLE CROW

Recently a photograph and a short description of a newly launched Spray replica appeared in the magazine *Wooden Boat.* After contacting the magazine I was put in touch with Frederik B Lawrence of Victoria County, Nova Scotia, Canada, who supplied me with the following information about his Spray replica:

'Enclosed are some photos of *Double Crow.* My family and I live in a small fishing village at Bay St Lawrence, on the northern tip of Cape Breton Island. My wife Margrit and I are commercial fishermen. Our building project started in 1985 when after much thought about vessel design we settled for a Spray because she was a wholesome blue water design, time tested, heavy displacement with big blocks and lines etc, essentially ship-like versus yacht-like. As a commercial fisherman I was also attracted by her fish boat ancestry and her shoal draft allows entry into most harbours.

The plans for my boat came from Pete Culler via Victor Slocum. The hull was constructed professionally by Cheticamp boatbuilders and myself as a member of the building crew. *Double Crow* is heavily framed and planked similar to the original Spray; however she is silicone bronze fastened and this was one of my few concessions to modern

A recently completed Spray replica (1993) afloat at Bay St Lawrence, Nova Scotia, Canada. Double Crow *was built from plans by Peter Culler and is owned by a commercial fishing partnership, Margrit and Frederik Lawrence of Nova Scotia.*

materials. Also of interest is that much of the hardware is from the ex vessel *Typhoon* which was constructed by Alexander Graham Bell at his shop for his chief pilot Casey Baldwin. I chose the original fisherman mainsail sloop rig which I believe you will see few of now.

Launching was on 1 August 1993, christened with champagne and witnessed by hundreds. Sea trials were conducted shortly afterwards and to my amazement everything worked perfectly, halyards, sheets, leads, sails, engine hull tight, all fine. She tacks neatly, lies hove to very comfortably, ghosts along well in light airs and loves 25 knots with full sail.'

On glancing through various editions of *The Spray*, which is the journal of the Slocum Society, there are special rosters of members who own Spray replicas; these lists include:

Double Crow's *joint owner, Frederik Lawrence.*

Stardust	Jim and Ruth Ainsworth
Narwal	Bill and Roni Callister
Osprey	Herman and Janet Conrader
Spray	Rocky Harris/Cameron Orcutt (Culler's Spray)
Delphinae	Peter D Norman (Roberts fibreglass Spray)
Anna Lee	Joseph W Rohloff
Un-Named	Keith and Kathy Palmerton (boat under construction)
Bertie	Peter and Dawn Bailey
Spray	Gregory Storozuk Jr
Dragon Hunter	George and Josephine Weyer
Fair Wind	George and Marianne Milburn
Slocum's Ghost	Rod Stuart
Gina B	Forrest A Beaton
Ella Zari	Ron Hackett (timber Spray replica in New Zealand)

This publication also listed six members with the name Slocum. One of these members, Colonel Donn C Slocum, is directly involved in reorganising the Slocum Society in time for the centenary of Joshua Slocum's departure on his singlehanded round-the-world voyage.

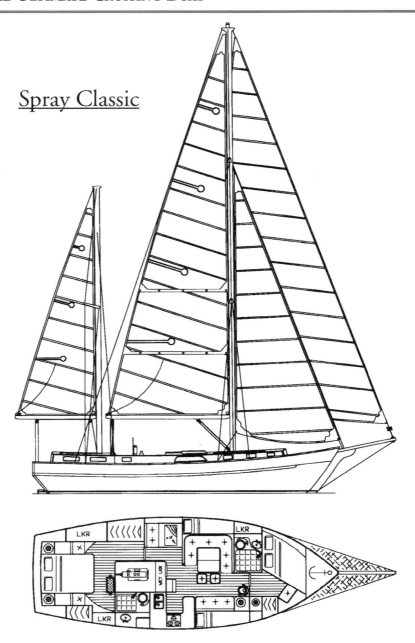

Spray Classic

This close replica of the Spray was designed by Bruce Roberts (USA) for Great Circle Yachts Ltd (see Appendix). Built in Sweden, this round bilge steel version will be fitted out for serious cruising and already the project has created serious interest amongst those British yachtsmen who have previewed the design. The basic dimensions are similar to the original Spray with only subtle differences in the treatment of the bow area. The draft has been increased by a few inches and as with most Spray replicas, several alternate sail plans will be available.

CHAPTER 6

Spray 40, Bruce Roberts' Version of the Original Spray

The Spray 40 was drawn by our design office in 1968 and was the first of the Spray series plans. The reason we called our design the Spray 40 was the way the boat was measured, rather than any difference in size between our Spray and the original as rebuilt by Slocum. Traditionally, a boat's length is denoted by the measurement between the transom and the deck line at the bow. There are many measurement systems, but leaving these aside, items such as bowsprits (and in the case of Spray, the cutwater) are normally not included, except when the measurement is quoted as length overall. This often causes confusion when comparing the length of any boat. Our Spray 40 is intended to be the same size as the original Spray. The dimensions shown below reflect the close similarity between the original vessel and our glassfibre version.

VERSION 'A'

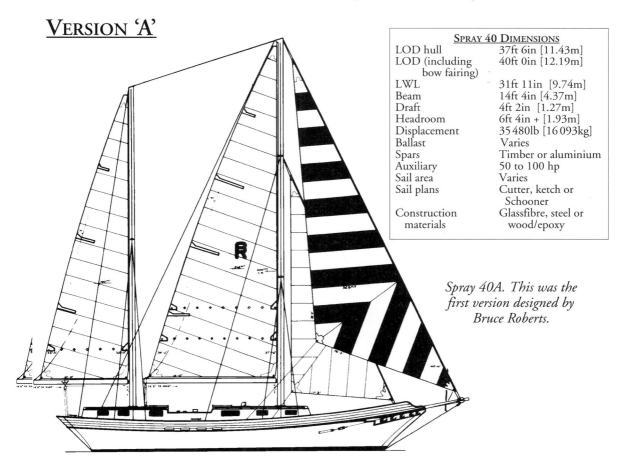

SPRAY 40 DIMENSIONS	
LOD hull	37ft 6in [11.43m]
LOD (including bow fairing)	40ft 0in [12.19m]
LWL	31ft 11in [9.74m]
Beam	14ft 4in [4.37m]
Draft	4ft 2in [1.27m]
Headroom	6ft 4in + [1.93m]
Displacement	35 480lb [16 093kg]
Ballast	Varies
Spars	Timber or aluminium
Auxiliary	50 to 100 hp
Sail area	Varies
Sail plans	Cutter, ketch or Schooner
Construction materials	Glassfibre, steel or wood/epoxy

Spray 40A. This was the first version designed by Bruce Roberts.

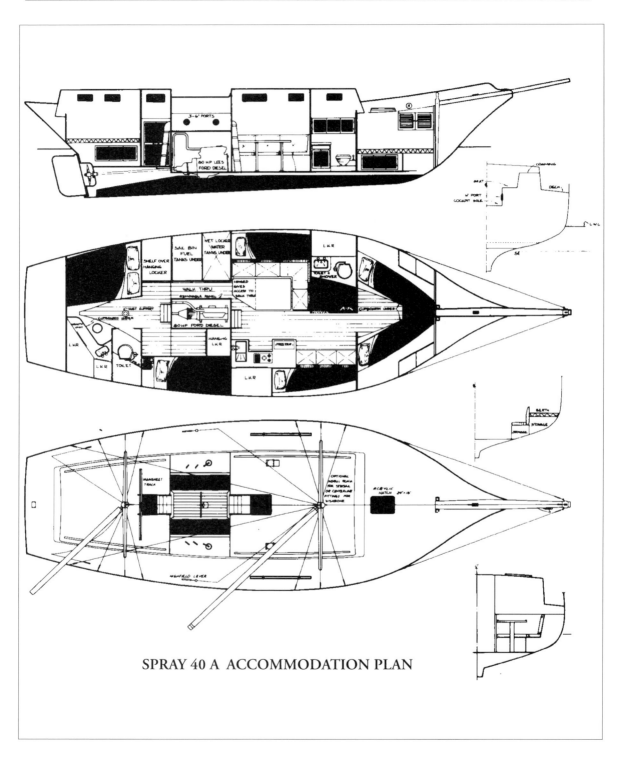

SPRAY 40 A ACCOMMODATION PLAN

JUPP SPRAY

Charlie Jupp was a paying customer, and was ready to proceed, so it was decided that his would be the first hull to be produced. We had completed drawing and fairing the lines, and had prepared the table of offsets. Although we modified the bow by fairing the topsides into the large cutwater, in other aspects we followed the original design as closely as possible. The next job was to draw out the lines full size. Here George Love and Barry Long really showed their worth, and produced a beautiful fully faired set of full-size patterns that we transferred to mylar plastic film. These same patterns have been used to produce over two hundred Spray 40 replicas.

Once we had the patterns for the frames, stem and keel, we were able to set up the male mould for the first foam sandwich glassfibre Spray 40. We next built a male mould, and laminated the first hull. What excitement there was when the hull was rolled upright, and we were able to inspect fully the Spray's beautiful form for the first time. One can study the lines and see the hull during construction, in this case upside down, but the first time we saw in full detail the beautiful lines of the Spray was a moment to be remembered always.

The first of many Spray 40s. Its owner, Charlie Jupp, proved that the Spray was indeed the ideal cruising boat.

Charlie Jupp took delivery of this first hull, which was finished outside with several coats of urethane paint. The hull was transported to Charlie's nearby home, where he proceeded to complete the interior and build the decks and superstructure according to the plans prepared for the glassfibre Spray 40. Charlie was working on his project full time, so I had my hands full keeping ahead and supplying the plan sheets in time for him. He actually got ahead of me at some stages, but this caused no problems, as Charlie was a trained carpenter and joiner.

It took Charlie about nine months to complete his Spray, and she was launched on our slipway with only two or three barrels of water as ballast. We knew that the original Spray was built and launched without any ballast at all, but since our Spray was much lighter we decided to use the barrels of water; this worked fine until we calculated the correct ballast amounts for this glassfibre Spray. Charlie even tried mineral sand from the nearby sand-dredging operation to see if he could have an easily movable ballast. We decided this was not heavy enough so in the end the scrap steel set in resin putty method proved to be the most effective as ballast.

The masts were timber, and the rigging galvanised plough steel wire. Charlie wanted to use the traditional deadeyes and lanyards to adjust the rigging. Although I was sceptical at the time, believing that the rigging would require frequent adjustment, I have since become convinced that within certain sensible limits, a person should rig their boat as they see fit. After all, boats are supposed to be fun, and we each enjoy them in our own way. We have a series of photos of Charlie Jupp's boat taken after he reached Lymington, England. The deadeyes and lanyards were still in place and Charlie reported that he had had no problems with his rig.

Charlie Jupp sailed from Brisbane, Australia early in 1976, and in November that year we received the first of several letters:

'I left for Mauritius, a voyage of 4500 miles, and 2000 miles off the Australian coast I had trouble with my appendix. I lay in my bunk for five days with all sail up, with a rising wind; Spray steered herself. When the pain eased, I sailed for Mauritius, and on arrival I let the anchor go. The yachties saw I was in trouble, and came and took the sail off. I had an operation, but felt very weak so I stayed another two weeks, then sailed for Durban. Lousy trip, last two days were storms and lightning. Had a glow at the masthead, rigging was very hot. I went below; I thought the boat was on fire. As I was coming down the coast, a helicopter flew very close and took photos of the Spray, and last night she was on TV here.

I will be leaving here at the end of December. Most yachts are taking on extra crew as far as Cape Town; they think I am mad, but if I can't get a good crew, I'm better off on my own. I had no worry about my Spray in the storm. It blew 50-60 knots, gusting to 70. I will let you know how things go around the Cape.'

Charlie Jupp's second letter came from St Helena:

'Thanks for your letter and all the help I received in South Africa. I am in St Helena, where there is no harbour, so it's a big job getting ashore. I met a lot of people building boats in South Africa, and over a hundred people came to see me off at Cape Town. My Spray sails very well, I sleep ten hours, and she stays on course all night. I hope to sail tomorrow, I will let you know how things go.'

The next letter from Charlie was when he reached England, dated 3 July 1977:

'I have just arrived in Falmouth after leaving the Virgin Islands. I was 40 days crossing; I had calms, head winds, fog and storms. People who draw upwind charts should try sailing with them. They show west wind; I went looking for it and I nearly saw polar bears I was that far north. As I came up the Channel the weather was perfect, not a cloud in the sky; it was warm seas, flat and a full moon. What more could I ask?

When I left South America for Barbados, I was 300 miles from Barbados when a foreign fishing boat with 12 crew came alongside and forced me up into the wind. Two crew came over the side ready to drop on to my deck, when a freak wave threw us apart. The skipper pulled a revolver and fired. I got one in the leg, and a few in the deck, so I shot at the two crew and got one in the skipper's arm. He got on the radio to his mate, but a naval patrol picked up his message, came and fired across his bows, and gave me an escort for the day. So for a week after, every time I heard a noise at night I would go on deck, with rifle in hand.

While in the Virgin Islands I did have an offer to skipper one of the charter yachts, but I'd made up my mind I wanted to go to England first. The Spray stood up very well in all weather. I carried sail, when in other yachts I would have reefed down, so over a long distance I am not behind other yachts, sometimes I would be a day before them.'

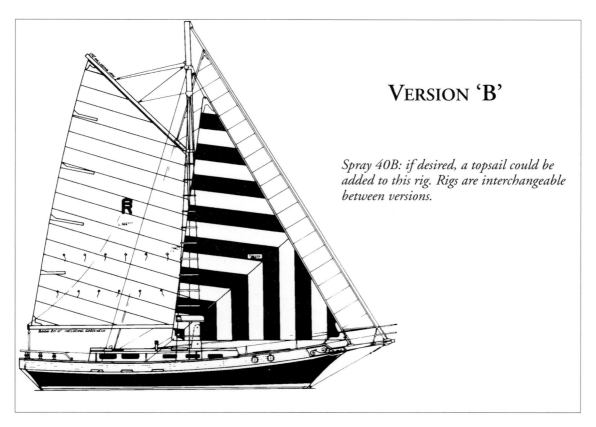

Version 'B'

Spray 40B: if desired, a topsail could be added to this rig. Rigs are interchangeable between versions.

In January 1978 we received a further letter from Charlie:

'I got a letter from a yacht club meeting in London to ask if I would go along and give a talk on my trip, and also, my easy method of navigation. Everything was to be laid on, food, drink and pay, but I had to decline the offer as I had very few photos and material to talk on, and so many people are sailing round the world and writing books nowadays. I have decided to keep the Spray, and you may see me on the west coast of the States this coming year. I have sailed and delivered a few yachts for owners, and so far I haven't sailed on a yacht as comfortable as the Spray. I think if ever I built another, it would be on the same lines. On the River Hamble here there are over 3000 yachts, but there's very few I'd swap my Spray for. I thought with all the racing yachts here I would be able to buy second-hand jibs, but there's none available and new ones are expensive.

The plans of my Spray show the draft at 4ft 2in [1.2m]. I changed mine, and put 12in [305mm] on the keel before I left Brisbane. It sails close to the wind and turns very nicely in the harbours, so I'm pleased I did it. I've met a number of people who are interested in building something they can take their families out sailing in. I'm sailing on a number of yachts, but they are very uncomfortable because there's a lump of ballast low down. However, if you spread the ballast the motion is much better. Other people may have different ideas.

Two young fellows thought they would like to race against my Spray from Falmouth. It was blowing hard, so they had to reef down. I was in Southampton five hours before them, so a heavy boat is OK.'

Charlie Jupp was a regular correspondent and we learned that he ballasted the hull with 9 tons of track pins taken from bulldozer tracks in a scrap yard, and screwed the floors down on top of them. He added a 12in [305mm] square wooden beam to the keel, and glassed it in without keel bolts. This altered the planned draft by 16in [406mm] which gave the boat a draft of 5ft 6in [1.6m]. He reckoned he could put a cup of coffee on his cabin table in a 30 knot wind, and it would stand without movement.

Like the original, this Spray will sail herself, although rigged as a Bermudan ketch she will hold a steady course for days on end unattended. In a storm the boat looks after herself better than the helmsman can with a storm jib to hold her steady. With a good trade wind blowing, Charlie set two jibs boomed out, with main and mizzen, and lashed the wheel, and left the ship to her own devices.

Also like the original vessel, Charlie has two separate cabins, with no cockpit; his wheel is amidships, sheltered by a canvas windscreen, and protected by ample bulwarks. 'There is none of this sitting up in the cold and wet on this boat,' says Charlie. 'As soon as it gets dark, I go to bed. I sleep ten hours every night and wait for the sun to come up before I get out of my bunk.'

Charlie sailed like this across the Indian Ocean in 1976, some 4500 miles from Australia to Mauritius, with the ship holding her own course. He did not touch the helm until he was in sight of the harbour, being tied to his bunk sojourn by the attack of appendicitis.

Charlie Jupp enjoyed no special advantages over anyone else in making his dreams come true. Twenty-seven years ago he was working as a labourer building sea walls in Essex when he made the decision to emigrate, choosing Australia because of the sun. His subsequent efforts at sugar cane farming convinced him there was no profit in small crop husbandry, so he got a job as a builders' labourer. After three years, he was building houses himself, which he did for a decade or more until the credit squeeze forced him to lower his selling prices. Spread over the five houses he had on the market, he just about broke even.

Charlie is not married and has done most of his sailing singlehanded. One of the reasons that many skippers are wary of taking on a crew came to Charlie's notice in Tahiti. Three men who had begged a passage from the West Indies then refused to go back to the yacht, saying they had had enough of the sea. The immigration authorities held the skipper of the yacht responsible and ordered him to pay their air passages home, two to England and one to South Africa.

Charlie arrived safely back in Brisbane after transiting the Panama Canal and sailing on into the Pacific. With about 2000 miles still to go, Charlie had lost the use of his rudder. Crevice corrosion in the stainless steel rudder shaft had caused the rudder to become inoperable. He managed to sail the boat for some weeks without a rudder, and steered the Spray quite successfully by adjusting the sails. Charlie is now back in Brisbane; he has sold the Spray and retired.

TRAH

The second Spray to be built on the male mould that had been used to produce Charlie Jupp's Spray, was a hull for Spray model builder, John Haskins. This vessel was called *Trah*.

John was working for us at that time, and the agreement was that he would help with the construction of his own hull and would be paid for his services, and the money would go towards the cost of his hull. John was a good worker, so everything was satisfactory to all concerned. It only took a few weeks to produce John's hull, and he elected to have his cored with end grain balsa rather than the foam core we had used for Charlie Jupp's hull. We were experimenting with different cores, and one of the first ones we tried was made of a PVC material, a similar product to Airex (tm). This core had properties that would make it suitable as a core for our glassfibre sandwich hulls. The manufacturers assured us that it would do the job, so we carried out some experiments making up test panels and subjecting these to various tests, some scientific and some not so scientific, to establish the suitability of the material. I have had the opportunity to inspect some boats using this Australian PVC core and they have stood up well. Unfortunately, the company that was manufacturing this material has now stopped making it as they decided that there was not a large enough market for it in Australia.

The next core we tried was a urethane-based foam. This material is made in a similar manner to Airex (tm) and other boatbuilding quality cores, but is not suitable as a structural core. However, it did prove to be quite satisfactory in providing a base on which to lay up the glass fibre hull. Later, when the hull is turned over and the mould removed, most of this foam is also taken out and stringers and other reinforcements are bonded in place. This foam material is really only used as a smooth former for laying up the outer glassfibre skin.

Another core material that was appearing in Australia for the first time was balsa core. This material consists of small blocks of balsa that are glued to a netting backing (something like a mosquito net material), to which the balsa squares are glued. The arrangement comes in sheets

Trah, *built by John Haskins in Australia. This was the second of the countless Spray 40s to be built in glassfibre.*

of 1ft 6in [457mm] x 3ft [914mm], and these sheets are used in a similar way to the foam core; that is, they are either sewn or tacked on to a male mould and then the outer glassfibre laminate is laid up over the core. One of the drawbacks with the balsa core was that it did not lay on the hull so fairly as foam sheeting. However, by putting extra cuts in the blocks and using other techniques that developed, we were able to use this material quite satisfactorily for hull construction. John Haskins opted for the balsa core in his hull, so that's the way his boat was laid up, and we actually developed the techniques of building balsa-cored hulls during this period. Balsa core is an excellent material for coring glassfibre decks, and has been widely used throughout the glassfibre boatbuilding industry for that purpose.

When John Haskins's hull was complete, he moved it into one of our boatbuilding sheds and proceeded to install the interior laminate and, as well as the bulkheads, web floors and other interior joinery. John then worked full time on his boat for some time while the cabin and decks were installed. He fitted a Lister diesel, which in its former life had been used to power a local dairy farmer's milking machine. The engine worked quite well until John replaced it some years later with a more modern marine diesel. John used his Spray as a family 'live-aboard', and his wife and three children lived happily on *Trah* while John worked the Marine Park boatyard.

John motored his Spray up to Cannes, a distance of about 1500 miles, where he cut down a tree and used this as his mast. He made a good job of converting the tree to a mast, and properly rigged the boat. John Haskins is certainly not the first person to go into the forest looking for a mast: many builders, not only of Sprays but of other vessels as well, have taken a similar route.

TERRY SPRAY
Brian Terry was the third customer at Marine Park who decided to have a Spray built from the existing male mould. Brian wanted a quick start, so our staff laid up his hull which he then fitted out himself. Brian then equipped his Spray with a large settee and other furniture and moved aboard.

OYSTERMAN
The next Spray replica to be taken from our male mould was one built for Roger and Riva Palmer. This couple hired the mould and built their own glassfibre hull; they certainly built it well and we all made jokes about it being bullet proof and how it would knock down any reef that it encountered.

Roger and Riva also built a Spray dinghy. They took the lines of the Spray, and then scaled them down to create a set of lines for a boat of about 9ft [2.7m] length overall. Next they proceeded to build this mini-Spray as a dinghy. However although the dinghy looked fine, it was a bit too buoyant to be a good dinghy. Roger and Riva made a few changes to the rig of their Spray, one of which was to fit booms to both foresails. Charlie Jupp, on seeing this arrangement, commented (as most of us had already done) that he thought this was dangerous, especially if you needed to work on the bowsprit. Also, by having the outer jib on a boom, it meant that the amount of sail area that could be carried with this particular headsail was limited.

Roger and Riva have since sold their Spray replica, and I assume that the new owners have changed the arrangement for the headsails. The rigging chosen by the Palmers was more than oversize, so no doubt this very well-built, heavily rigged Spray is still happily cruising today.

After the completion of these first four Spray replicas from the mould we built at Marine Park, there was such a rush of plan sales that it is impossible to list all of the boats built in chronological order. Consequently, I will select some of the Spray replicas at random, detailing the experiences of the owners, and commenting on the individual boats.

It is necessary to sort the various Sprays into sizes, because after the success of the Spray 40 design we then proceeded to prepare plans of other sizes for the Spray. These other boats

Oysterman, *Spray 40 built by Roger and Riva Palmer using Bruce Roberts' plans. They hired the mould and built a very substantial glassfibre hull themselves.*

which came to make up the Spray series were scaled up and down from the original plans. Generally speaking, we tried to keep as close to the proportions of the original boat as possible, but of course there were always customers who decided that they would purchase a plan for one size, and then stretch it one way or another to suit their own needs. Some of these boats are very successful, proving that the Spray is an incredibly versatile design. No matter what criticisms have been levelled at the original Spray, and some of the replicas, I feel that most of these criticisms cannot possibly be justified in the light of the comments and experiences of owners with whom we have been in contact.

SALTY SPRAY

We all well remember the day that Howie Franklin walked into our office in Vancouver, Canada. The design office had not long been moved from Gabriola Island, and Howie came to see us and said that he would like to build a Spray. Howie had seen a boat that featured an unusual poop arrangement, and he decided that this would fit nicely on the Spray hull. He asked us to prepare plans for a semi-custom Spray design incorporating his own ideas of the poop stern and a small pilot house. So shortly after this, we started making plans to meet Howie's requirements.

At the time, we considered Howie's ideas 'a bit much', and we displayed our feelings when

drawing up the sail plan by putting a pirate flag at the top of the mast! As events turned out, we had nothing to complain about when it came to Howie Franklin's *Salty Spray*. Not only has Howie kept in touch with us over the years, relating the various experiences he has had with his boat, but also he has proved that there are a lot of people out there who want something just a little different, because the Spray Version C (as it became known) proved to be a very popular arrangement for the Spray 40, and indeed for some of the smaller versions as well.

Salty Spray was one of the first steel Sprays built from the plans that we drew up for building this steel multi-chine version of the Spray. We simply took the original lines of Spray and redrew them to a multi-chine configuration. This retained the design parameters of the original, but made it possible to build the boat in sheet steel. There had already been round-bilge Spray hulls built in steel; however, round-bilge steel construction is beyond the ability of most amateur builders. For this

This steel Spray 40, Salty Spray, *was built in 1975 by Howie Franklin in Canada and is still cruised by Howie and his family.*

reason we decided to produce plans for a multi-chine steel version.

We drew up the plans for the steel Spray at about the same time as we were drawing plans for several other new steel designs. This was in 1974, and anyone involved in the marine industry (or any other industry then where glassfibre resins and other petroleum-based materials were required) will remember that it was a time when anything manufactured from petroleum was in short supply. Consequently, we found that we had many successful designs that could be built in glassfibre, but unfortunately the glassfibre, or at least the resin components, were almost impossible to obtain. In a way, this situation did us a favour, because it forced us to design boats that could be built in other materials. As it has turned out, steel now represents just over half of the boats built from our plans.

Howie Franklin took his plans back to Toronto, where he had the hull and deck professionally built; he then proceeded to fit out the boat himself. All the while he was in touch with us, and sent photographs of the boat at all stages of the construction process. We received one letter from Howie that reads as follows:

'On 14 August 1978, we were out sailing on Lake Simcoe, which is just north of Toronto. It was a warm and pleasant day, but I was concerned about the possibility of thunderstorms. About 1630 and on our way home, the sky darkened and it was obvious we were going to be hit by a storm. Since there was little wind, I had decided to sail on jib-staysail and mizzen. The main was down and stowed. Soon the rain became heavy, and visibility was down to 50ft [15.25m]. Things were still OK, until all of a sudden the wind velocity increased from 10 knots to about 80 knots in less than 15 seconds, and *Salty Spray* was knocked down. The storm was part thunderstorm, part tornado, and we didn't have the time to release sheets. It all happened so quickly.

I am telling you this story because I want you and your customers to know of the incredible integrity of the Spray. In our knockdown, I think the masthead touched the sea, and yet she rolled back up with no damage done, except to the captain's pride. She had water inboard, but that was later discovered to have come from the freshwater tank; it had siphoned itself up through the galley tap. It was an unfortunate incident, which could have been much more serious if not for the incredible integrity of the Spray design; I had 12 souls on board that day, and we all went out again the next day because of the faith we all have (even stronger now) in the design of *Salty Spray*. Although it frightened us at the time, the incident did not deter us from proceeding with our plans for the future with the Spray. I just wanted you to know how proud we are of our boat.'

Howie is a former airline captain so is used to dealing with crisis situations. Some years ago he sailed *Salty Spray* from Canada down the east coast of the USA to Florida, and we lost track of him for some time. However in December 1993 we received another letter that read as follows:

'Do you remember one of the first Spray 40s that you featured in your catalogue way back in 1980? Well, *Salty Spray* is still going and has just finished a total refit job with new rigging, new bowsprit, new bow rail, new wheelhouse and new engine. I fitted an 85 hp Perkins diesel. She is in very good shape at this time. We are still enjoying the boat, but would consider selling her at about $70 000.'

Further correspondence with Howie produced the following comments:

'What I can do is tell you of all the good things we like about *Salty Spray,* starting with that nasty double knockdown we had in August 1978 when she was maybe only half finished and half ballasted. Her survival was a fine display of her great integral stability. Since then we have had many good times, including a trip down the Mississippi river to New Orleans, then over to Florida where she now resides at Key Largo. What I like about the Spray is that most other people like her too. Spray seems to be like a story book dreamboat, yet here she is for real.

She is a great live-aboard and when we get together with friends with their boats, someone always says, 'Bring your boat, we need the poop deck for dancing." Although *Salty Spray* is not the boat for winning races, she is certainly comfortable, stable, likeable and a lot of fun. There is one other Spray owner here in Key Largo. He bought it from the builder when it was a schooner, then he changed it to a sloop.'

LYNCH SPRAY

Virgil Lynch operated an engineering business in the mid-west: and, like many people who live far from the water, he had a strong desire to own a boat and go cruising. Unlike so many people who never realise their dreams, Virgil decided to do something about it, and came to see us when we were located in California. Virgil purchased two sets of plans because he had a friend who also wanted to build a Spray 40 in steel. Over the years we received several letters and pictures from Virgil, mainly showing construction details and how he was looking to improve the methods of fabrication that we had shown in the plans. I must confess that we have learned as much from the builders of our boats as they have learned from us. We are forever indebted to the many builders who have shared their ideas with us, especially when we were constantly developing the building techniques. Virgil Lynch subsequently completed his steel Spray 40 and rigged her as a schooner. In fact, I remember he engaged us to custom design the schooner rig for his Spray.

I assume that the Spray that is moored next to Howie Franklin's *Salty Spray* is the same one that was built by Virgil Lynch, so obviously this Spray has been re-sold and re-rigged as described in the letter from Howie Franklin.

JUMBLY GIRL

Recently, in response to my notices in various yachting magazines, the following letter arrived. Before going into detail concerning the contents, one must speculate about the name of this particular Spray. This boat was built by Michael S Rigg, and although he does not say in his letter what inspired the name for his boat, we all suspect it might be the fact that in Britain sales of used and surplus marine fittings and equipment are generally known as boat jumbles. Here is what Mr Rigg has to say about his vessel:

Jumbly Girl, *a steel-hulled Spray 40 built by Michael Rigg in England. This Spray with its 'go anywhere' commercial coaster look has a beauty all its own.*

'I own a Spray 40, version C, Bermudan ketch built to your plans. I bought the bare hull in 1983 and spent nine years of my spare time fitting her out. She is built of steel, $^3/_{16}$in [5mm] hull, $^1/_8$in [3mm] decks and superstructure, and has hollow wooden masts and galvanised rigging. I have installed quite an old, but reliable, Ford 57 hp diesel engine, which drives the boat at 8 knots. The hull was built by an amateur boatbuilder near Manchester, and I did much of the fitting out in Whitby, which is where I lived before moving to Ipswich. The furthest I have been so far was a trip last summer across to Denmark. We went through the Limfjorden south through the Baltic, and back to Ipswich through the Kiel Canal. It has always been my intention eventually to depart on a long voyage, and we have finally decided to leave the UK this September.

Concerning the boat, she sails with a very small angle of heel, and has a very easily driven hull for a heavy boat. I have only three tons of ballast in her, and even then she is over her design draft of 4ft 2in [1.28m], due I think to her heavy construction. However I don't think of this as a detriment.'

The photographs of *Jumbly Girl* show that she looks like a coaster. I use this term in its most complimentary manner, because one often sees small chunky vessels trading around the coasts of Europe that give the appearance of no-nonsense, go-anywhere boats. This of course is in keeping with the heritage of Slocum's Spray. As we know, the original vessel was a commercial vessel, not only before Slocum rebuilt her, but also during her trip around the world with Slocum as her skipper. Quite often, he used Spray to carry cargo and for other money-making ventures, so when I see a Spray that has commercial overtones, I feel that the boat is in the spirit of the original.

SHINDERA

This glassfibre Spray 40 was built by Larry and Karen Mahoney of Grand Rapids, Michigan; Mr and Mrs Mahoney have sent me a fine selection of construction photos, plus a couple of photographs of their boat under sail. The Mahoneys have made a great job of building their Spray, and have been regularly cruising Lake Michigan. Although they do not elaborate on their future plans for the boat, the construction photos reveal that the boat is intended for long-distance cruising.

MILE HIGH

One of the many interesting customers who walked into my office during the period we were living in Newport Beach, California, was James Kirby. Jim was a real-estate broker who lived in

Valyermo, California, and operated the Mile High ranch, which (as its name suggests) was up in the mountains of California. Jim is an interesting person, and one with whom I enjoyed working. He had the hull professionally built, then finished it in a boatyard in Costa Mesa. As this yard was close to my office. I was able to visit the yard frequently to keep an eye on Jim's project. He did a fine job of fitting out the boat, and made his own mast from solid timber. It was interesting to watch as he started off with a square balk and taking advantage of the modern electric tools, gradually transformed this into a main mast for his Spray.

Jim kept in touch with us after his boat was launched:

'Just a quick note to let you know how she handles. We launched 28 July 1981, and had her sailing within two weeks.

Mile High, *a Spray 40 built by James D Kirby in California, was recently sold after over 12 years of extensive cruising by her original builder.*

Last weekend we came back from the Ismus in 15-18 knot winds, and she averaged 6 ½ knots under drifter, main and mizzen. I am extremely happy with the boat. It is much better than I expected. As people sail by us on our mooring, which is two blocks east of the Pavilion in Newport Harbour, we get nothing but compliments. Come out and see us.'

On 1 November 1981 Jim got in touch again:

'With our big drifter in medium air she does really well. We averaged 7 knots on one of our return trips from the west end of Catalina in 20-22 knot winds, and on a return leg from Dana Point we averaged 6½ knots to windward with the main

Building your own boat brings rewards. Jim Kirby and his family sailing Mile High, *off the coast of Mexico.*

mizzen and jib in 28 knot winds and 6ft [1.8m] seas. Caught many fish with four poles trailing off the stern. The boat seems to steer herself no matter in what direction we are sailing, with a few minor sail adjustments. I just want to thank you again for all your help during construction, and if I had it to do all over again, I would not change a thing.'

On 2 February 1982 Jim wrote again, telling us of all the compliments the boat was still receiving. He also told us he had added polyurethane to all the topside teak. It is becoming a real show boat.

'Saw another Spray in Catalina made out of wood. The builder was from Long Beach, California. He stretched the boat out to 46ft [14m] with a 16ft [4.8m] beam. I tried to tell everybody not to mess with the original lines, but many people change them around. We are still outfitting, and plan to leave for Mexico in November 1982 and then jump off for the South Pacific in May of 1983.'

The 46ft [14m] long and 16ft [4.8m] boat that Jim Kirby mentioned was the first Spray that we designed for strip plank construction. The builder had some ideas of his own, so he asked me if it was OK to lengthen the boat to 46ft [14m] and also he suggested that as he was going to be building in strip plank it would not be too much of a problem to slightly alter the mould formers to make the boat a little beamier, and thus maintain the proportions. We have not heard any more about that particular strip plank Spray, except for the mention in Jim Kirby's letter.

SPIRITWIND
The following report was sent to us by Earl Maupin Snr:

'We would like to update you on our progress and send you some pictures. We have been building our Spray 40 foot steel Version C for eight years this July. To give you a brief history of our boat, *Spiritwind*, we received your plans and laid the keel and then began the framework in the Fall of 1987. We rented some farm property in a small rural community of Washington State called Kingston, which is just west of Seattle. At this time, we joined the newly founded Metal Boat Society, and for the next $2^1/_2$ years, with the help of your material and boatbuilding books, we laboured on. In the spring of 1990, *Spiritwind* was shipped by truck to San Diego, California, and hit the water for the first time. We moved aboard and began finishing the inside. During this time, we were raising a family (two children), boatbuilding, and finishing a naval career. Since that time, the boat has been back to the Puget Sound area, where we continued to live aboard for three years, and our live-aboard home became a sailboat for the first time. *Spiritwind*, though built on a shoestring budget, has turned into a comfortable and seaworthy vessel. She was a participant in last Fall's annual Metal Boat festival, and received excellent comments from all who boarded her.'

Earl told us that the inside of the hull was sandblasted and painted with coal tar epoxy. The outside received coats of zinc-enriched epoxy, epoxy high-build and enamel, and has caused no problems. Inside the boat, they welded 300 2in x 3in [50mm x 75mm] steel tabs to which they attached 2in x 2in [50mm x 50mm] cedar strips, then they installed rigid foam, sealing the backs and sides. This has worked quite well for them. The bulkheads are constructed of plywood, cedar and mahogany. They did not install the after-cabin hatch. Instead, they have only one hatch entering the boat, and by bringing the sides of the cabin and coachroof back flush with frame number 18, they created a walk-through on the port side to the aft cabin.

On the starboard side, they stopped the coachroof and sides at frame number 17, giving them a walk-through to the cockpit on the main deck into their enclosed pilot house. For ballast, they used concrete and steel, giving them 15 000lb [6804kg].Their mast and rigging are made from aluminium street lighting poles, originally from the highway Interstate 5. The main mast is 40ft [12.1m] and the mizzen is 30ft [9.1m]. The rigging is $^7/_{16}$in [11mm] galvanised wire eye-looped with stainless steel 50 ton pressed fasteners. The total estimated cost of their rigging is $1 500 [£1 000 approx]. They chose the Marconi rig and have two after running backstays. Their bowsprit is made of $2^1/_2$in [35mm] diameter schedule 80 pipe which they heated and bent around a tree into a loop. It is welded to the hull, on which they welded deck plate and chain link fence rollers for anchor rollers. The engine is a 75 hp GM diesel with Borg-Warner velvet drive transmission.

The boat has three staterooms, and a large enclosed horseshoe galley. The main salon has an L-shaped couch and table for eating, and a wood stove. Earl chose to eliminate the head in the aft stateroom, opting instead for a long closet on the port side and a full-sized bed on the starboard. This also gives them room for a love seat aft, and a sit-down make-up vanity area forward on frame number 18 Earl continued:

'*Spiritwind* was built on a shoestring budget. We estimate that over the last seven years we have spent approximately $35 000 [£23 333] to this point. Our cruising plans are to sail the boat south after our retirement from the Navy in the Fall of 1995.

We are always excited to see and hear from other Spray owners. To our knowledge, during the time we spent in Washington State, we know of five Sprays and have made friends with their owners. One wood and the rest were made of steel. We have also met a Spray owner in San Francisco at the Alameda Air Station. His wooden Spray looks like Slocum's boat. Here in San Diego I only know of three, all steel; and, to our surprise, a new arrival at the marina where we live is the new owner of the 40ft [12.1m] version 'C' steel Spray, *Mile High,* which is featured in your publication. We have not seen another version 'C' Spray 40 on the west coast so were delighted to meet the very excited new owners, who were also delighted to meet us.

In closing, after nearly eight years of boat building and blood, sweat and tears, we are still content with our choice of the Spray design and the help you have given us. We would do it all over again.'

ARA-A-KIWA
Ron and Joyce Macmillan commented:

'Our Spray was built in Wellington (New Zealand) by Stain, Ward and Jones, launched and registered in 1980, and brought to Auckland, sold to a Mr M C Hornsby who fitted her out, and sailed to Fiji and Vanuatu and New Caledonia in 1982. Then she was virtually unused until we acquired her in 1991, when a major refit was necessary. Our voyages include the North Islands, and in 1992 we sailed to Tonga, the Heiapaignvavau Groups, then to Vitulevu in Fiji for the Suva regatta on the Vitulevu and Musatt Cove at Malololailai Islands for the Fiji regatta and the Fiji-Vila race. Then reluctantly we went back to New Zealand ahead of the hurricane season.

In the last year we have worked towards early retirement, and we are fitting out *Ara-A-Kiwa* as a long-term live-aboard. The vessel is what we expect of her, no ocean greyhound, but comfy as old armchairs. She sails well, and we have added a bit to the rudder to track better. The multi-chine steel hull is 42ft [12.8m] on deck, 14ft 6in [4.4m] beam and 4ft 6in [1.3m] draft. Overall length is 48ft 6in [14.7m]. We have added the wood capped rail on steel stanchions, and recently the afterdeck canopy that performs as shade, water collection, solar panels on top and easy furling for the mizzen. We have seen three other Sprays. One from Canada, *Spray Venture,* and *Blue Beard* and *Susan II* on the New Zealand coast, though I believe at least another four are around here somewhere. Our interpreta-

New Zealanders Ron and Joyce Macmillan plan to fit out their Spray as a retirement live-aboard. Ara-A-Kiwa *('Wake of the Navigator' in Polynesian) has been cruised extensively throughout the Pacific.*

tion of Ara-A-Kiwa is "Wake of the Navigator" in Polynesian.

Recently, we were "shaking down" after an almost complete refit, and *Ara-A-Kiwa* was behaving great. Our new GPS and radar were the latest toys; the new mainsail set really well. On top of this, both of us were feeling really smug, having passed the Yacht Master coastal exams together.

We visited Mayor Islands, and then decided to head north for the Great Barrier Islands. The weather was good and the wind fair. A night's anchorage at Slipper Islands was planned and a short cut to the bay between the south end of the island and Penguin Island was there – narrow, but there. Our cruising guide indicated 12ft [3.6m] of water in the gap, not a problem for the Spray.

The following breeze pushed us along at about 5 knots, but as we approached the gap I started the engine just in case. Joyce went forward to the bowsprit to see if the bottom became visible, and I watched the depth sounder as it rapidly decreased: 15, 12, 10, 5, 3, 2 fathoms, then 1 fathom (1 fathom equals 6ft or 1.83m). Joyce began gesturing, she had spotted large boulders that were getting closer; we had misjudged and were about to pay the price.

The engine roared in reverse, but *Ara-A-Kiwa* is almost 20 tons and the sails were still pulling well; we were stuck with a grating and sickening crunch and came to a halt. The following swell was about 3ft [less than 1m], but it began to pick the ship and force her further on to the rocks. The lifting and dropping could be likened to a pile driver. The incredible jarring had the booms jumping and the timber dinghy in the davits was attempting to turn itself over.

The tide is ebbing, it's a beautiful day, and we are having a terrible experience! We handed the sails as quickly as we could and took stock. The following swell meant that efforts to reverse off were negated, and the rudder was being knocked around a bit. There remained only one way off that I thought we could try. I gave the helm hard over and pushed the throttle further than it had ever been before or after.

The Leyland's 130 horses roared, smoke poured, the engine temperature soared, and *Ara-A-Kiwa* began to shudder forwards and to turn! Gradually and almost painfully, the ship made her way, grinding over the stones until her bows again pointed seawards. After what seemed a punishingly long interval, we broke free. Hurriedly, Joyce took over the helm while I searched the bilges, surely we would be taking water; there must be a broken weld, there ought to be, but there wasn't. Good old Spray, I do not know of any other boat I have owned or sailed that could take that amount of punishment and survive.

There was some damage; the lower edge of the rudder was mangled and punctured, the shoe bent, and the 2in [50mm] stainless shaft was "screwed" at the tiller bar. Our "shakedown" cruise had become a "shake-up" cruise. We rigged the emergency tiller and continued with our intended voyage, even crossing the Hanahe Gulf on a beam reach with the remnants of Cyclone Betsy still blowing 28 to 30 knots. We did over 8 1/2 knots and were comfy and proud.'

LOWREY SPRAY

The following was an article in the New Zealand magazine *Sea Spray*:
'Wellington fireman Chris Lowrey says: "If you are prepared to rummage through scrap bins

and put in a day's work in exchange for materials, you could get the boat you want at a price you can afford." And to prove it, he picked up his hull plating for nothing, made his blocks from old bedroom furniture, sewed his own sails, had a brother-in-law make one SSB radio out of two DSB rejects, and sheathed his cabin top with 35ft [11m] of brown striped nylon dress material. The result: a 16 metre cruiser for NZ $20 000 [£7000]! One of the greatest hassles of building boats is paying for them, but Chris Lowrey has found a way around the crippling costs. Over the past four years he has created a magnificent oceangoing cruising yacht, a 40ft [16m] Roberts Spray design, for just NZ $20 000. The way he went about it was a simple process, and one he would like to pass on to anyone with big dreams and small pockets. To this end, he is writing a book as construction takes place.'

The article went on to explain that four years before, Chris, a Stokes Valley fireman, had been dreaming of an ocean cruising yacht. He and his wife Sue had reached the dangerous age of discontent when the family became self-sufficient, and the mortgage was manageable. Chris has been a sailor since schooldays. As a small boy, he joined the sea cadets, the merchant navy at 15, and was never far from something afloat. Six years previously, as owner of a Silhouette, a 16ft [5m] dinghy with a lid, he crossed Cook Strait singlehanded one afternoon on an impulse. There he tied up alongside a race finish of Wellington keel boats. 'That was it for me,' he recalls. Chris just had to have a 'real yacht.'

Chris had always loved traditional boats, and his initial thoughts were for something in timber, and about 36ft [11m] long. He made sketches, and took them to a Petone boatyard. 'How much to build this?' he asked. 'One hundred and ten thousand dollars,' came the reply. That poured cold reality all over his dreams, but Chris is not a man to give up easily; he had once conducted a five-day vigil on Wellington harbour to protest against a nuclear ship's visit. For a cost of NZ $600 [£300] he bought a set of plans from two men who had decided against building a ferro-cement Spray. The article continued:

'Then, through consultation with designer Bruce Roberts, he exchanged the ferro lines for steel. "All I could do for six months was study the drawings," he says. "I didn't have any money, but decided there had to be ways of doing it." To Chris, that meant picking up materials at the right price and building the boat himself. Soon after, his first deal transpired. As payment for spray-painting a demolition yard owner's car, Chris accepted two truckloads of kauri, oregon, pipe, iron and valves. One piece of oregon, 46ft [14m] long, 8in [203mm] octagonal, is now his mast. It was a magnificent piece of timber, not one knot in it. He set to work with a timber jack plane, bought a drum of linseed oil, and for 25 nights swabbed it down. Now 42ft [12.8mm] long, it will carry the gaff topsail rig. "It has to be the most expensive mast in the country, counting the hours I've spent on it," says Chris. "But it's some mast, my pride and joy; if it ever breaks, I will just put in a bigger engine."'

The article explained that the steel for the hull plating came from a diesel storage tank at Miramar. The twenty lumps of steel, all corten, low carbon content steel, cost nothing. 'It looked dreadful,' said Chris. But once the hull was constructed, he and friends sandblasted it inside and out, submerging the Lowrey household and surrounding neighbour-hood in a fine-dust cloud for five days. 'One thing you need for this boatbuilding lark,' said Chris, 'is heaps of cheek. Never be afraid to walk into an engineering firm with a bin outside, and ask to have a rummage. It is amazing what is thrown out.'

Chris scored 1640ft [500m] of tongue and groove flooring this way, at a quarter of the price. For ballast, Chris worked for three days lifting 4900ft [1500m] of railway lines. He weighed the ballast into 50lb [23kg] lots, and divided the weight across the bottom of each keel section. Even the engine had a history: a Thorneycroft, it originally belonged to the New Zealand Navy. Chris came by it in the hands of one of the men he bought the Spray plans from. It was completely rebuilt, and Chris only had to tidy it up. It took six off-duty firemen to lift it, but it puts out 40 hp, has an oil controlled gearbox, and two to one reduction. The big plus is that it can be hand cranked if necessary.

A toolmaking apprenticeship served years ago came to Chris's aid. With the help of a forge, made with the vacuum cleaner reversed, and a drum full of firebricks, he cast and made all his own fittings. He also made hatches from teak, dorade vents from mahogany and kauri laminated, and he made himself a lathe for the taff-rail. From old oak bedroom furniture came 52 wooden blocks, and he even turned his own axle pins and sheaves. The majority of hardwood on the boat is African iroko. Deck cleats at a cost of $1.50 each and jaws for the boom were from a selected jarrah railway sleeper.

Sticking fairly rigidly to tradition, there are no winches on deck. Sail handling is with tackles. The staysail is self-tending. He has one big headsail, though, to pull the boat along in light weather, so he may relent later and have a couple of single-action winches. He is looking out for a second-hand anchor winch, but is prepared to make one of those too. From lengthy discussions with similar-minded alternative-lifestyle cruising folk, Chris had deduced that when one closes the door on jobs and regular pay cheques, replacing worn-out gear such as sails becomes an impossible task. So, for the sails, which can be expected to last at best about five years, he has picked up an old sewing machine from a farm, bor-rowed a work table, and is negotiating with an Auckland importer to supply him with tan-bark sailcloth. Sailmaking holds no mysteries for Chris. 'You just mount the machine on the table with a motor and clutch, and buy lots of books. I figure if you can't make it in the workshop, there is no way you'll afford an expert when you are cruising.'

Obviously there are certain things one must buy, but the single sideband radio was not one of them. From two acquired double sideband rejects, a 'radio nut' brother-in-law made one single sideband pretty cheaply.

The 118sq ft [11sq m] of glass sheathing for the deck and cabin top, at $45 a metre, was a difficult one, but Chris found out what the cloth was made from and bought the equiva-lent in brown-striped nylon dress material for less than NZ $1.00 a metre. He glued a test piece on to ply, boiled it, hammered it, and once convinced it was as good as you would get, down it went. 'It was harder to wet-out,' says Chris, 'but I defy anyone to knock it. You don't have to fill it, just paint over the top.' Chris emphasises, though, that you cannot build a boat for nothing. 'You can't make welding rods, silicon brass nails, paint. You have to buy the stuff, and it costs.' Chris also believes that a would-be builder need not be as fancy as he has been, with ornately carved dolphins either side of the pushpit, and three bulletproof work-of-art hatches.

Below decks the accommodation sleeps seven, and has a private owner's cabin aft, and another to forward. There is provision for a potbelly between the galley and the main saloon. Naturally enough, Chris is making the stove. 'I was not keen on gas [firemen are all safety first], and it's not easy to get fills in some parts of the Pacific.' A kerosene cooker with an oven would have cost NZ $1200. So, from an old gas range, he made patterns, salvaging the racks and panels. Chris has installed a ring circuit around the interior. He salvaged four brass lamps from an old railway carriage to provide electric power over strategic spots such as chart table and galley, but the balance will come from kerosene lanterns.

SENTA

Kenneth P Latham Jr of Rockport, Maine, arranged to have his steel Spray 40 hull and deck professionally built in Canada. The frame spacing was increased from 1ft 6in [457mm] to 1ft 8in [508mm]

effectively increasing the hull length to 43ft [13.11m]. Kenneth chose the gaff schooner rig and the photographs reveal a well proportioned sail plan; the main carries a topmast that often carries the topsail in lighter weather.

The pilot house was designed by the owner and provides extra comfort when the north east coast weather turns nasty. The auxiliary engine is a 3QM30 Yanmar fitted with a 3:1 reduction transmission and gives 6 knots. (Designer's comment: Normally I would recommend a larger engine than the one fitted here; however the 3:1 reduction somewhat compensates for the lower horsepower rating.) The fuel tanks are integral (they use hull skin as one side of the tank) and provide 150 US gal [567 lit] plus the water tanks hold 400 US gal [1514 lit] divided between four tanks.

Senta is a steel-hulled Spray 40 with an increased length of 43ft. Her owner, Kenneth Latham, chose to fit her as a 19th C coaster with a gaff schooner rig and designed a pilot house to give extra comfort and protection from NE winds on her New England cruising grounds.

When the steel work was completed, in Port Credit, Ontario, Canada, Kenneth motored the bare hull down the Erie Canal to Boston, Massachusetts, where he finished off the fitting out over a two year period. Kenneth stated:

'I think the hardest part was building the rig. The spars are aluminium tubes, painted with Allgrip (with a brush!) and I recommend the finish which has lasted well over several years. The rig is that of a 19th Century Coaster with a single jib. All the blocks are rope stropped, the standing rigging is galvanised, hand spliced and tarred. The running rigging runs to pin-rails in the shrouds. The steering is by rope and drum. Nothing fancy, but cheap, reliable and easy to repair.

The extended cruising has not happened; although we did live aboard for four years, cruising New England coastline as time permitted. We are now settled in Maine and I am modifying the interior to suit her use as a coastal cruiser. For example what had been a workshop in the forepeak is now a two berth cabin for guests.'

WALPURGA
Mike and Christine Platzer wrote to us as follows:

'It may please you to hear of another Spray that turned out well. She is built to your steel Spray 40 design, with slight modifications. My wife and I built her; we always wanted a floating home that was more of a cruising yacht, rather than one developed from a racing design. After reading Slocum's book, Pete Culler's *Building and Sailing a Spray,* and Kenneth Slack's *In the Wake of the Spray,* the decision was quite easy, and we don't regret it. Our Spray is called *Walpurga,* which was a Bavarian witch in ancient times, and we have lived on her now for more than three years.'

Walpurga, a German-built Spray 40, named for a Bavarian witch, fascinated her owners Mike and Christine Platzer with her magical ability to steer herself from Lisbon to Lanzarote.

After a season of trials in the German Bite, Mike and Christine left their home of Port Wilhelmshaven in the summer of 1991 and cruised the Baltic Sea until November. They then wintered in Hamburg and worked there on land. They left Hamburg in spring 1992 and visited many ports in Holland, the south coast of England, Brittany and the whole north coast of Spain, where in November they found a little fishing port near Coruña to spend another winter and work on the land again. Mike and Christine left in the spring and sailed comfortably along the west coast of Spain and Portugal, and crossed from Lisbon to Lanzarote in the Canary Islands in $5^1/_2$ days. They continued:

'Here our boat, for the first time, could really stand up to her reputation. She steered herself all the way, sometimes in strong winds, in exactly the same manner that Slocum's *Spray* and all the famous replicas did. She did it of course on other occasions, but only for hours at a time, on this occasion she had the opportunity to show her paces for a longer period. She does it on all courses and also under different sails.

We want to stay in the Canaries for at least a year, and do a bit of charter work in the winter.'

CHEZ MOI
This Spray replica is currently owned by John Guimont, who sent us the following account:

'*Chez Moi,* currently at the Oyster Point marina in south San Francisco, California, is a Spray based on your design. I am the second owner. She is constructed in steel with some modifications. Don Lefler was the builder. Don is a retired custom home builder, who began construction of the Spray in 1981 in Oregon. He contracted the hull and deck welding project, and then moved her into his back yard where he spent several years completing the project. She was completed in Richmond, California, in 1987, and christened *Shibumi,* and sailed to Mexico, Hawaii, and then returned to California. The interior was photographed by Steve Dashu en route. (Steve Dashu is a famous American yachtsman who designs, builds and sails fast cruising boats, and is a prolific yachting journalist and well-known figure on the American cruising/yachting scene.) She was sold to me in 1991. The plan is to finish some upgrading in the next few years and retire for an extended cruise.'

Chez Moi has a steel hull, a staysail ketch rig, and the interior is fitted out with Honduras mahogany. She was finished by a custom home builder, who did a wonderful job; this kind of interior is effectively unavailable from any commercial builder. Don made a number of design changes. She is powered by a 20hp China diesel, which is marginal. The raised portion of her cabin was extended forward for additional headroom. The

The beautiful interior of this Spray 40, Chez Moi, *was built from Honduras mahogany by her original owner and builder Don Lefler. Photograph by Steve Dashu.*

masts were raised 6ft [1.8m], and 6in [152mm] were added to the keel. John bought *Chez Moi* for the safety and comfort of the design, and the steel for long-distance offshore ventures. To date this experience has been in San Francisco Bay and the surrounding coast. John feels that the only drawback of such a heavy, stiff design is that the genoa will blow out before she feels overpowered enough to reef. This was his learning experience on a trip to Drake's Bay.

Instead of a conventional V berth forward, Don, the original owner and builder, built one on the starboard side, and then installed a complete head and sail stowage area on the port. In the main cabin there is a U-shaped settee to port and two swivel chairs to starboard near the heater and bookshelves. The galley is to starboard, and the navigational station to port. The aft cabin has an athwartships berth, which is usable under almost any conditions. Don built pilot berths into both sides of the main cabin but John says there's been no need for them. He plans to remove the one on the port side to use it for an entertainments centre, TV, VCR tape storage, etc. The overall design concept was set up for extended offshore work by a couple with the option of having a single crew member in separate quarters forward for long passages. John's plans are essentially the same.

Fuel capacity is 2 x 45 gal [2 x 204 lit] tanks with a 10 gal [45 lit] day tank mounted above the engine. There are four water tanks totalling 150 gal [682 lit], and there is another 45 gal [204 lit] tank that has never been used. Don was not sure which fluid he would run out of first, so he kept the last tank in reserve to be adapted to water or diesel as needed. He never came up short on either one. John plans to carry a water maker so he expects to increase the diesel capacity.

Don kept the construction simple and cheap, no refrigeration, but there are two huge ice boxes that are very well insulated. It is basically a no-frills construction. Don had Loran, HAM, VHF, Satnav, supported by three batteries in two banks. John has added radar, and plans to add GPS, two of them, electric windlass, three more batteries as a third bank, inverters, scuba compressor, and salt water wash down. 'That's more than enough complication for me,' he says.

John continued:

'When I bought *Chez Moi* I was single and planned to cruise alone. If I had known I would marry again, I would have named her *Chez Nous*. I will probably change the name when we repaint the entire boat prior to departure.'

The Spray is a comfortable cruising boat, and one that can carry a lot of extra gear and equipment without adversely affecting performance. When fitted with the slightly deeper keel that some owners have opted to install on their Spray replicas, the boat does go to windward better than one would expect. Also, the rig is an important factor; and, as the reader will observe, many owners have opted for gaff ketches, gaff schooners and the like, so you cannot expect impeccable windward performance using these rigs. Various owners go into some detail about the rigs they have chosen, and try to assess the value of each in relation to the Spray design.

FLORISSANT

Last year when visiting Australia, my attention was drawn to a publication called *Trade a Boat,* which contains hundreds of boats for sale. I decided to write to all of the brokers who had Spray replicas on their books; the first reply was from John Latchford at Whitsunday Marine Brokerage of Airlie Beach, Queensland:

'We regularly see Sprays here in our marina, particularly during the cruising season, and we are always interested to see how different boats of the same design can be. They certainly are boats designed for the individual! The *Florissant* is a Roberts Spray 40, built of solid glass fibre. The owners live on *Florissant* permanently, and also run their business on board. She is cutter rigged with two furling headsails. The main has Dutchman reefing. A storm sail is fitted and a 2200 sq ft [204 sqm] MPS, which I assume is a cruising spinnaker. The engine is a Ford 85 hp diesel, and the boat cruises at 8 knots. This particular Spray is well fitted out with Autohelm, wind speed indicators, depth indicators, log and radar. She has a full range of navigation equipment, including a GPS Navstar. Safety equipment includes dry chemical fire extinguishers, and a good selection of anchor gear, chain etc.'

Subsequently, a letter arrived from the owners of *Florissant* which stated:

'We were very excited regarding your plans for the forthcoming book about the beautiful Spray, and to know that our own yacht *Florissant* will take part.

We bought Auntie, as we now affectionately call her, in the beautiful Whitsunday's Airlie Beach to be precise, which is part of the magnificent Barrier Reef on north-eastern Australia. It was an instant love affair; and after an inspection and a test sail a deposit was placed, and the arrangements made for a survey.

In shock from our unexpectedly rash decision, we raced back to Sydney to finalize the sale of our home, which was to finance the purchase.

It was love at first sight when Gorge and Gorgine Lippis saw this handsome cutter-rigged Spray 40, Florissant. *Her owners live aboard and also run their business from her.*

As nature would have it, we commenced our delivery voyage from Airlie Beach to our boat's new home in Sydney, a voyage of approximately 1100 nautical miles, at the worst possible time of the year for the prevailing winds. The wind was on the nose at regular forces of 25 to 40 knots. Rain squalls and large swells, possibly 16ft [5m] on occasions, added to our time of about three weeks for the trip, which normally takes about ten days.'

Their greatest problem was of the manmade variety. About 15 miles off the coast opposite the sleepy little village of Ballina, on one very stormy night, a huge container ship mistook their yacht as a rendezvous vessel for, they suspect, illegal drug trading or illegal migrants. Their radar screen picked him up about 6 miles away heading north to south, but instead of continuing on his way after passing them, he turned and circled *Florissant* in ever-decreasing circles until he was no further away than about 100yds [92m].

The letter continued:

'Repeatedly we called on the VHF for the ship to recognize us and signal his intentions, but we were met with only the chilling response "We have no course", which was spoken in such a cold and cruel tone that we will never forget it. Eventually our local volunteer Coast Guard came to the rescue via the VHF, and as soon as the ship knew he was monitored by the authorities he sped off at a great rate in a southerly direction. Naturally, reports were made to the Customs and other authorities.

On our arrival back home in Sydney, we had time to reflect upon our adventures and to realize what a wonderful yacht *Florissant* truly is, that is, a magnificently strong, stable and seakindly lady. We would have no hesitation in sailing her in anything Mother Nature cares to conjure up, and to recommend her design to anyone contemplating purchasing a Spray.'

ARNAK

The owner writes:

'My wife Linda and I have now been living on board our Spray *Arnak* for the past 14 years, and, after a shake-down cruise around New Zealand in 1980, have cruised the south-west Pacific including Fiji, New Caledonia, Vanuatu, Solomons, Papua New Guinea and Australia.

We departed Australia in 1987 bound west across the Indian Ocean, visiting Christmas Island, Cocos Keeling Islands, Chagos Archipelago, Sri Lanka, India,

Arnak, a glassfibre Spray 40, was built in New Zealand by Geoff Gentil who lived aboard for 14 years, wandering through the world's seas with his wife Linda.

Oman, South Yemen, Djibouti, Sudan and Egypt, then through the Suez Canal in May of 1988 to visit Israel, Cyprus, Lebanon, Turkey, Greece, Italy, Malta, Tunisia, Spain, Gibraltar and Morocco. We visited many ports on the Algarve coast of Spain and Portugal, then sailed to Madeira and the Canary Islands, thence to Senegal and Gambia on the West African coast where we sailed up the Gambia and Casamance rivers, perhaps the first Spray and New Zealand vessel to do so.'

Their next stop was the Cape Verde Islands off the African coast and then across the 'pond' to Barbados, Bequia, and south through the Grenadines to Trinidad and Venezuela, where they explored as far as they could up the San Juan river in the Gulf of Paria. Next they went west to Bonaire and Curacao, and on to the Bay Islands of Honduras. Their next stop was the Rio Dulce in Guatemala, where they explored far inland, then Belize, Mexico and the USA, which is where they are at present.

They called their Spray a 'Spray type', as a replica would indicate an exact copy, which theirs is not. The owner says he has heard the term 'Spray class' used, which may be relevant.

The letter continued:

'We bought your plans for the glassfibre Spray 40 and a copy of Ken Slack's book *In the Wake of the Spray* in 1975. After making some minor modifications and designing the cabin and interior layout to our liking, we built our Spray, completing the project in 1980. This is a rather sad time for us as we have decided to sell *Arnak* and live ashore for a while, during which time I will build another Spray. Tomorrow, *Arnak* will have a new owner, who will retain the old name and be using the vessel in his marine biology studies around New Zealand, so she will complete her circumnavigation and be an ideal platform and home for him and his wife. People often ask me what I think of the Spray, and my answer is, "I am building another one".'

After cruising and working in many countries, *Arnak*'s owner believes that the Spray is the ideal vessel. To start with, a well-proven working boat type, modified slightly for ocean sailing, is a great compromise. The stability and balance of the Spray are legendary. What a lot of people don't realise is that there

Arnak. *The attractive interior of this glassfibre Spray 40 as installed by owner/builder Geoff Gentil.*

is no perfect boat, only boats most suited to the work you put them to. You can't have 14ft 4in [4.4m] beam and 4ft [1.2m] draft, and go to windward like a witch, just as you can't have 10ft [3m] beam and 7ft [2.1m] draft and have initial stability and live aboard comfortably on a small vessel around 40ft [12.1m]. The letter said:

'Looking back over the last 14 years in black and white, we have spent 80 per cent of our time at anchor or in port, 19 per cent sailing off the wind and 1 per cent on the wind. How much compromise should you make for windward performance? Of course, this is only the use we put our vessel to, which is, live-aboard ocean cruising. We have spent a lot of time exploring rivers and creeks as well as coral atolls and islands, a lot of which are uncharted, and our 4ft [1.2m] draft was of great value. In the open ocean, again our draft has been of benefit, giving to the seas rather than being held when a large wave hits. Running dead downwind with our great beam has been very comfortable with no rolling from gunwale to gunwale. This is a point of sail most cruising sailors hate, but one generally found on ocean passages in the tropics. I believe there are basically three items that should be addressed when choosing a sailing vessel. Firstly, *seaworthiness*: a proven design or type. Second, *windward performance*; look at where you will be cruising or sailing. Third, *comfort*: look at how long you want to live on board, initial stability/stiffness, roominess and displacement. The Spray is exceptionally well balanced, and *Arnak* is no exception.'

Arnak's hull is built in solid glassfibre using C-Flex (tm) as the base material with alternating chopped strand mat and woven roving lay up. The hull laminate tapers from $1^1/_4$ in [31mm] keel to the 14in [355mm] high bulwarks which are $^3/_4$in [20mm] thick. The hull is divided up into 6ft [1.8m] square sections using hollow glassfibre frames and stringers to give an extremely strong and stiff hull. Ballast is $4^1/_2$ tons [4572kg] of cast iron securely glassed in. All full and partial bulkheads land on frames, and are locked and keyed in place with a substantial glass laminate. Below the waterline there are four thick layers of epoxy tar to prevent osmosis, followed by a waterproof barrier coat, then three coats of copper antifouling. The coamings, cockpit and cabin top are finished in epoxy saturated, laminated plywood, covered with a 6oz [170g] glass cloth and epoxy resin followed by a two-pot polyurethane paint system for very low maintenance.

The deck shelf is laminated New Zealand kauri epoxy glued and through-bolted with 3/8in [9mm] bronze bolts, which pass through the hull and the rubbing strake. The deck beams are 4in [100mm] and 2in [50mm] kauri, checked into the deck shelf and carline, which is again laminated kauri. The decks are constructed using $^1/_2$in [12mm] epoxy-saturated ply with 2in x 1in [50 x 25mm] teak over. The cabin sides are $1^1/_2$in [37mm] laminated ply, and the cabin top is 1in [25mm] laminated ply over laminated beams. The king plank is 10in x $1^1/_2$in [250mm x 37mm] in kauri, through which the anchor winch and large bronze bollard are bolted. There are six dorade vents on the cabin top, giving excellent ventilation in hot weather. All deck hardware, including portholes, winches, cleats, bollards and turn-buckles are bronze. There are no plastic fittings, and even the sail slides are stainless steel. The sails are all triple-stitched Dacron, made by Lidgard Rudling Sails of New Zealand. All working sails are tan in colour; the large cruising spinnaker and mizzen staysail are gold. These sails are still in very good condition. The rigging is hand spliced and swaged 7 x 7 stainless steel, oversized, and supporting a large section double-spreader mainmast and single-spreader mizzen; a track holds the permanently mounted spinnaker pole. The headsail is rolled around a furling gear that is strong and reliable and can be reefed from the cockpit. All other sails are hoisted using double braid terylene, all rope halyards leading on to New Zealand made bronze Murray bottom action winches.

The davits are a heavy section 2in [50mm] pipe and carry the 10ft [3m] aluminium dinghy. The outboard motor locks on to a pushpit bracket, and there are strong hardwood grab rails on the cabin top. The spray dodger, which covers half the cockpit, has zipped windows for extra ventilation. There are two large cockpit lockers. A large awning also doubles as an efficient rain water catcher with flexible down pipes. The bronze steering wheel is attached to the tiller arm with a $1^{1}/_{2}$in [37mm] shaft, chain, cable and steering box, which is next to a robust autopilot motor. This gives a very positive and strong steering system without the loss of feel. The emergency steering drops straight on to the top of the flanged 2 inch rudder shaft for tiller steering. Spare steering cables are only part of the extensive spares carried to make this yacht self-sufficient. Under the cockpit floor is the main engine, a Ford 4 cylinder 60 hp engine (diesel), completely rebuilt with new cylinder liners, pistons, rings, bearings etc in June/July 1992. It is a slow revving and reliable motor, which has always started at first turn of the key. *Arnak*'s owner has maintained this engine in top condition and kept a full log of all maintenance. Coupled to this engine is a large, two to one Paragon mechanical gearbox driving double universals and stainless steel shaft, which is held solid by a heavy thrust bearing. The stern gland is bronze and the stern bearing is of the rubber cutlass type. The three-blade propeller gives a cruising speed of 6 knots, with 8 knots maximum. At cruising revs, 1500 rpm, the fuel consumption is about 1 gallon per hour, giving a cruising range of about 600 miles [965km]. Fuel is carried in two separate integral tanks of approximately 60 gal [270 lit] each with spare containers on deck. Situated in the engine room is a 12 gal [54 lit] hot water cylinder, which heats off the engine or via the AC system to which it is wired directly.

A lay shaft alongside the engine drives a 75 amp alternator and the compressor for the 4cu ft [0.36cu m] freezer and the 2cu ft [0.18cu m] fridge. There are spare pulleys fitted to take any other equipment that could be fitted at a later date. The freshwater pressure system is also mounted here, along with the automatic and manual bilge pumps. There is good access to the engine, and all regular maintenance areas can be easily reached. Two BCF fire extinguishers are fitted close to the engine room. Outboard of the engine on either side are the fuel and water tanks, with sight gauges and good access for cleaning.

Water tanks are approximately 60 gal [270 lit] each, and the batteries are above the water tank in a dry and easily serviced area. The switch panel fronts the main saloon over the chart table, which hinges up for access to the fridge/freezer.The navigation equipment is also in this area, including autopilot, VHF, Satnav, RDF, depth sounder and instruments. The sounder swings out for easy helmsman's viewing.

All the bulkheads are 1in [25mm] laminated ply, faced with New Zealand honeysuckle and sapele mahogany. The cabin sides are fitted with polished brass grab rails and the main saloon table is mahogany with a unique cork inlay, and seats six. Cupboards and under seats provide plenty of storage space, and cupboard doors are fitted with rattan/cane for ventilation. The floors are ply with cork overlay, easy to keep clean, and warm. Forward of the forward cabin is a chain and rope locker with plenty of room for spare chain and rope, etc. The forward cabin has two V berths with separate reading lights and storage under and alongside. The galley is fitted with a stainless steel sink and tiled bench and upstand with a New Zealand-made stainless steel, three-burner stove, and efficient oven. There is also a DC to AC invertor fitted to run normal domestic appliances. There is excellent storage space for food and crockery, etc in cupboards and drawers. In the aft section of the boat on the starboard side is the master cabin, with a comfortable double bed and vanity unit with hanging locker and plenty of drawers. On the port side is the roomy shower and toilet area, with shower curtain and hot-and-cold pressure water. Forward of this is the sail locker with storage under.

Arnak's owner said:

'In 14 years of live-aboard cruising, during which she has carried us effortlessly three-quarters of the way around the world, *Arnak* has proved herself especially comfortable at sea, rarely heeling more than 10 degrees, and easy to sail for two persons in all weathers. Had we not decided to have a break ashore for a few years, *Arnak* would not be for sale. In fact, that period ashore will be spent building a new vessel, identical to *Arnak,* but slightly bigger.'

Norwegian Kjell Zetterstrom built his own Spray 40, Capt J Slocum, *with a substantial steel hull made from 5mm plate. He modified the cabin and cockpit design to suit the Norwegian climate and chose a rig which could be adapted for singlehanded sailing.*

Capt J Slocum

Kjell Zetterstrom of Norway has told us his experiences of building and sailing his steel Spray 40, Version C:

'Way back in 1980 I received the boatbuilding package and started building shortly afterwards. I decided to weld the hull, since I had done some amateur work in the field and had access to left over 5mm steel plates from a shipyard. Your specification was 4mm (these two mm sizes fall one each side of $^3/_{16}$ in inch), but I estimated the extra weight not to represent a problem.

Bearing in mind that I live in a cold and rainy country, I changed the upper decks and cabin and cockpit. The cabin and cockpit were $1/8$in [3mm] steel plated, on which $1/4$in [6mm] plywood was glued with polyurethane. In turn, $1/2$in [12mm] teak was glued to the plywood with epoxy. Next change was the rig. Several old sailors advised me not to use the wooden gaff rig, and I'm glad I didn't, even though it would look more classic. I installed a new 6 cylinder Ford diesel that I was able to obtain very cheaply, and also installed hydraulic steering and aft deck mechanical steering. Also, I installed a 3 kw diesel-powered generator, electric bow steering, and a 1500 Watt winch. Also included are two 132 gal [500 lit] stainless steel water tanks. The hull was completely foamed internally with polyurethane foam, and all of the interior was fitted out with teak; it is heated using a diesel heater and an electric oven. You can probably imagine that it has become 1.2 tons too heavy. On the other hand, less ballast was required, so the total weight is approximately 18 tons.

Since I mostly sail alone, in moderate winds though, I saw the necessity of handling the boat from the aft deck. The solution was a roller sail system, and a genoa foresail using profurl. This gave an effect that gave me more weather helm than I would like, so I found the obvious answer, and that was to extend the bowsprit. Now she sails beautifully. I don't mind challenges, and I believe problems are there to be solved, and the satisfaction in solving them justifies all the headaches. I will not hesitate to tell you that my Spray is admired wherever we go, and I can only guess how many hundreds of photographs have been taken of her by admirers. It probably does not surprise you when I say that she was christened *Capt J Slocum,* and that I am very proud of my Spray.'

MIROUANGA

Ulrich Kronenberg contacted me by fax to say he was the owner of a Spray 40, and that he was building it from early 1985 until 1990. He said that he had two friends with Sprays, *Cornchri* and *Walpurga. Cornchri* was standing in Wilhelmshaven and *Walpurga* was in the Grand Canaries.

Naturally, I was most excited at receiving Ulrich Kronenberg's fax. Not only had I discovered one more Spray in Germany, but another three boats had come to light. Shortly after this, the postman delivered a large envelope, which contained a copy of the magazine *Palstek,* which specialises in the practical needs of sailing people. There are lots of 'Do It Yourself articles', and stories of the cruises undertaken by the readers of the magazine. Ulrich Kronenberg is the editor of *Palstek* and has written several building and cruising articles that feature his Spray called *Mirouanga.* In one of the articles Ulrich talks about the early days of building the Spray hull and points out that everyone has to make sacrifices if they are going to build a boat successfully. He says, 'You yourself will have to take a long period of deprivation. It is usually even worse for the family. No more visits to Granny's. The dog will be chased instead of walked. The theatre is a thing of the past, and conversations are just boring breaks that disrupt work, unless of course, they are about your own boat.'

Ulrich Kronenberg's article goes on to lay out step by step how he built the boat, and some of his comments are worth noting: 'With all purchases, the best advice is to have barbed wire in your pocket.' On building a steel boat, Ulrich says, 'The building site should not be too close to a residential area, for most of the work is done at weekends, when other people, believe it or not, want peace and quiet.' On working under cover, Ulrich says, 'The minimum covering is a tent roof. We were very happy with our "Scottish" tent. In Germany, where 10 per cent of the building value is due in fees, the "Scottish" tent is most suitable.'

Mirouanga, another German-built Spray 40. This steel-hulled Spray with the classic gaff rig took its builder-owner five years to complete; a dedicated project that made great inroads into his family life.

When discussing obtaining some of the materials for the setting up and the strong back, Ulrich says, 'You can get all the beams from the scrap heap. New ones would be too expensive and would not carry out their function any better. They will land up on the scrap heap again anyway. Prices are according to market conditions, sympathies and moods. Here you need to use the international boat construction currency: beer for small change, brandy for banknotes.' On buying the materials to build the boat, Ulrich says:

'A sad chapter is the purchasing of materials and the acquisition of tools. It is sensible to order large quantities, because small orders are usually over-priced. Things that are used up like welding wire, grinding disks, etc, should never be bought individually, but you should try to negotiate prices for a large quantity to be delivered. Do not forget that high-quality tools are the only ones that last. Cheap DIY items seem enticing, but are only suitable for DIY home handyman use. We are not putting together a hobby room, but building a boat. A service network is important, although this can give you grey hair too. Good planning is especially important, because shops may be closed at the weekend when you do most of your work.'

Ulrich feels very strongly about personal safety and says, 'Be careful with your eyes. Think of accident prevention. My two visits to the eye clinic have strengthened my conviction that you cannot make savings here.'

PEGGOTTY
As is evident from the text, most of the Sprays are scattered far and wide around the world. There are Sprays in almost every country; and, as we wanted to include the details of as many of these boats as possible, we did not stint in our efforts to track down individual examples of the Spray design.

The story of *Peggotty* originally appeared in the *Eastern Daily Press,* a newspaper that covers

Norfolk and Suffolk. Via a phone call to the newspaper, I obtained the original photographs that appeared with the article; shortly after filing the information away, a letter arrived from Alan Sendall, totally independently of the information via the newspaper article. Alan and his wife are the owners of *Peggotty*. Alan wrote:

'A little over ten years ago, my wife and I decided to build a yacht and go cruising. Like most people who intend to build their own yachts, we looked at as many books of plans and study sheets as we could lay our hands on. We wandered up and down marina docks and dreamed, read of other people's voyages, and books about yachts. At the end of it all I bought a set of plans from your Australian office to build a Spray; it was to be just a floating home for my wife and I, and any children we might have along the way. The Spray seemed to be what we needed, and it is pretty as well. Even from the time that she was just a set of frames, she looked and felt right.

I made one or two slight alterations to your hull plans. As an engineer, I felt entitled to do so. None of the interior layouts that were offered were suitable for our needs as they were. Version C was closest. I felt it was a shame to cut up the interior of the Spray into small compartments, as one of the advantages is the great volume below. I kept the interior as open as possible. Living space while on long passages, even for a family of three, is so important. Much more so than a second head, or having seven permanent berths. The former is ridiculous on a 40ft [12.19m] yacht, unless it is for chartering. The latter uses great space and encourages guests to stay longer than they would if they had to make up their berth each night.'

Alan Sendall decided that he wanted to rig his yacht as a gaff topsail cutter. However, at the time that he wrote to us about this, we did not have the sail plan readily available. We have since designed additional sail plans to suit the Spray 40, but Alan was able to design his own, which, judging from the information he has sent us, turned out very well. He goes on to report that they built *Peggotty* below some willow and fig trees on the edge of Tauranga Harbour Bay of Plenty, New Zealand. During the spring tides her keel got salty, and when there was a small whirlwind one night that sent a large part of one of the willow trees

Peggotty, *built by New Zealand engineer Alan Sendall. Her original ill-fitting, second hand sails, seen here, still gave her a speed of 8 knots. Photo by courtesy of Alan Sendall.*

Alan Sendall on board his steel Spray 40 during a visit to his former home port in England.

crashing into her then unplated stern, there was a couple of days of clearing debris and frame straightening to be done. It took three years of weekends and evenings before *Peggotty* was ready to launch.

Alan explains that Clara Peggotty was a character from one of Charles Dickens' novels. She was David Copperfield's nanny, and lived in an upside-down boat on Great Yarmouth beach, which is where Alan comes from and where the boat is registered. By this time, Alan had given up trying to find information from which to make a wooden mast, so he looked at making a steel mast; a mast from 8in x $^1/_8$ in [203mm x 3mm] wall, spiral wound pipe worked out stronger and lighter than its wooden equivalent, was very cheap, and took just eight hours to complete, including all the fittings for the housing topmast. To begin with, Alan thought of this steel mast as a temporary affair to see them by until a decent piece of wood could be found, but as time and miles went by, they grew to like its strength and even its looks. The top mast was made of New Zealand tanikaha.

The launching was an event in its own right, because *Peggotty* had to get a crane or low loader within reach. During spring tides there was 2–2ft 6in [610–762mm] of water in the inlet; there was clearly not enough water for a yacht of this size. These things caused a lot of speculation among the residents about Alan's sanity, and the chances of 'it' ever floating. However this dilemma was solved by using railway irons and sleepers. They built a little railway and dragged *Peggotty* for 450yds [411m] until the water was about 3ft 3in [990mm] on a king tide.

Before starting to build, Alan built a 20:1 scale model and used this to calculate the draft of the yacht in a semi-finished and completely unballasted state. He also found this model useful in determining the best size of plates to buy, as well as deciding on certain aesthetic features. For a long time, one side was black and the other white, until they could decide on a colour. With an all-up weight of 10 tons *Peggotty* should have floated on the king tide, and after seven days of gruelling work winching and carrying railway irons and heavy sleepers through the thick, gooey mud, and with ten strong men pushing under the transom, and another ten hauling her over with a halyard, eventually she did. Alan was extremely relieved. He was unsure how tender she would be without any ballast, but she seemed fine, and within the hour they had sailed on, and gone gently through Tauranga Harbour.

For the next two years they sailed the coast of the north island of New Zealand, and for the first nine months they still had no ballast and she stood up to it very well, although they didn't

Built for endurance, the gaff topsail cutter Peggotty, *in the icy waters of the Antarctic.*

have the topmast in. When they put the ballast in, it was only 3 tons [3048kg], and with full tanks, they sat right on the marks. By May 1990, they were ready to go off-shore, so they provisioned, said goodbye, and left. The plan was to go to England via Aus-tralia, Indian Ocean, Cape Town, and Atlantic. All of their sails, except the storm trysail, were second-hand. The mainsail was made from an old Bermudan main elon-gated with a vertical panel set in from the luff. About 150 miles north-east of North Cape they experienced their first gale, and were very satisfied with the way *Peggotty* handled things, except that she did not heave-to well, but insisted on lying almost beam-on to the wind. (Later, changes to the sail arrangement eliminated this problem.) Their only new sail was of no real use to them. They spent the next few months cruising in Fiji and New Caledonia, and by the time they reached Australia in December they knew that they had made the right choice of yacht. However, their plans had changed slightly. Alan continued:

'It was obvious to us that *Peggotty* was well suited to strong winds, and handled rough condi-tions very well. While I was building *Peggotty* I tried to imagine her in the worst seas and wind, and how she would fare if rolled or pitch-poled, and I tried to design all her fittings and fixtures accordingly. Always in the back of my mind I had the idea of sailing the Southern Ocean to round Cape Horn. Another desire of mine was to some day see the Antarctic conti-nent, and it seemed logical to do that at the same time, seeing as we would be so close; and now in Sydney we started to prepare for the long trek across the Southern Ocean. We had new sails made, and incorporated a trysail into the main so that we would have a gaff-headed trysail, which I hoped would cause her to heave-to better. The new staysail had one reef which was probably a waste of time; we have only used it reefed a few times, preferring to use the storm jib.'

A year after arriving in Australia, they left and crossed the Tasman Sea to Nelson, New Zealand, which gave them a chance to test their new systems and the new sails. Heaving-to now with the new mainsail was much improved; they lay 50-60 degrees off the wind, were 'very comfortable' and it was so much quicker than setting the trysail. The next months in New Zealand were spent in preparation and waiting for November, the time they had chosen to leave. Alan commented that another advantage of a Spray is the ability to stow 12 months'

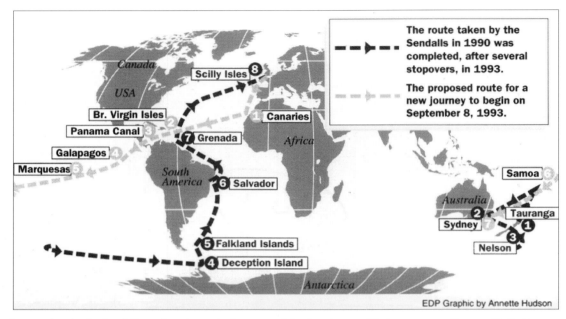

Route taken by the Sendalls in their Spray 40 Peggotty. *Map by Annette Hudson, courtesy* Eastern Daily Press .

supply of food and all the spares and tools needed for such a voyage. Alan said:

'We left New Zealand on 11 November 1992, and during the next 12 months we sailed 24 000 miles. We sailed over 5000 miles direct to the Antarctic and cruised there for three to four weeks before heading north to the Falkland Islands where we stayed for another four weeks before heading to the UK via Brazil and Granada. We left England in October 1993 and sailed to Antigua via the Canaries. During all these miles *Peggotty* took good care of us, and we had no really anxious moments (except for a few close calls with ships in the English Channel), whether it was beating clear of Elephant and Clarence Islands in the icy waters of the Antarctic, or drifting along in the Inter coastal Waterway. In the big following seas of the Southern Ocean, we lay below reading. With the storm jib poled out and her long keel, there was little enough for the steering gear to do. The only breakage we had was a gaff fitting that broke 300 miles south of Port Stanley.'

HARRY B

Roland Latina of Illinois, USA, built his boat using some unusual boatbuilding techniques, which seem to have worked out well in practice. Bob's Spray 40 is not the first boat to be built using the multi-chine steel patterns as the basis for building a glassfibre boat, but some of the techniques Bob has used are a little unusual. He purchased the patterns for the 40ft [12.1m] multi-chine hull Spray replica sometime in 1978, choosing the multi-chine patterns so that he could use the material that was available for frames.

He worked for the Rawlings Sporting Goods Company, and when they dropped their hockey line, he made them an offer for all the left-over hockey sticks. He used the ash handles, four in a bundle epoxy glued and bolted, for his frames. Roland was very pleased with the results. He then planked the hull, deck and cabin using C-Flex (tm) glassfibre planking, which was monel stapled to the frames, and inside the hull he backed this up by using epoxy fillets and additional glassfibre to attach and bond the frames into the hull structure. He discovered in order to keep costs down, you had to be a great scrounger. Roland used just about every type of wood available for the interior. He laminated his cabin and deck beams, mast, boom and gaff from clear Douglas fir and epoxy.

Roland made his mast and boom hollow, but had a tough time getting the wood to give him an 8in [203mm] round mast and a 6in [150mm] round boom. Roland filled the hollow parts of the mast with crushed aluminium foil, to ensure that he would be picked up on radar. He used railroad tie plates for his ballast and bedded them in epoxy. His vessel has a 50 hp Perkins diesel, an auxiliary engine and a three-bladed prop. When all this work was finished, Roland had the boat hauled on a hydraulic trailer from Belleville, Indiana, to Berkeley Lake, Kentucky.

After a shake-down, Roland and his wife left Berkeley and headed south through Kentucky Lake, Tennessee River, Pickwick Dam and Lake Cistlok, and then down the Ten-Tom Waterway to the coast. The last two years they have been cruising the Gulf Coast from Biloxi, Mississippi, and also around Ocean Springs, Pennecola, Pestin, and were now at a marina in Niceville, Florida. They love the boat! Lots of room down below, and they live aboard quite a bit. Roland and his wife can easily handle the Spray (they are aged 69 and 66 years) and she stays stable under sail. The boat is rigged as a gaff cutter with the foresail on a boom.

OSPRAY

Mellor, the builder of the steel Spray 40 *Ospray,* wrote in March 1982 providing considerable detail about the building of his boat. Jim also wrote several articles for the UK boating magazine *Practical Boat Owner,* which were run in the January, February and March 1981 issues. The articles and letters that Jim sent to me reveal that he was a very resourceful builder and thought through each stage of the building programme, and developed some useful building techniques as well as ways to save on the costs. For instance, when it came to obtaining the timber for his mast, Jim researched the matter thoroughly and found that there was a stand of suitable timber up on the Welsh mountainside only 30 miles [48km] from his home. He said that for some reason or other this particular stand of timber had not been thinned out and the trunks of the trees grew straight and tall. Jim and another builder, who was also looking for mast timber, went off to inspect these trees. Accompanied by a forester, he was advised that providing he was willing to pay a little over the commercial price, he would be able to purchase one of these trees for himself. In effect, when the time came to choose the trees, he and his companion chose three for the two masts they needed, the idea being that if one proved unsuitable then they would have a spare. The cost was £80 for three splendid masts. The trees were felled without delay, and by good fortune a timber merchant working in the area agreed to haul the timber home for £35. The same person had a 100 hp Ford diesel engine available, and Jim was able to purchase this for £50. As he says, 'thus by one stroke of luck did we acquire the basis of two forms of motive power.' Jim launched *Ospray,* and was in touch with us during the sailing trials and later reported:

'I am glad to say that *Ospray* has fulfilled all our hopes and expectations! After several grand little cruises to the Hebrides, West of Scotland and Ireland, Else and I took a year off and did a round trip to the West Indies, going via the Scillies, Northern Spain, Madeira, the Canaries, Cape Verde Islands and then across to Else's birthplace – Trinidad, where I can tell you, there was a great reception from the family. We sailed in through the "Dragons Mouth" just as dawn was breaking to the weird screams of the Howler monkeys, and the rich steamy smells of the jungle only a few hundred yards away. An osprey swooped down and flew over his namesake which we took to be a good omen.

After enjoying Christmas with the family we spent the next six months cruising the tropical paradise of the Grenadines, the Windward and Leeward Islands and then on to the British Virgins. The snorkelling was terrific and the variety and colour of the fish has to be seen to be believed. We swam and dived in the "champagne" off Parumica where strings of bubbles trickle upwards from the sea bed as a result of volcanic activity beneath the sea.

We had some close encounters with sperm whales who grabbed our attention by throwing their great flukes in the air only a few yards from the boat. The hand of god was what the old whalers called it. Mostly throughout the islands we anchored close in with a stern line tied to a palm tree. Talk about idyllic! Boat boys would swarm alongside, sometimes too many, bringing hands of bananas and other provisions. *Ospray* was the centre of attention wherever we went and we made many friends along the way.

Having built my Spray with the help of my sons I was very proud that two of them were able to join us. All too soon it was time to make sail for old England via Bermuda, The Azores and Ireland. The twenty day crossing from Bermuda to Horta was a rough one, three gales and of the seventeen vessels that arrived in the Azores from Bermuda during that period, *Ospray* was one of only two that arrived undamaged; she looked after us wonderfully well and in the big following seas she was brilliant; no yawing or corkscrewing as I have struck in other boats.

On the way back we were guided by "Herb", a radio ham and meteorologist from Bermuda. Each night Herb would call his "ducklings" in listed order and give and receive weather information, telling us which way to head to avoid the worst of the weather. Over the years Herb must have saved many lives with his selfless all for nothing service, God bless him.

We saw whales almost every day and one day a trio of fin whales, which we estimated to be nearly 70ft [21.3m] long, against *Ospray*'s 40ft [12.2m], swam up to us, one swimming under the boat while we looked on with some apprehension, truly a magnificent sight.'

TANIMARA

This glassfibre Spray 40 was built in Belgium by Jack Daneels, who writes:

'Regards your calling all Sprays, I built *Tanimara* (the name is Comanche for Northern Wind, Lonesome Wind) in Antwerp, Belgium, after work and during weekends and holidays. I started in 1978 with a companion called Frank Nys. Preliminary study of the subject via your booklet *Build for Less*, and the Spray study plans plus Ken Slack's book *In the Wake of the Spray* finally set our minds on the idea.'

The detailed construction plans and full-size patterns were received in the summer of 1978. They were to build one mould and two balsa sandwich hulls together, sharing all costs. When the first hull was finished and turned over in 1981, Jack's partner Frank lost heart. Realising that the project was

Tanimara, a Belgian glassfibre Spray 40, built by Jack Daneels, leaving harbour.

going to take up all of his free time and disrupt family life, he decided to give up. So Jack was on his own. He decided to use the hull as a mould for the second hull after he won the toss for the first hull. With the help of his wife, this second hull was completed in 1982.

Jack slightly modified the bow, starting at station one-half, to give *Tanimara* an increase in the clipper bow, making her LOA 44ft [13.4m]; the keel line was lowered by 5in [127mm] to accept 6.5 tons [6604kg] of lead ballast and to allow for the slightly higher masts. Jack goes on to list all of the equipment aboard his boat and then states, 'The boat was built as a "live-aboard" for four in great comfort, with room for another two occasionally.'

Tanimara was finally launched in September 1991 and did not need trim ballast at all; she sailed her maiden trip on the North Sea in 1992. Although Jack and his wife do not have long-distance cruising experience, this is for them in the near future; they are hoping to circumnavigate – they can already confirm some virtues of apparently all of the Sprays: excellent balance on all points of sail, very seakindly, and safe motion even in very chaotic seas. *Tanimara* is easy on the rudder, but needs a lot of practice to manoeuvre out of the small, crowded and confined harbours of Belgium.

Jack's partner Frank found a courageous buyer for his hull in 1987. Since then the boat has been completed and Jack saw her sailing on the River Schelde on a return trip to his home port of Antwerp. This Spray is called *Jan Wandelaar* (Johnny Walker). Jack says he is con-vinced that all proud builders and owners of the Bruce Roberts Sprays will give 'equally enthusiastic experiences in reply to your call'.

CANORES

My initial information about this Spray replica came from the passage notes column that appeared in a recent edition of the American boating magazine *Cruising World*. I quote from the report:

The stylish modern interior of Tanimara *with beautiful iroko woodwork. Photo by courtesy of Jack Daneels.*

'*Canores*, a 40ft [12.1m] Bruce Roberts version of Joshua Slocum's Spray, with Floridians Julia and Jim Pensioner aboard, called at Barbados last spring, bound for the Grenadines and Venezuela. Jim and Julia have lived aboard *Canores* since she was launched in 1989, and have cruised the US east coast, Gulf coast and Bahamas with her. The Pensioners, who built their dream ship in eight years, prefer steel construction for its strength in comparison with other materials. They recycled some 5000 lead wheel counterweights for ballast and used masts resurrected from another boat.'

Jim and Julia provided the US Bruce Roberts office with a brochure that details some of the features of *Canores*. Obviously they plan some chartering, as this brochure details all of the attractive features of the yacht that would appeal to would-be charterers. On deck they detail that the boat is equipped with two anchors that are housed on the bow with bow rollers, and an anchor windlass, for each. Some 200ft [61m] of anchor chain comes through the deck at the windlass and the second anchor has a 50ft [15m] chain and 200ft [61m] nylon rode. Teak anchor chocks are provided for on-deck storage for the two main CQR and Danforth anchors. A deck box behind the bowsprit contains mooring lines and anchor floats. The bulwarks of this Spray are 18in [457mm] high and these are topped off with stanchions and lifelines. The good-sized, comfortable, midship cockpit is covered with a permanent, but removable, sunbrella awning with roll-up acrylic windows all round. This of course is a very 'Floridian' type of arrangement, as most of the boats that operate around Florida and the Caribbean make plenty of provision for protection from the sun, and often the cockpit areas are capable of being temporarily fully enclosed, so as to afford protection from the numerous insects that prevail at certain times of the year in that area.

SPRAY OF DELL QUAY

Built from 1985 to 1987, using Bruce Roberts plans, by Trinity House pilot Brian Reed of Liverpool, this steel Spray 40 is currently owned by John Corello of Chichester. The Spray is fitted with a 80 hp Watermota diesel. The sails and rigging were made by James Lawrence of Brightlingsea; the mast and spars by Collar of Oxford.

All the above detail was supplied by the current owner, and looking at the photos of the boat I can see why he has gone to some trouble to give credit to the various suppliers. This is a beautiful example of the Spray 40,

The splendid workmanship by builder Brian Reed was complimented in a recent survey of John Corello's Spray of Dell Quay.

as an excerpt from a recent survey report conducted for an insurance company reads: 'Workmanship throughout the vessel is all of good standard, with every care being given to all aspects of construction to give a strongly built craft with scantlings in excess of normal yacht construction. The fitting of the plating is reflected in the fact that no filling of the topsides has been necessary.'

Owing to the frequent difficulty of obtaining crew, John Corello has mostly sailed the boat singlehanded. Poole, Portland and the areas around the Solent have been John's cruising grounds. John stated:

'She is a magnificent sea boat under sail or power (I've owned or built a total of 37 craft), and I am very happy sailing her on my own, but now long for a companion. For some years I sailed the famous Gold Belt, a coasting barge carrying foodstuffs around the coast; she likewise has great seagoing properties, riding out many storms.'

DELPHINAE

This is one of several glassfibre Spray 40s built by Peter D Norman from a female mould he constructed in Vancouver in Canada in 1974. During the period when I was opening the Bruce Roberts design office in Vancouver, Peter occupied an adjoining office, where he carried on his practice as an insurance adjuster. I remember Peter was well respected in his profession and was always in demand, flying here and there to inspect the latest major disaster.

Peter approached our design office and purchased a set of Spray 40 glassfibre plans and patterns. A female mould was to be built, and it was hoped several hulls could be sold. To my knowledge, about a dozen hulls were built from this mould – and maybe many more. A photo taken back in 1976 reveals several hulls being fitted out at that time. Hearsay leads me to believe that the moulds were still in use until recent times. We would like to hear about some of the other Sprays whose hulls were laid up in the same female fibreglass mould.

DRIFTER WAY

Frank Thiessen, an airline pilot/training captain who is stationed in Taiwan, writes:

'I leased a mould from Peter Norman in British Columbia Canada in 1979 and we laid up a Spray 40 hull. Subsequently, I finished the ketch design with centre cockpit. The boat was finished beside my house in Whistler in British Columbia, and we named the boat *Drifter Way*. My wife completed the interior fabric work and like every sailor's wife, was a terrific support person throughout the project. *Drifter Way* is presently located at Mosquito Creek Marina in North Vancouver. Our plans are that as soon as Taiwan allows private yacht ownership, we shall park the boat here for a while.'

DERWENT ENDEAVOUR

This is another Australian-based glassfibre Roberts Spray 40, which took Ronald Moss four and a half years part-time work to complete. *Derwent Endeavour* was built in Tasmania close to the banks of the Derwent river, hence the name. As the boat was intended for the Queensland charter trade, she was built to the strict survey requirements required by the Queensland authorities. The hull was constructed using C-Flex (tm) glassfibre as the basis for a hand-laid-up all-solid glassfibre hull. In May 1982 *Derwent Endeavour* set sail from Hobart with her first planned port of call, Port Macquarie, which is on the New South Wales coast. After the several hundred mile uneventful trip, *Derwent Endeavour* tied up at the marina in Port Macquarie. Ronald was very pleased with his new boat, for she had behaved very well when the boat was struck by heavy winds, just north of Newcastle.

The Australian east coast is famous for the dangerous sand bars that attempt to deny entrance to the safe harbours in this area. Many boats have come to grief when attempting to traverse these bars, which can present a boiling cauldron to any yachtsman daring to cross in the wrong wind and sea conditions. Ronald discovered that if he opened up the engine, he could surf in over these bars. He stated, 'I realise I should have reversed the engine and cleared the broken water as quickly as possible, but the Spray seemed to delight in this surfing; no doubt the hull design, long straight keel and an 80 hp diesel engine contributed to the success of this action.'

Ronald felt that the craft had still not as yet proved herself, but on a trip to Lord Howe Island the boat was to remove any doubts as to her ability. Ronald and his son, together with two friends, sailed out of Port Macquarie. At first the weather conditions were reasonable, as had been forecast; however, about 60 miles out, the wind veered and blew up. This caused a confused sea condition, and the Spray was indeed in the middle of a sizeable storm. The storm lasted all through the five days it took to reach Lord Howe Island, and the local met office on Lord Howe recorded wind speeds of 60 knots. As can be imagined, Ronald reported conditions on board were pretty hectic, but the boat behaved beautifully, and the only damage was a torn mainsail.

After an uneventful sail back to Port Macquarie, the next trip planned for *Derwent Endeavour* was from Port Macquarie to Southport. Owing to business commitments, the crew who took the boat to Lord Howe were not available, so Ronald signed one young totally inexperienced crew (he refers to this young man as a 'hairdresser') and another older person with some offshore powerboat experience as crew. In June 1983 the Spray was sailed out over the turbulent river bar at Port Macquarie and headed north. The weather forecast was not particularly favourable, but as Ronald's son and one of the crew had a tight time schedule, it was decided to make for Southport in one hop.

With a 20 knot easterly, the boat was making good progress; but as the weather looked threatening and as a seam in the jib looked suspect, it was lowered. It was decided to go into Coffs Harbour to get the sail repaired. The next day it poured with rain as *Derwent Endeavour* left Coffs Harbour. The weather forecast was for more rain, and north-east winds of 15 to 20 knots. Soon after leaving harbour, the winds freshened and backed to the north. Under all plain sail, the Spray handled the conditions well. Mr Moss reported:

'At 4 pm I awoke, the craft was being thrown around; I put my head through the hatch and the "hairdresser" who had been on watch said, "She has been going off the clock", and promptly put his head over the side to be sick. The log read up to 12 knots, the sea was menacing, and I remember thinking, "I hope it does not get worse." Well, as later reported by all of the crew, it did get worse, a lot worse. Although a lot of spray was coming over the cockpit, no sea was coming on board. After checking the Satnav to assure there was plenty of sea room, everything was battened down and all of the crew took to their bunks, only stirring to take it in turns to be sick.'

By this time it was pitch black outside, the wind shrieked as only it can, and the waves appeared to be massive. Ronald was wedged in his bunk in the stern cabin when he heard a strange noise, loud enough to be heard above the din of the storm. On looking through the perspex overhead hatch, he realised that the mizzen was flapping free. With some effort, Ronald released himself from his wedged position, and his son was already taking care of the immediate problem while shouting to the two crew in the forward cabin to put on their life-lines before coming up on deck to help. In Ronald's words, the young hairdresser was 'past it', but the older crew member 'was game'. After some hair-raising experiences, the skipper and the two crew were able to secure the aft boom and remove the large chunk of stern rail that had been torn out of its sockets and threatening to decapitate all concerned. After the strain of these efforts, it was decided to take off all sail and let the Spray lay to under bare poles. After a severe battering that lasted all night, it was a relief to see by first light that the conditions had improved. There were still big seas rolling in from the east, but these were only breaking occa-sionally. The position was now checked, and as the boat was now only 30 miles east of Ballina, it was decided to make for that port to get some rest and food.

When *Derwent Endeavour* reached the area outside the Ballina bar, a shocking sight greeted their eyes. There had been a lot of rain, so the river was running out at flood level and the breakers were rolling in through the entrance. After trying to make contact with the harbour authorities to get permission and some advice, and due to a mix-up over the response, it was decided to risk going in over the bar. With the two crew battened down below, Ronald and his son Chris headed the boat in. The first wave caught the Spray as she was just outside the entrance; the skipper could hear it coming. It lifted the boat, drove it forward, and with a rush of white water was past. The second wave caught the Spray just past the entrance; Chris yelled to the skipper that there was a big one coming. They could hear it roaring, so they opened up the motor and surfed in with it for about 100yds [91m] and reached clear water. About this time, they became aware of the crowds lining the north breakwater, they were applauding. The captain and crew of *Derwent Endeavour* later learned they had been in a cyclone!

The above experiences encountered by *Derwent Endeavour* were reported in the Australian boating magazine *Cruising Helmsman*. This magazine specialises in reporting cruising experi-ences, and in it all sorts of helpful advice is given to the cruising yachtsman. In the same issue as the report from the skipper of *Derwent Endeavour*, which under the circumstances, was a very low-key description of events, was another report by Anne Clode, a bystander on the breakwater. Anne Clode reported:

'The gale warning had kept all local and visiting craft in Ballina for nearly a week. The Richmond river was in full flood and several boats had been damaged at the wharf. As the fenders and barge boards could not cope with the pounding, it was not much better out at anchor, with logs and debris coming downstream. One fellow yachtsman gloomily remarked that the last time he had been in Ballina he had been "weathered in" for 17 days.

There had not been much talk on the 27 meg radio, for no one was going anywhere in these trying conditions. Unexpectedly, a yacht was heard calling Ballina Coastguard for information on the bar. Surely no one could be mad enough to attempt it under these conditions? There had been a gale warning for the past three days, and there was no improvement in sight.

The conversation between *Derwent Endeavour* and the Coastguard revealed that the yacht had been sitting out the storm for two days and the crew had about all they could take. With two inexperienced crew and all on board seasick, they wanted to attempt the entrance in the hope of getting some relief from the awful conditions outside. The Coastguard advised against them making the run over the bar; however, the skipper of *Derwent Endeavour* insisted, so the Coastguard officer gave all the help and advice that he could. The skipper sounded confident, knowing of the Spray's log keel and a 80 hp diesel. Appalled at the thought of any boat attempting that entrance in these conditions, the club bar emptied, and, along with half the town's population, headed for the breakwater to watch the saga unfold. The bar was a mass of boiling and breaking waves, line after line of breakers, surely no one would be mad enough to attempt to make the harbour in these conditions?

It seemed as though every house in Ballina had a 27 meg radio, for the word spread so quickly. Cars from all directions converged on the breakwater. This is a fishing town, and all the locals are very much aware of the bar entrance to their harbour and its well-earned reputation.

As *Derwent Endeavour* approached the bar, she began to be picked up by the breaking waves that thrust her forward at accelerated speed before sliding off the back of the wave. Closer to the bar as the seas got steeper, the onlookers expected to see her broach, but it seemed that the long keel kept her heading in the right direction. The flat transom caused her stern to lift, and the waves were lifting her as she surged forward on each succeeding breaker.

An exceptionally large wave picked her up, right at the start of the breakwater and at that moment the watching crowd could hear the helmsman give her full throttle. The Spray took off like a surfboat, disappearing in a sea of foam, and she surfed in at what was reliably estimated by the many experienced onlookers at an incredible 15 knots. During the entry, her fibreglass dinghy, which was mounted on the stern in davits, filled with water, tearing the stern out of it. *Derwent Endeavour* herself suffered no damage, and a spontaneous cheer and applause showed the relief of the watching crowd.'

Anne Clode completes her record of the events with the comments, 'Anyone who watched *Derwent Endeavour* can hold no doubts as to her seaworthiness and the skill of her captain. Her full bow would not allow her to bury her nose, and the stern lifted exceptionally well in the following sea. My mind balks at the thought of what would have happened to a fine fin-keeler. The enthusiasm of one fellow watcher knew no bounds; he had recently launched his own Spray in Sydney, and boy! Would he have something to tell the "knockers" back home.'

WAGONGA

In *Cruising Helmsman* magazine, the headline for the article by Bob Reynolds that described the building of a Roberts Spray was 'Wagonga, The Boat from the Bush'. Bob Bettini used a set of Roberts Spray 40 glassfibre plans as the basis for building his Spray replica. Thus the wheel had turned a full circle. Plans had been drawn up to build glassfibre Sprays from the original timber Spray, and now these glass-

Glassfibre Spray 40, by unknown Australian builder, in Antipodean waters.

fibre plans had been used to build a timber Spray. It is interesting to note that Bob retained the Roberts Spray bow, and several other updated features of the Spray 40 design. As we have said before, Slocum improved the original Spray when he rebuilt her, and we in our own way tried to improve the boat without losing the many features of the original Spray. It is for the owners and crew of the many Spray replicas to decide if we have succeeded.

RESOLVE

Rick and Mary Smith are completing this steel Spray 40 at Mariners Farm Boatyard in Rainham, Kent, in the UK. Rick's steel work and attention to detail are superb examples of what can be achieved by a careful builder.

BAGGINS

This ferrocement Spray is owned by Wayne Marshall; the plastering was undertaken by Colin Brooks. Wayne obtained his plans from our Australian office some years ago, after we had designed the Spray Variant, for which plans were available for ferro construction. At present, *Baggins* is kept on the Medway in Kent in the UK.

CASTELGATE SPRAY

Many Spray replicas have been used for worthy purposes, and none more so than this steel, three-masted, schooner-rigged, Roberts Spray 40. This boat was built for the Castlegate Quay Heritage Centre, which forms part of the 'Vision 2000'. The Castlegate Quay is situated in Stockton-on-Tees, Cleveland, England. This project consists of a large wharfside development that includes a floating, full-size replica of Captain Cook's *Endeavour*, plus the *Castlegate Spray* youth sail training schooner and a number of other vessels and associated co-ordinated facilities.

Throughout the UK there are many waterfront redevelopment schemes and the Vision 2000 Castlegate Quay water activities centre has made the Maritime Youth Training Centre one of the centre points. The first project to get started was the Roberts Spray 40 youth training schooner, and after the recent crop of modern sail boats and powerboats that my office has

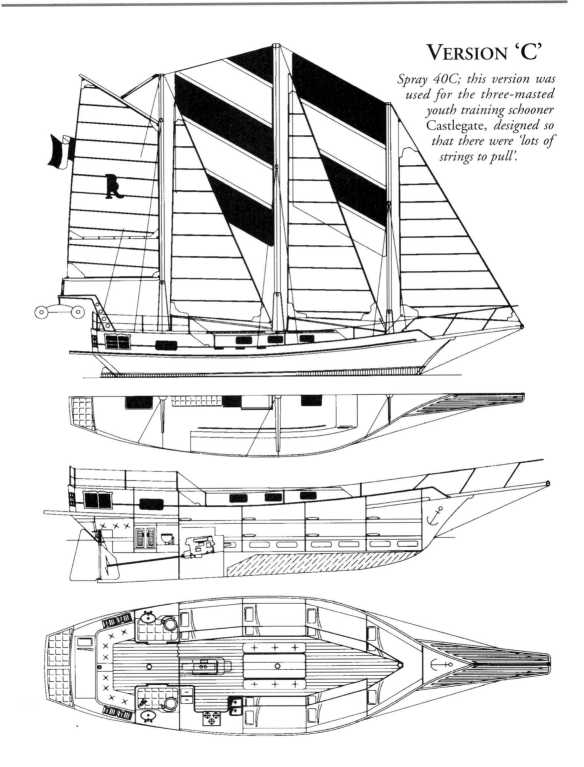

VERSION 'C'

Spray 40C; this version was used for the three-masted youth training schooner Castlegate, designed so that there were 'lots of strings to pull'.

recently designed, it was refreshing to be asked to draw a special version of the Roberts Spray 40 for use as a sail training vessel. The object was to provide a sailboat suitable for maritime youth activities; the boat had to be capable of accommodating ten young people for training cruises up to several days long.

It was important to provide for handicapped youngsters, as well as make sure there were 'plenty of strings to pull', so as many youngsters as possible could become involved at one time. Another requirement was that the boat had to be capable of being short-handed in the event of seriously adverse weather conditions that made some of the young crew inoperative due to severe sickness, or for some other reason. The sail plan was designed to fulfil the foregoing requirements. The boat also had to be suitable for accommodating disabled persons, and allowing them to share fully in the activities.

The Spray sail training schooner is currently nearing completion, and we are looking forward to seeing her fulfilling her designed role of offering a seagoing experience to the youth of Stockton-on-Tees.

MOULDED SPRAY

Allan Roper of Box Hill, in New South Wales in Australia, informed me that he has a female moulded glassfibre Roberts Spray 40. From the plans and full-size patterns a strip plank male mould plug was built and a split mould was built on this plug.

The basic dimensions of the finished hulls are as follows: length of hull including bow fairing, 42ft 7½in [12.9m] waterline length, 33ft 1½in [10m], and beam 14ft 6in [4.4m]. Five solid glassfibre hulls were built from the mould. According to Allan, 'I have sailed on several of these completed boats and they are quite impressive and enjoyable, especially in heavy weather.' Allan is a boatbuilder by trade and a very experienced seaman, having sailed around Cape Horn. According to him: 'the Sprays I have sailed on fulfil all my requirements.'

BELGIUM SPRAY

I recently received a fax from Van Hoof of Mol, Belgium:

'I have a question about the boat I'm building, the glassfibre Spray 40; in particular the reinforcing of chainplates, because I want to build traditional. I maybe want to work with deadeyes instead of rigging screws. My question is how to reinforce the chainplates if they are outside the boat, even if I work with rigging screws.'

Mr Van Hoof is building a glassfibre hulled Roberts Spray 40, and I must say I was pleased to receive his fax not only to learn of another Spray being built, but because it is good to hear builders asking the designer questions, rather than just charging ahead and doing something on their own that may cause problems later. I duly faxed the following reply to Mr Van Hoof's questions:

'There are several ways to reinforce chainplates in a glassfibre boat and they do need reinforcing no matter if the plates are inside the hull, through the deck or outside for all to see. One of the best methods is to weld up a steel strap structure using say 2in x ¼in [50 x 6mm] flat bar, the strap thickness and size will vary depending on the size of the boat. The vertical flat bar has short fore and aft bars welded at regular intervals and the whole arrangement is laminated inside the hull. This backing arrangement will spread the load when the chainplates are through bolted from the outside. A similar arrangement can be used for through-the-deck chainplates or chain plates attached to cabin sides where no bulkhead is conveniently located to accept the extra loading.'

Regarding the proposed plywood deck on Mr Van Hoof's boat: those who know me are aware that I am no lover of plywood decks and/or superstructures. Most decks built of this material eventually suffer from some form of rot which eventually requires replacing all or part of the deck. Unfortunately this usually happens sooner rather than later. Some builders are determined to use plywood for building decks and superstructures so we do try to offer advice of how best to build a long lasting plywood structure. Sheathing in glassfibre helps; epoxy resins should always be used in conjunction with the chosen glass fabric.

PIMENTA SPRAY
The availability of suitable boatbuilding timbers in Brazil makes wood the natural choice of materials for intending boat owners who live in that country. Carlos Montaury Pimenta of Rio de

Janeiro is one of those who has chosen to build a wooden Spray. He used the Roberts Spray 40 plans, which are available as a strip plank option, and sent us a photograph in March 1982 showing the various stages of the hull being set up and planked using the strip plank method.

GILLIRE SPRAY
Gillan C Oran wrote that he was delivering a Roberts 40 Spray to the British Virgin Islands to enlist in the crewed charter service. He thought perhaps some people were interested in chartering, especially those who were building Sprays, or plan to, or already have one. It took Gillan five years to build the steel version, and has on board all the tools except the welder used to build her, along with the plans and step-by-step photos, and would be glad to offer assistance and advice to travelling guests.

DUNCAN SPRAY
This Spray 40 is being built by Mr R Duncan of Shipley, West Yorkshire, in the UK, and his letter was accompanied by a thick wad of photographs, showing all stages of the construction of his steel boat.

HOMEWARD BOUND
This glassfibre foam sandwich Spray 40 was built by Richard White of Cincinnati, Ohio, who sent a sketch of his boat and his ballasting arrangements:

Another Spray 40 using the Bruce Roberts 'one off' glassfibre method. This one was built by Jim Gladstone.

'Enclosed find a sketch of my Spray 40 showing the location of the major weight items and the ballast that is already installed. The ballast is lead pigs cast to fit the sections between the solid floors, bonded in with resin and glassed over. Each section was weighed as it went in. The hull is glass with ¹/₂in [12mm] balsa core and 10oz [283g] of fab-mat on the inside. The lay-up on the outside is pretty much as specified on the plans. As my sketch shows, the keel is extended adding some weight in glass, but is all enclosed, and not an outside bolt-on arrangement. The deck and cabins are timber, as shown in your plans for wood. The aft end of the cabin has been shortened 6in [150mm] and the cockpit shortened to make room for a 12in [300mm] bridgedeck.'

PLEIADES II

This Spray 40 was built using glassfibre by Thomas R Scott (Bob) of Columbia, South Carolina, USA, who has made a nice job of it. Bob Scott recalls that as a youngster in Galveston, Texas, he once went down to the beach and built boats out of sand. With the help of his five-year-old imagination, Bob sailed his make-believe boats around the world, stopping along the way to improve and enlarge his vessels with sand from exotic beaches and distant shores.

Almost half a century and half a continent removed from that scene on Galveston Bay, Scott has built a real boat in his Columbia backyard, and he still dreams of sailing around the world. His childhood fantasy has materialised as the 41ft [12.5m] glassfibre hull of an oceangoing cruiser *Pleiades II*. 'When I remembered that incident on the beach, it gave me a sort of spooky feeling,' said Scott, 'because a glassfibre boat is made of sand too; sand and oil.'

Bob Scott's boat became a reality when he launched *Pleiades II* in July of 1987. Since then Bob has lived aboard for the past seven years and cruised the east coast of the USA and the Caribbean. Ports of call have included Bermuda, Abaco, Eteuthera, Berry Islands, New Providence Island and Bimini, to name just a few. To quote Bob:

'I had something of an adventure between Dry Tortugas and Havana when at around two in the morning I ran head on into the biggest wave I have ever seen. The green water came over the bow and filled the cockpit in a second. It felt like I ran into a brick wall; I

As a small boy, Bob Scott of Columbia, South Carolina, used to build boats of sand on the beach; in 1987 his dreams became reality when he completed his 41ft glassfibre Spray 40, Pleiades II.

guess when you run into a huge wave like that it is pretty solid; thank goodness I had installed four large drains in the cockpit.

Due to various circumstances, including my crew having the need to return to work to top up their finances, I have done a lot of single handing in my boat. The amazing directional stability of the Spray made my single handed passages considerably easier since I was able to put her on "automatic pilot". My automatic pilot consists of two lines led from the tiller to cleats at the side of the cockpit; I just set up the sails to suit the conditions and let her rip.'

When Bob built *Pleiades II,* he added 10in [254mm] to the depth of the keel; he credits this change for much of the exceptional windward ability of his boat. As for stability, Bob regularly sails right through thunderstorms and 40 knot winds, he does not need to shorten sail; the rail goes almost under but water never makes it on to the decks.

HALE SPRAY

This steel Spray 40 is being built by Art Hale, of Brenerton, Washington State, USA. In 1991 he sent some photos: 'Here are some pictures of one of your 40ft [12m] Sprays in steel. I am building Version C, and I am not really big on all this high-tech rigging bull; I would like to go a little more old-fashioned on the sail rig to complement the particular version of this fine vessel, say a schooner rig or maybe a 1901 Amundsen's sloop. I would like to use $^1/_2$in [12mm] steel cable, greased and sewn over with canvas the way it was done in yesteryear. Here is a picture of what I want for the sail plan. Would you please look this over and let me know if it will

fly.' But alas, the sail plan is now separated from the photos and the letter, and I'm not sure if it would have flown or not.

VARIENT

This is one of the few boats I've ever designed for building in ferro-cement. As most of my clients and many others are aware, I am not a lover of this material. Fortunately, my yacht design career began in earnest around 1968, and this was towards the end of the ferro-cement era. Not long after I had designed the glassfibre Spray 40, a client approached me requesting a variation in the design in that he wanted to have an outboard rudder. His idea was that he wanted to use mechanical wind-driven, self-steering gear that is common on boats that don't have the self-steering qualities of the Spray. He want-

Information would be welcome on this Australian glass-fibre Spray 40, possibly called Id, *as shown on the bow.*

ed to incorporate the self-steering: I guess he had a 'belt and braces' approach, wanting to cover all possibilities. Anyway, he convinced me to design this ferro-cement version, with an altered transom to allow the installation of the self-steering arrangement. As considerable numbers of ferro-cement boats were still being constructed at that time, I felt justified in preparing the plans, as that is what my customer wanted. I used the construction methods pioneered by Richard Hartley, the New Zealand designer of plywood and ferro-cement boats; that is, to use a web frame and a lot of steel rods combined with several layers of chicken wire mesh as the armature. I saw this boat through to the plastering stage, so I know that as far as is possible with ferro-cement, this was a good, strong, seaworthy hull.

WEISE SPRAY

Several builders have stretched the Roberts Spray 40 to various lengths, including 45ft [13.7m], 47ft [14.3m] and 50ft [15.2m]. Many of these boats have been redesigned after the builders have contacted us for suggestions, and to obtain our approval for the design changes they propose to make to the Spray 40 design. We have provided additional sheets of drawings to some of these builders. In some cases we have designated the design as the Spray 45, Spray 47 and Spray 50, and so forth.

One stretched boat was built by Mr Weise, who requested plans for increasing the length of the glassfibre Spray 40 to 47ft [14.3m]. At the same time, he asked us to design a larger sail plan.The Spray 47 was a great boat, tons of room, wide side decks with adequate, confidence-inspiring bulwarks.

BURMA SPRAY

Bo Colomby reported from Myanmar (Burma) about a recently launched Roberts Spray 40. Bo's company builds boats in Burmese hardwoods, using quarter sawn teak above the waterline and for decks, cabin tops and interiors.

Burmese forestry practices are very sound; there is no strip cutting and logging is still done by elephant and ox cart. The felled trees have to be dragged to the river and then have to wait for the monsoons so there is enough water to tow them down to the places where they can be collected or trucked out for cutting or shipping. The wood that is not used for boatbuilding is used for framing sheds; what is left over is then used by the workers for cooking their meals. The sawdust and shavings fire the primitive heating system used for applying direct heat to the planks when bending them on the frames. There is no waste in this operation.

The shipwrights of South Asian Nautical Explorations Ltd stand before the framework of Burma Spray. *From left to right: Tan Chawn, Tin Myint, Myint Swe, Htay Win, Aung Zaw, Thein Soe and U Pyone.*

THE BIG SPRAYS

SPRAY 45

LOA	45ft 0in	13.72m
LWL	35ft 10in	10.93m
Beam	14ft 6in	4.42m
Draft	5ft 0in	1.52m
Displ.	40 000	18 144kg
Ballast	12 000	5443kg

Construction: Steel

The Spray 45, a stretched Spray 40, was designed for Mr and Mrs Hill, an experienced couple who required a spacious life-style. The first steel version is being built by Richard E Flowers of Custom Steel Boats, Arapahoe, North Carolina, USA. It is available with draft options and this first example will draw 5ft [1.5m].

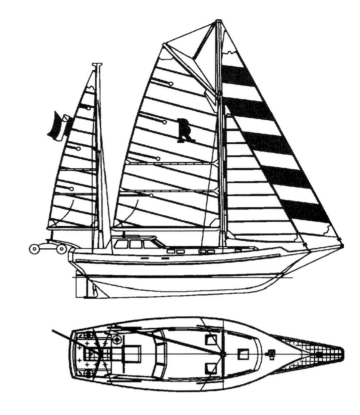

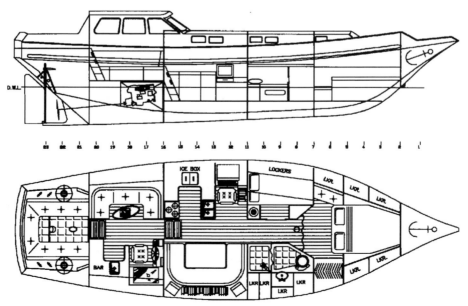

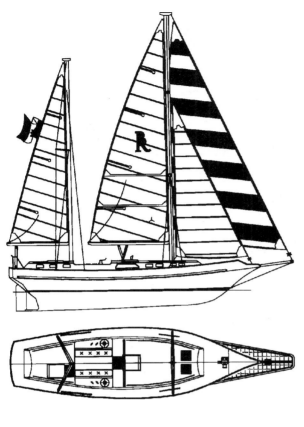

SPRAY 50

LOA	50ft 0in	15.24m
LWL	39ft 6in	12.04m
Beam	14ft 6in	4.42m
Draft	5ft 0in	1.52m
Displ.	45 000	20 412kg
Ballast	12 000	5443kg

Construction: Steel

Spray 50 is another straight 'stretch' of the Spray 40, and is certainly the maximum we would recommend without increasing the overall beam if one is to retain the benefits of the original concept.

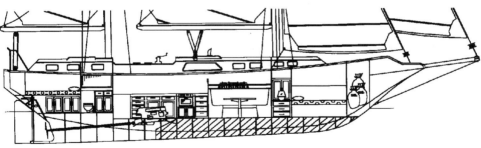

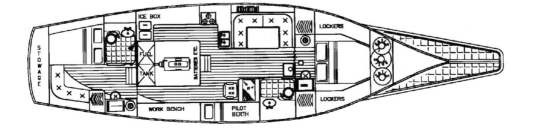

Spray 55

LOA	55ft 0in	18.7m
LWL	46ft 6in	14.17m
Beam	18ft 0in	5.46m
Draft	5ft 3in	1.60m
Displ.	75 000	34 020kg
Ballast	28 250	11 907kg

Construction: Steel or glassfibre
Sail plan: cutter, ketch, schooner

Spray 55 was created as a custom design for Robert T (Bob) Murkland, a civilian employee of the US military in Kuwait. This steel Spray will prove popular with anyone looking for a larger Spray type for either charter or cargo use. The enormous interior space offers several accommodation alternatives.

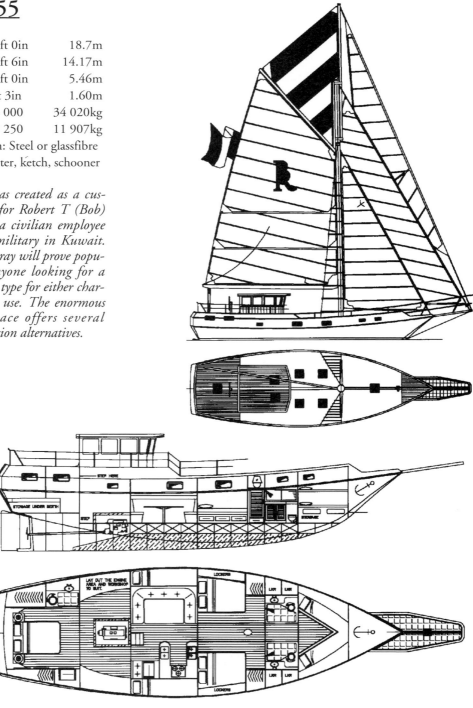

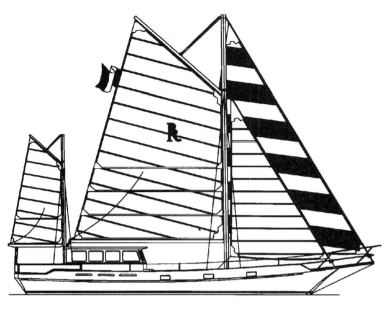

SPRAY 75

LOA	75ft 11in	23.16m
LWL	65ft 2in	19.87m
Beam	22ft 7in	6.89m
Draft	6ft 0in	1.83m
Displ.	135 632	61 623 kg
Ballast	34 000	15 422kg
Sail Area	2 367ft²	219.89m²

Construction: Steel or glassfibre
Sail plan: cutter, ketch, schooner

The Spray 75 is the largest of the Bruce Roberts designed Sprays. This motor-sailer version has been ordered as a custom design for Walter Manning Jr, an American client who currently resides in Indonesia. With its wide beam and shallow draft, this boat is a roomy charter vessel capable of exploring all but the shallowest waters.

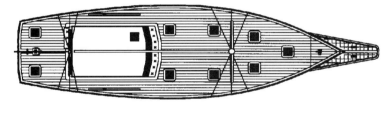

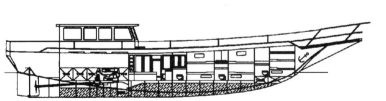

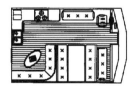

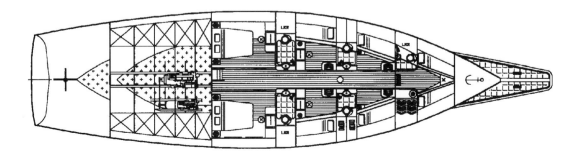

CHAPTER 7

Spray 38 – Near Full Size Roberts Spray

ROBERTS SPRAY 38

LOD	38ft 10in	11.8m
LWL	31ft 8in	9.6m
Beam	13ft 0in	3.96m
Draft 4ft (5ft)		1.22m (1.52m)
Headroom 6ft 4in+		1.93m
Displ.	29 000	13 154kg
Ballast:		Varies
Spars:	Timber or aluminium	
Auxiliary:		50-85 hp
Sail Area:		Varies
Construction: Steel or aluminium		
Sail plan: cutter, ketch, schooner		

The Spray 38 was originally designed as a ketch, and has successfully carried a variety of rigs.

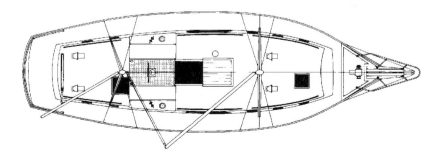

Spray 38

*The centre cockpit arrangement shown here is
only one of many possibilities for this sailboat.*

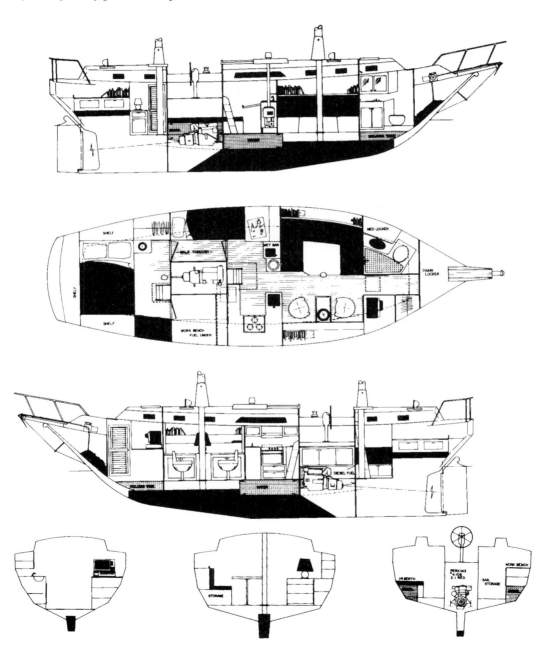

This design for the Roberts Spray 38 was prepared early in 1980 when one customer, who had considered the plans for the Roberts Spray 36, felt he wanted a little more room in the aft cabin. In order to attain his wishes, we felt that a new design was called for, and hence the Spray 38 was the result. As this was originally a custom design, and as no other client has come forward requiring a boat to be built in any material other than steel, these plans were only made available in steel. Nevertheless, they have been quite popular, and seem to fill the gap between the Spray 36 and the full-size Spray 40. The Spray 38 also has a limited number of versions available. However, owner/builders have purchased the plans for this design and made their own changes.

RAVEN
This steel Roberts Spray 38 was built by Stuart J D'Arcy-Hyder, who commented:

'For your information, we cut the first steel in May 1988 and moved on board in March 1989. We had our first small cruise last year, 1990. The boat performs superbly. She is by and large true to the Roberts's drawings, but with lots of detail changes. By altering the shape and size of the cockpit, we have a full headroom walk-through arrangement with pilot berth under one coaming. The galley is under the other coaming.

We did put on the controversial bilge keels, but have never regretted the decision. The sail plan is altered, the area being increased. She is rigged as a Galios cutter-headed ketch, with squaresail on the main. Much easier to handle than a spinnaker, and most attractive. The transom and poop deck shape have been slightly modified and the bow shape has the understated clipper line to it.

Machinery is a 72 hp Ford by way of a 2:1 Borg Warner, and a 23in x 16in [584mm x 406mm] pitch propeller. Steering is by Servi hydraulic system. *Raven* is amazingly stiff, and in January when we sailed on the back of an easterly gale, my young son painted in the saloon, and not a drop of water was spilled. She is surprisingly fast and responsive. The finished boat cost something over £25000 including absolutely everything, and was completed in under a year. The fact that I'm in the trade probably helped in both these respects, but none the less, it can be done.'

We next heard from Stuart D'Arcy-Hyder in April 1991 when he said:

'I concur with Paul Fay's comments (Paul Fay built and sailed his own Spray 36, and details of his experiences appear in Chapter 8) on the squaresail being a lifting sail as opposed to the hard pressure of a spinnaker, and yes, keeping the yard tight into the stick is a problem that is still under development. The sheer efficiency of a squaresail down wind is quite awe-inspiring to a man used to the more modern fore and aft arrangement. Basically, the route we are working on is as follows; we have aluminium spars, the sail yard is raised up a heavy genoa track fixed to the fore side of the main mast. The fixing of the yard to this track is by way of cannibalised stainless fittings, variously cut and welded together. There is no reefing. The sail is up or it is down. It is controlled by lines that open or close it like theatre curtains. The sail is currently 240sq ft [22.3sq m]. I was also concerned about the extra pressure on the mast, and have added an extra shroud. Our costs were low; for example, our aluminium spars and standing rigging cost only £350, an insurance write-off. The main and mizzen masts were originally 10ft [3m] longer, keel stepped spars, a crane had driven over their heels, so we cut them off and deck stepped them. As a consequence, our main is 43ft [13m], our mizzen mast is 35ft [10.6m]. We lashed some wheels on the butt ends and towed them home. Why we didn't get stopped by the police still amazes me, we had to physically carry them around the roundabouts!

Our boat is called *Raven*. This year we only anticipate short voyages: the Scillies, Ireland and Brittany. Next year we hope to go to the east coast of the USA via the West Indies. I live aboard *Raven*, and I have rigged her for easy singlehanded sailing and find her quite manageable. We haven't as yet done any long passages, but we have sailed recently from here to mainland England and up the south coast and across to south Brittany in France.'

Stuart supplied us with some details of modifications. He has increased draft to 5ft 6in [1.6m] overall, and has twin bilge keels of ¹/₂in [12mm] plate. The bilge keels and the main keel have full-length sacrificial wooden shoes. The masts and bowsprit are somewhat larger than the original design recommended, thus the sail area is greater. The vessel carries 4 tons [4064kg] of ballast, 200 gal [909 lit] of water, and 120 gal [545 lit] of fuel. *Raven* is a cutter-headed ketch at the present time. This summer Stuart will continue to experiment with the squaresail. He says he prefers it to the spinnaker for downwind sailing. He also carries a substantial mizzen staysail, which in the right conditions is a wonderful sail. Stuart told us that the boat balances wonderfully under almost any point of sail: stiff, comfortable and surprisingly fast.

'It is our intention to make a centenary celebration circumnavigation, starting in 1995 via Panama. Is anyone else interested? It would be lovely to cruise in company with other Sprays. Our best run was from St Mary, Isles of Scilly, to Falmouth before a south-west force 7, average 8.4 knots, would have been faster but for the turning tide at the Lizard. If you ever get this way, welcome aboard! We are the only live-aboards on the Isles of Scilly, thus locally world famous, or infamous. You have to be slightly mad to live on a boat here in the winter.'

Towards the end of March 1994 I again heard from Stuart, when he commented:

'You may wonder at the rig I have. This somewhat antiquated vessel actually sails an awful lot better than she looks, like she ought to. A friend built the jib furling sail. He cut it out of different weights of cloth, so that when almost fully furled it is a flying storm jib. This then becomes progressively lighter as it is unfurled for different sizes of jib/genoa. Finally, when fully unfurled a large balloon comes out of the top, giving me a sort of cruising chute/pseudo spinnaker. It is an enormously powerful sail. Whilst running before a gale of wind a couple of years ago, the poor old log kept bending the needle on the pin at 10 knots. We broke our bowsprit, a 6in x 6in [150mm x 150mm] section of Douglas fir. It was only a short thing too, and extended about 4ft 6in [1.3m] out from the stemhead. The new one is a bit longer and made of 9in x 8in [230mm x 203mm] section. Originally I was going to have a nice modest gaff rig with tarred rigging and timber spars, all lagged. However things didn't happen that way. I got to hear about those damaged spars that I bought cheap. The engine, twice your recommended size, was another lucky find, 17 years old, but had done less than 500 hours. Beautifully maintained too, it was an auxiliary generator engine at Treliske Hospital in case of power cuts. It was sold by tender, and as a 17-years-old generator no one was interested in it, so my silly offer was accepted. My main problem now was trying to convince people I am not an eccentric, wealthy man. They will just not believe that *Raven* was built in its entirety in a little over 12 months for something just over £25 000.'

SEA PEA II

Chris Parnham contacted us about his Roberts steel Spray 38, which was built in Kingswinford in the UK by master steel boatbuilder, Philip Grosvenor. Phil has built several of the Spray models, plus other steel powerboats designed by Bruce Roberts. This Spray 38 is fitted with bilge keels. *Sea Pea II* was fitted out over a 3^1/$_2$ year period and was

Sea Pea II, a Roberts steel Spray 38 owned by Chris Parnham of Boston, Lincolnshire, England, has bilge keels fitted, so she can stand firmly on a dry mooring.

launched in August 1993 at Newark on the River Trent. After a week on the river, the mast was stepped and rigging installed, and the boat was sailed round to the mooring at Boston, Lincolnshire. Chris Parnham is planning some blue water cruising, possibly a circumnavigation. The boat was built with blue water in mind and he says it is a 'belt and braces' job with steel, watertight bulkheads, in-mast roller reefing, oversize rigging, polycarbonate windows, Decca, GPS, SSB/VHF radios, bow thruster, power anchor winch, 300ft of ^{1}/$_2$in [12mm] chain, 35, 60 and 140lb CQR anchors, bilge pumps, full burglar alarm, Ampair wind/water generators, Mase diesel generator, Whitlock 'Mamber', and cable steering, Cetrek Autochart Pilot, 'Hydrovane' wind vane steering, keel cooling, 'Striver' Aquadrive, etc, etc. All this has had an effect on the waterline; he reckons it will draw about 5ft [1.5m]. It tips the scales at about 16 tons [16 256kg].

In contrast to some of the more modestly built boats, Sea Pea II is having £200 worth of gold leaf applied to the bow by Kerry Parks.

Chris Parnham wrote recently, telling us that he plans to follow in Slocum's wake, one hundred years on exactly, and will be leaving from Boston, England, via Gibraltar etc, following his route, but calling in at a few additional places.

GEORDIE LAD

Mr Lowther said that he spent a year deciding which design to build. He was only going to build one vessel so it had to be right. He chose the Spray because it looked right. The building of the *Geordie Lad* started in June 1986 and was finished in July 1992; the hull and fitting out was done by Mr Lowther himself.

'The remainder of the season of '92, I spent in trials off the north east coast, and most of the '93 season we spent getting to know each other, then in August we went to the Ijsselmeer in Holland for a month. My only sailing prior to this was a two-week sail in the Western Isles. Going to Holland was quite an experience. I had two crew, one 71 years old and one 41 years old, neither of them experienced. The yacht handled beautifully and looked after us; never gave us a bad moment. This

The completion of a six year project inspired by a two week cruise, Geordie Lad *safely carried her owner-builder and two inexperienced crew to Holland the following year.*

year I hope to lift her out and fit a bow thruster, and head for warmer climates. I am at the moment taking my Yacht Masters, so wish me luck.'

I note from one of the photographs that Mr Lowther sent, that he has painted the port side of his deck red, and the starboard side green. I imagine this was to assist some of his inexperienced crew in identifying port and starboard. This reminds me of an American yacht I once saw in Australia. This boat had every possible piece of gear fully labelled. The inside steering was clearly marked port and starboard, left and right, and all of the other equipment and fittings on the boat were clearly identified. Although this may sound a rather unnecessary arrangement, I am sure that it could have some benefits, especially in an emergency when sailing with inexperienced crew.

EAGLE SPRAY

Recently I received a photograph of a completed Spray 38, together with a long letter from Alain Guichard:

'Many people have written about how the Spray stands up very well in rough waters, or how she seems to steer herself with a few minor sail adjustments no matter in which direction she is sailing, but nothing has been written about her aesthetics, and the following qualities are equally endearing. As an author and professional diver for three decades, it took me two years to decide on all the requirements for my ideal boat. A sailing boat is a bride. You marry her for better or worse, and it is important to know the qualities before you go ahead. I knew as soon as I studied your plan that the Spray would anticipate some of my minor distractions on a singlehanded cruise, and at that time I hadn't yet read all the Slocum books. So what else made me choose the steel Spray 38, apart from my budget, and an analysis of the future cost and maintenance? What we call *l'assiette*, French for plate, describes how she sits in the water. I didn't want a racing boat.

If you are going to spend a long period living on a boat, you must have a very large deck to give freedom of movement without knocking over your shipmate while running around the side-decks. The Spray 38, with its 14ft [4.2m] beam which runs more or less the total length

Alain Guichard intends to use his self-built Spray 38, Eagle Spray, *as a base for his professional diving and writing operations.*

of the boat, gives tremendous space and comfort both inside and outside. Where, alas, would you find a sailing boat of this size where you can fit two toilets, one at each end with ample headroom. "Ah," some people may say, "what about the speed with such displacement?" Well, who cares when you don't have to be in the office by 9.00 am each morning!'

Although Alain Guichard's Spray 38 is almost completed and about to be launched, he has as yet no experience of sailing a Spray. Once he reads the favourable remarks made about the Spray's performance, as voiced by so many owners of these boats, then he will no doubt add performance to his list of favourable points. Alain went on to say:

'For my personal use I wanted a very large rear platform on the deck above the aft cabin for diving, and had to be able to enjoy a good meal with friends, under a canopy, of course. The Spray gives me almost 100sq ft [9sq m] of space. All Sprays are so well balanced and have such a low centre of gravity that they can be rigged as a ketch sloop or cutter. I have chosen a cutter because it facilitates a singlehanded trip, gives me more room on the rear deck, and is much cheaper than a ketch to install. If you intend to sail around the Med or around the coast of Europe as I do, you must give some thought to the cost of mooring in these expensive marinas. A 38ft [11.5m] boat, being under 12m, makes a lot of difference to the cost per night, believe me. So Bruce, if I cannot tell you right now how she will perform at sea, I can at least say at Ridge Wharf Yacht Centre, near Wareham in Dorset, there is no shortage of admirers for this beautiful boat, from both would-be and experienced seafaring folk.'

AMANDA JANE

Larry R Randall built his Spray 38 mostly in Oklahoma, which, as most of you will be aware, is a very much landlocked state in the centre of the USA. Some of Larry's comments follow:

'Thank you for the chance to brag about my boat, *Amanda Jane*. We don't get enough opportunities to do that. As a former marine mechanic I had many bad experiences with what I refer to as production "Tupperware" hulls. The keel of *Amanda Jane* was laid in Oklahoma in 1984 by a very good friend of mine by the name of Kendall Keeton. She was to be his retirement home on the water. She was trucked to Washington State in 1984 for the fitting and commissioning, and she was finally launched at Point Roberts, Washington State in

Two good examples of the sleek lines of the Spray. The Spray 38 shown above was professionally built by Philip Grosvenor in the UK. Below: one of the many Spray 38s built by Watercraft of Diglis, England.

1989. Kendall's intention was to sail to Alaska from Washington for the summer and then, like most sensible people, sail south in the winter. Unfortunately for him the sailing gods decided that it was not to be. While he was aboard her for the summer season in Alaska, fate changed his plans when his wife suffered a heart attack. Returning to Port Roberts he realised that his dreams of retirement as a live-aboard world sailor were not to be. That is when I was blessed with the chance to acquire *Amanda Jane*. My wife and I are still attempting to get to know her. We are finding that she is a very forgiving lady, with the heart of a lion, a big steel lion.

As you can gather, I think she's a fine vessel and we are looking forward to many happy days aboard her with the wind in our faces. That's how you generally end up sailing in the north west.'

BLAIR SPRAY

Jim Blair of Margate, Tasmania, Australia, wrote:

'My Spray 38 is under construction at present and steel work is 90 per cent complete. Regarding the sail area displacement ratio of the Spray 38: of course with the standard ketch rig, she has quite a low sail area displacement ratio and would take a larger sail plan. However, many people with families prefer to be slightly undercanvased than overcanvased, but it would not be a problem to design a larger rig for this boat; and as you see by the information supplied by some other builders, larger sail plans have been installed on the Spray 38 with considerable success.'

ROSENDAKI SPRAY
Robert Rosendaki of Spring Field, Missouri, is building a Roberts Spray 38 in steel, and he commented as follows:

'On my Spray 38, the transom is done and most plating on. The pictures are 90 days old, and we are snowed in today. I have used a trolley developed from angle iron track and four roller skate wheels, about 400lb [181kg] only, most helpful in frame erection, etc. I'm painting all new oiled steel with aluminised asphalt paint. Accepts welds, and sandblasts off easily, and prevents rust until I'm ready to blast and paint.'

SIABAN
Sirius Yachts of Stourport-on-Severn in the UK built the hull and deck of this Spray 38 for Angus Mackinnon of Milford Haven. Angus told me that the name he has chosen for his Spray means 'Spray' in Gaelic.

HALF PAST
This boat is owned by Captain Harold Barbour who had the hull and deck built by Dragon Marine UK. Captain Barbour also informed me that he first picked up one of my design catalogues in Australia about thirty years ago and at that time he thought the Spray 40 too large for his needs; when the Spray 38 became available he decided to have a Spray for himself.

This Spray was commenced in 1989 and completed in 1990. The hull is spar galvanised outside and the entire interior is epoxy coated. Spray on insulation was added to the interior. Captain Barbour is 6ft 4in tall [1.93m] so on our advice, he increased the freeboard of the hull by 3in [75mm] and reports that he finds sailing with 4 to 6 people just about right.

This Spray 38, Half Past, *was completed by Captain Harold Barbour from a steel hull built by Dragon Marine, UK.*

CHAPTER 8
Spray 36 – Developed from the Roberts Spray 33

Originally, we prepared plans for this design because a few customers lengthened the Spray 33 to get extra room and in some cases desired a centre cockpit arrangement. After some of these stretched boats were completed we were able to determine that this design would work quite well, so we decided to prepare a complete set of plans for the Spray 36 for construction in either glassfibre, steel or wood/epoxy.

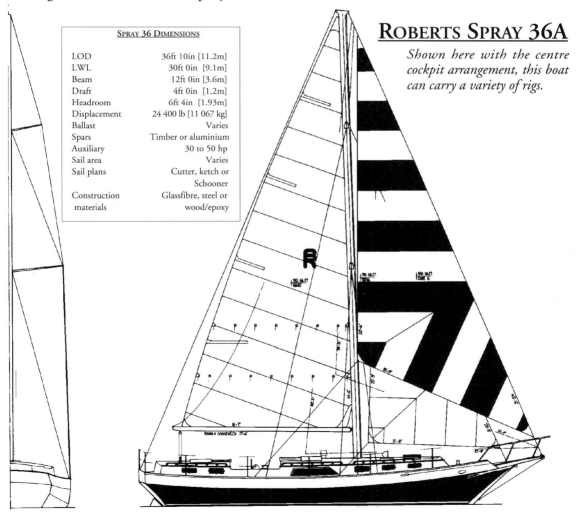

SPRAY 36 DIMENSIONS	
LOD	36ft 10in [11.2m]
LWL	30ft 0in [9.1m]
Beam	12ft 0in [3.6m]
Draft	4ft 0in [1.2m]
Headroom	6ft 4in [1.93m]
Displacement	24 400 lb [11 067 kg]
Ballast	Varies
Spars	Timber or aluminium
Auxiliary	30 to 50 hp
Sail area	Varies
Sail plans	Cutter, ketch or Schooner
Construction materials	Glassfibre, steel or wood/epoxy

ROBERTS SPRAY 36A

Shown here with the centre cockpit arrangement, this boat can carry a variety of rigs.

ROBERTS SPRAY 36A

This accommodation plan works out well, although some may object to the athwartship aft double berth.

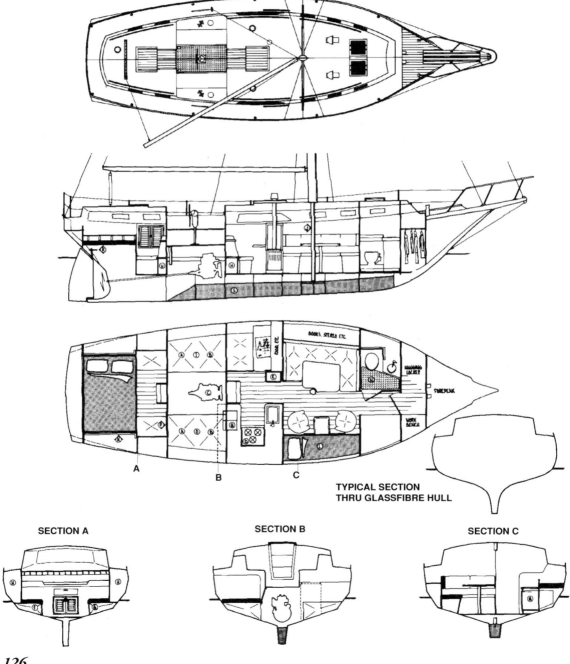

TYPICAL SECTION
THRU GLASSFIBRE HULL

SECTION A   SECTION B   SECTION C

ROBERTS SPRAY 36B

Despite its 'pirate ship' appearance, Spray 36B has proved very popular and this is a well-proven arrangement.

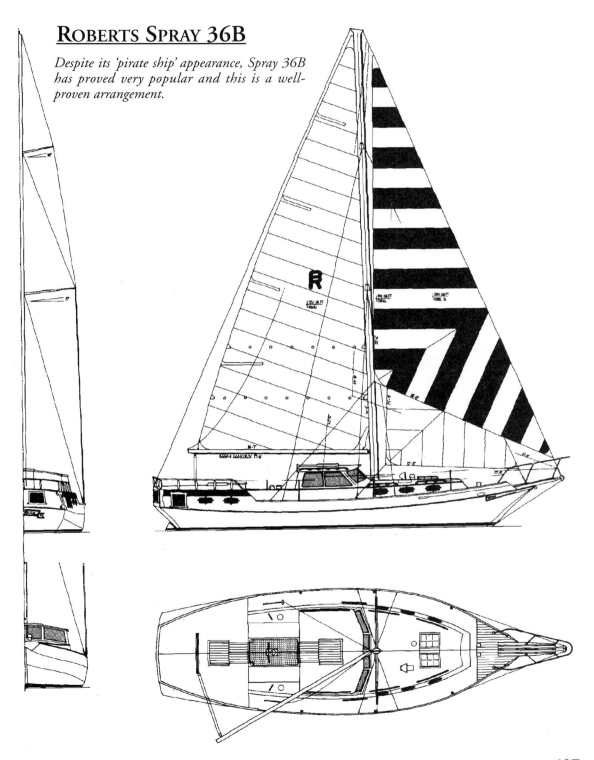

Roberts Spray 36B

The accommodation arrangement of the Spray 36B is similar to version A but some of the elements can be 'mixed and matched' between the various layouts.

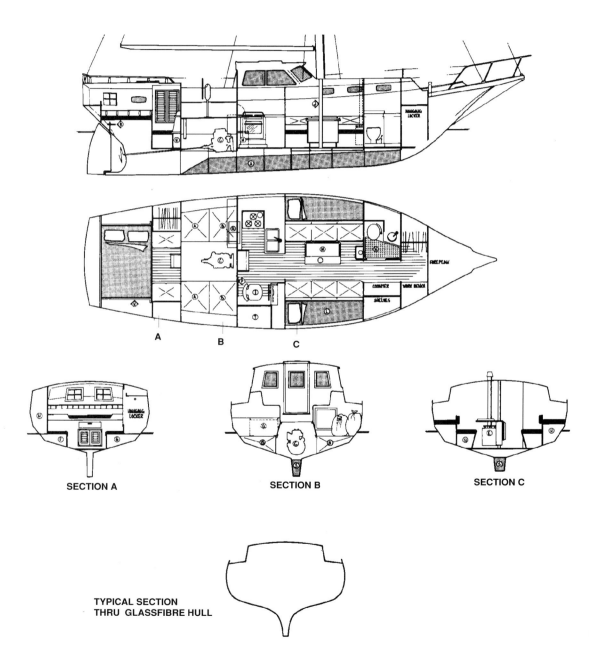

SECTION A

SECTION B

SECTION C

TYPICAL SECTION THRU GLASSFIBRE HULL

ROBERTS SPRAY 36C

The pilot house configuration has always proven popular amongst serious and experienced sailors.

ROBERTS SPRAY 36C

*Two variations are suggested for this layout
of the pilot house version.*

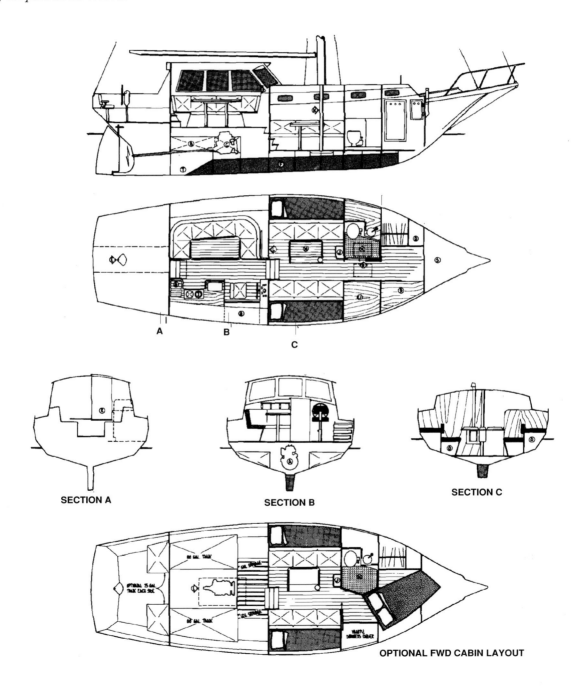

A   B

C

SECTION A   **SECTION B**   **SECTION C**

OPTIONAL FWD CABIN LAYOUT

SWEDISH SPRAY

On one of my first visits to Europe, I went to Sweden and I stayed with my long-established plans agent Sven Pettersen. At that time, Sven was an officer in the Swedish army. Many of our designs were built in Sweden, including several Sprays. Some were built at Sven Pettersen's factory at Kelmar, and others were built by individuals and various professional boatbuilders throughout Sweden. One of the first boats I had the opportunity to see was the Spray that was being built by Christos Athanasopoulous, a Greek professional jazz piano player who lived in Stockholm. First, Christos built a model of the boat he intended to build. The pilot house followed the typical Scandinavian styling and he blended this in with other features of the Spray 36. The whole worked out very well and we later incorporated the arrangement into the standard plans. When I visited Christos Athanasopoulous's boat, the hull, decks and superstructure were completed and work had just started on the interior. Christos was very proud of what he had achieved to date. About two years later a letter arrived from Christos:

'You perhaps have been wondering if I will show up again. Well, here I am, after four years of building my Spray 36, and all in my spare time. I was able to launch her at the beginning of last summer. I named her *Spray* and have enjoyed cruising in the Archipelago around Stockholm. She is just a wonderful boat. She is still unfinished in some details, like the decorative painting, the teak trim on deck, etc. Inside, though, she is just about complete. I have altered the interi-

Jazz piano player Christos Athanasopoulous turned his dexterous talents to building this fine Spray 36, Swedish Spray. *After cruising her extensively around Europe she was sold to an American buyer.*

or, as you can see in the photos; her great space inside gives a home-like feeling.

Unfortunately, I cannot say much about her performance under sail, simply because I have not had her rigged until now. However, the spars are now ready, although there is no chance of enjoying sailing as the boat is laid up for the winter. I can say a little about her motoring abilities, though. I have installed a Kabota 6 cylinder diesel, developing 58 hp, and 2600 rpm. My first propeller, which was 19in x 13in [475mm x 325mm] was giving 5 knots at an idle speed of 800 rpm. By that time, my optimistic waterline was disappearing under water as she was weighing 26 455lb [12 000kg], so I took her up on the land for a new antifouling job and changed the propeller to another that is 19in x 10in [475mm x 250mm]. It was at that time I discovered the rudder was full of water due to bad welding, so repairs took place at that time. I managed also to fit a greaser to the rudder stock for easier turning of the wheel. Motoring now at 1400 rpm gives a good 6 knots and 7 knots at 1700 rpm, still having plenty of margin for adverse conditions. Maximum speed so far is 9 knots at 2400 rpm. I very much appreciate your time spent helping me, mostly for my peace of mind.'

From the above, you can see how important it is to fit the correct propeller to your boat: 1in [25mm] in pitch can make a lot of difference, and even after having calculated and recommended hundreds of propeller sizes over the years, I think trial and error seems to be the only way to get the perfect propeller combination. This can be expensive if the error is too great, as the propeller has to be changed rather than altered. Even with computer aided design, we still cannot guarantee a perfect match every time.

It was another two years before I heard from Christos Athanasopoulous again. This time the letter was from Athens, 1988:

'I arrived in the port of Athens at the end of last summer. *Spray* has proved to be a marvellous boat. She is now under Greek flag ready to be chartered.' Finally, he wrote 'she is stable, like a rock, large and strong. She gave me many thousands of hours of pleasure in return for the time I took to build her. I have now sold *Spray* and I will miss her a lot.'

Many builders who have sold their Sprays have commented that they regret selling the boat or that they are building a replacement Spray.

HOPEFUL

This steel Spray 36 belongs to James and Joan Moysey, who purchased their plans when we were exhibiting at the Newport, Rhode Island, Boat Show. We heard nothing from them for two or three years, but then we received news that they were having the hull, deck and superstructure built by a professional builder. Shortly after this, we received regular progress reports:

'*Hopeful* has been launched and christened, but I am getting ahead of myself. The keel was laid in 1981 in Gulfport, Mississippi, by Ray Merrell and his sons. They constructed the hull including decks, engine formers, prop tube, rudder, window and portlight cutouts. She was flame sprayed, zinc and primed when I received her by truck on 10 October 1981 at my residence in Grangeville, New York.

Hopeful, a Spray 36 completed at last after 12 years by James and Joan Moysey. Perhaps 'Tenacity' would have been a more apt name!

I was working full time, and during the next five years not much progress was made. I took early retirement, and in October 1988 I shipped her back to Ray Merrell, who was now located in Pass Christian, Mississippi. My wife Joan and I had put our home of 26 years on the market. We followed closely behind *Hopeful* and moved south to enter another phase of our lives. In Mississippi I worked full time on the boat, and received direction and encouragement from Ray and his sons.'

Hopeful was launched on 29 June 1992 at Misc Marine in Gulfport, Mississippi. After a week of sea trials, James and John motored her over to Florida via the Intercoastal Waterway to Hernando Beach on the west coast of Florida. *Hopeful* was not rigged at that stage, but she was at their dock in their back/front yard. James said: 'If you thought I worked slowly up to this point, I really slowed down. Finally on 13 June 1993 the mast was raised with the help of four others plus myself. When it came to raising the mast, it went very smoothly and was completely uneventful. After a last-minute clean-up and some accessory additions, it seemed like time to have a christening.' This was held in October 1993. *Hopeful* has now been sailed, but not yet fully trialled. James is very pleased with the way his vessel has turned out and has received excellent reviews from everyone who has been aboard.

It is amazing how some builders can build a complete boat from scratch on their own in one year, when another builder will take up to ten years to fit out a hull. When I first became interested in boats some thirty years ago, I used to marvel at the various boatbuilding projects around Brisbane, which seemed to take for ever to complete. My own first boat, a 28ft [8.53m] sailboat, was built in under a year; however my neighbour Bill Haslet took about eight years to build a 30ft [9.14m] planked motorsailer. Bill has now had that boat for about twenty-two years.

FAIZARK

This Spray 36 was built in steel by Paul Fay, who has gone on to become a professional boatbuilder. To quote Paul:

'Before building our Roberts Spray 36 in steel, I read Jim Mellor's articles in the English boating magazine *Practical Boat Owner*. I read these articles very carefully, and bought a copy of Mike Pratt's *Own a Steel Boat*. I also read every book in the local library on boatbuilding, regardless of the type of material it was referring to. We found that useful information on general methods of building could be learned from all of them. We bought a copy of *Boat World*, which is a wonderful annual publication listing all of the manufacturers of marine parts in the UK. Over a period of about two months, we used it to find the makers of most of the items we would need to fit out our boat. We then wrote almost 300 letters (not all at once), asking for details and prices. Savings made here allowed us to spend more on other things. The best example of this were anchors and chain, which were bought at half the normal price. We also saved money by regularly visiting various second-hand dealers and going to marine auctions.'

Faizark, a handsome steel-hulled Spray 36 built in his Devonshire garden by Paul Fay and his family and friends. So successful was this project that Paul became a professional boatbuilder.

Paul, Fay, their family and friends built the hull themselves, though they did need help in carrying the 5 tons [5080kg] of steel from the delivery truck to the garden. The cost of the hull was £4100, and this included the deck and cabin, and four steel bulkheads, two water tanks and a diesel fuel tank, as well as the welding rods, grinding discs and gas used for cutting. They bought several tools that the average handyman probably wouldn't have, like a grinder, oxyacetylene cutter and some smaller hand tools. The price of £4100 for the hull included the cost of grit blasting and painting. The paint scheme is epoxy tar for the inside and outside up to

134

deck level, and then epoxy resin over the deck. Regarding the rig, they bought a Sitka spruce tree for the mast, which needed to be left to season and then planed down to shape. The rigging wire is completely galvanised, except for two forestays. These need to be stainless, otherwise the sail hanks would quickly wear away the galvanising. They made all the mast fittings themselves, except for the blocks and rigging screws, and then had all the fittings galvanised. All the running rigging is $\frac{1}{2}$in [12mm], which should be obtainable at a discount price if bought by the reel. (Regarding making your own fittings, if you are capable of welding up a steel boat, you are certainly capable of making all the fittings that are needed to complete the project, and it is worth remarking again that with a boat like the Spray, she looks best if the fittings have that slightly rugged commercial or handmade look. A Spray looks all wrong when she is glossily finished and fitted out with all off-the-shelf gear and equipment. It is best if some of the vessel's workboat heritage shows through.) Paul Fay's original estimate of how much the boat would cost to build was £9500, with only the cost of grit blasting and painting to be added. Nevertheless, they added £3500 for luck to make a total of £13 000. In the event, the total cost will probably rise to nearly £1000 above this because they have added to their original specification. For example, having bought a few windows from the auction, they decided that the overall appearance of the boat would be enhanced if the rest matched. They also bought a radio after being lectured by a coastguard friend. Paul wrote:

'For anyone who would like to build a boat of this size, but cannot afford that sort of money, don't be put off. I am convinced that an amateur who is prepared to spend more time making things himself can build a strong, seaworthy boat about 35ft-40ft [10.6-12.1m] for about £10 000, especially if he has bought a set of Bruce Roberts's plans, which are full of money saving ideas. We bought ours long before we were ready to build. After studying the plans thoroughly, we wrote to 20 steel stockholders asking for quotes "to include delivery for the 5 tons [5080 kg] of steel we needed". This is one area where great savings can be made, by buying as much as possible in one go. When we received all the quotes, we were amazed to find that they varied from £1700 to £2250. Our local stockholders were some of the most expensive, so our steel came all the way from the Midlands to the West Country and was still £500 cheaper than we could buy it round the corner. As you may have realised, we don't have a bottomless pocket. Like most amateur boatbuilders, we have to watch the pennies very carefully, so for those of you thinking of doing something similar, we have quoted figures that are applicable to the early 1980s. Of course, prices will change, but if you just add in something for inflation, you should be able to come up with an estimate that is fairly close.'

Faizark's engine is a 4 cylinder, 42 hp Volvo Penta with a propeller bought from a second-hand dealer. They bought a new sterntube and shaft. They have three anchors, 240ft [73.1m] of chain, two anchor warps and a very pretty anchor winch, which Paul doesn't believe will last very long. There are six sheet winches, all of which were bought second-hand. The reason for the number of winches is because they believe that the weakest member of the crew should be able to handle the boat. Paul says that plenty of mechanical advantages are needed but that the rest of the deck fittings were made by them and then galvanised. 'As you can see from this list the basic boat, in what can be called sailaway trim, can be built quite cheaply,' he said.

Faizark was launched on 22 June 1983 into the river at Bideford, Devon, UK and despite the slight change I made to the design, she floated dead level, about 2¹/₂in [60mm] higher than the design waterline (it's always nice to have some waterline to spare!). Paul reports being extremely pleased with the way she handles and the speed achieved even in light winds. She is very stiff, and even though there is more ballast to add, she has proved very comfortable to sail in. Apparently she punches through the horrible Bristol Channel chop like a dream. The deck layout has been altered by taking the poop stern 5ft [1.5m] forward, and the deck used as cockpit seats, with simply a coaming around the cockpit. There is full headroom throughout the boat. She certainly has as much accommodation as most 45ft [13.7m] boats. The engine is under the cockpit well, so there is plenty of room to move about.

Paul Fay and his family have extensively cruised their Spray 36 and some of their experiences were chronicled in letters and phone calls:

'We left Bideford on 5 September bound for Spain across Biscay. The first night going down the Cornish coast we averaged 5 knots, rounding the end of Cornwall next morning. Then we crossed the Western Approaches. The wind fell light until we were totally becalmed for the next night. The following day we moored for a while until a little wind came. After this, only the log can tell the story, as the wind increased to force 7, quickly going from south-west to north-west, causing a very confused sea that impeded our sailing. Later, the wind swung back to the south-west, and increased to a force 8 for a while, but this time the seas were more regular; and, under deep-reefed main and staysail *Faizark* worked up to windward magnificently, giving us great confidence if ever we get caught on a lee shore. During all of this, the only water we had on deck was when going to windward, when she occasionally scooped up a dollop along the bows. After this, we were again becalmed, eventually moping for 100 miles [161km]. The last night was really grand sailing, with winds of force 6 on the beam; we arrived at La Coruna on the 12th, which seems a long time for this distance, but speaking to others who crossed at the same time, it seems we did very well.'

Since then, Paul and his family have taken a slow cruise down the coast of Spain and Portugal. At the moment they are in Lisbon, and the next stop is the Canaries. In every port they arrive at, *Faizark* causes quite a stir: 'There are always several people who come up to us with the expression "She's a Spray, isn't she?" We have met a Norwegian who has a deep keel yacht in steel. He has problems with water coming into his boat, and when I took a look I found that his skeg was falling off, so between us we dried his boat out and did a major repair on the beach in Lisbon. After getting to know *Faizark* well, our Norwegian friend is interested in owning a Spray of his own, so perhaps you will send me some information that I can pass on.'

Paul's comments about the Spray working to windward were later confirmed during several conversations. The addition of a slightly deeper keel on some Sprays makes a world of difference to their windward ability. This has also been backed up by comments of many other Spray owners including Charlie Jupp, who added about 1ft [305mm] to the draft of his Spray 40, and also by owners of some of the older Sprays that were built in the 1930s, 1940s and 1950s, many of which also had slightly more draft than the original Spray. With our smaller Spray designs, that is, the ones smaller than the normal full-size Spray 40, we always design in a little more depth of keel. This seems to have greatly improved the windward performance of these boats.

Paul also has some other useful information to pass on:

'After our recent crossing we decided to try a squaresail, so we cut down a piece of parachute that we had used as a spinnaker and made it from that. It sits right at the top of the mast. So far, for downwind work we have set twin headsails and the squaresail above them. I have been so impressed with it that any boat I have in the future will have to have a rig designed to carry one properly, i.e. swept-back crosstrees, etc. Although ours is only 180sq ft [16.7sq m] it is much more powerful than a jib at 250sq ft [23.2sq m]. Using it on the trip from St Barts to here, we averaged 5 knots, and the only boats that passed us were a couple of large Swan, and they were motoring.

We well understand why the Spray is so popular, as we have found her to be fantastically comfortable in any type of sea, even running before a bad storm, which another yacht equipped with accurate wind instruments reported as force 10 for a while. I went to sleep on the cockpit floor. On top of all that she still punches up to windward when everyone else is hove-to.'

Paul Fay subsequently returned to Devon in the UK, where he built a steel Roberts 345 that was sold, and then, pleased with the success and profits he had made from previous boatbuilding ventures, decided to become a full-time steel boatbuilder. Paul has recently completed a steel Spray 33 that is mentioned later. As for *Faizark,* this Spray 36 was sold to an Australian, who sailed it home to Brisbane, Queensland, and this vessel is now happily cruising the Australian coast.

HORNICKE SPRAY

Recently, a large package popped through my letter box from Hans-Jurgen Hornicke of Vasteras, Sweden. This package contained a beautifully presented set of photographs covering the entire building process of Hans's glassfibre Spray 36. To quote Hans:

'I started to build my Spray 36 at Christmastime in 1988. I started by making the frames in May 1989, and by 27 July I had completed all the glassfibre. I then began to fair the outside of the hull, and the turning over was a happy day because for the first time I can see the whole hull, and it is beautiful. The same time as I built the hull, I made many items, including blocks, mast fittings, rudder, pedestal steering and the wheel, and many other items. I work on the boat every Tuesday and Thursday after my ordinary work is complete. I am a glass blower for neon lights. I also work on the boat on Saturdays for a full day.

Another thing of interest was that I had to attach the foam myself without any assistance, so I used pipe cleaners that I bent into a U-shape and inserted through the foam so that each side of the U was each side of a batten. I then twitched the pipe cleaners together from inside the mould. The whole thing worked beautifully. The pipe cleaners are very kind to the polyurethane sheets, and there's very little risk of drawing them right through the foam. Finally, I hope you can understand most of this letter for my English is not good.'

Swedish yachtsman Goran Kjerrman (above) combined his favourite interests, sailing and steam engines, in this superbly crafted Spray 36, Steam Lady. Below: the 54 hp steam auxiliary engine built to Goran's specification. It has a diesel oil burner but can also run on wood or coal.

STEAM LADY

For many years, Goran Kjerrman in Gavle, Sweden, thought about building a Spray. He had read Slocum's book, and he wanted to combine sails and steam power because his two big interests in life are sailing and steam engines. Of course, the combination of sails and steam is a very old idea; when Slocum decided to sail around the world, the steam engine was then very modern and also becoming very common. Goran decided to build a Spray 36, fitted with a steam engine auxiliary. He considered that this boat had all of the features to be a good sailer, and he thought the boat very beautiful. When people hear the words 'steam engine', it often conjures up thoughts about coal dust, soot and smoke, and

a stoker shovelling coal in the front of a hot boiler. However this is not necessary with a small, modern steam engine. In Nkyvarn in Sweden there is a small factory that specialises in building small steam engines; most of these are custom built. This factory, HF-Maskiner, was able to build Goran's steam engine just as he wanted it. It is a triple expansion engine working at a steam pressure of 426lb/in² [30kp/cm²]. The engine weight excluding the boiler, but including feed pump and lubricator, is about 1322lb [600kg]. The engine develops 54 hp, and the maximum number of revolutions is 400 rpm. The diameter of the high-pressure cylinder is 3in [76mm], medium-pressure cylinder 5in [132mm], and the low-pressure cylinder, 9in [228mm]. Goran Kjerrman is a licensed welder, and he made the boiler himself. He started with a water tube boiler, but this type took up a great deal of room and he soon changed his mind and made another one, a small fire tube one, very like the famous Scotch Steam Ship boiler. To this boiler he adapted a super heater, a feed water heater, a condenser and an evaporator for the production of drinking water from sea water. The boiler has a diesel oil burner, but it can also fire the boiler with coal or wood. The weight of the boiler and steam engine together is about 2645lb [1200kg]. Goran has insulated the boat for living aboard in all seasons, and the whole interior is fitted out with oak. The entire vessel is a masterpiece, and perhaps this *Steam Lady* is the only steam engine Spray in the world.

LADY HAWK

This Spray 36 was built by Paul and Pamela Hawkins of Palatine Bridge, New York:

'Our Spray 36 took us eight summers of weekends to complete. We might have been able to build the entire boat in less than 16 months if we had worked on it full time. We enjoy the boat very much, and can't believe just how much boat we have until we compare it to O'Days and Hunters of the same length owned by our friends. The overall performance of the boat is outstanding. She easily handles 20 knots of wind under full main, and 150 per cent Genoa. In 25 knots we routinely set the staysail and full main. On Lake Ontario we have 5ft [1.5m] waves and our friends are amazed at how well she handles these. The only changes that we would recommend are a larger diesel, around 45 hp, a 6ft [1.8m] cockpit, and a 3ft 6in [1.1m] wide cockpit sole, to give better clearance around the wheel.'

The Spray 36 Lady Hawk, *built by Paul and Pamela Hawkins of Palatine Bridge, New York. They were delighted by the performance of their Spray, seen here during her first sail.*

Paul Francis was so impressed by his initial Spray 33 that he commissioned her builder, Jack Read, to build a Spray 36, Hazebra Pride. *Paul and his wife Chris think that* Hazebra Pride *is a lovely sea boat – very safe and seakindly.*

Regarding cockpit sizes, it is always something of a decision as to what width your cockpit should be. If you have it too wide, then you cannot sit on one seat and rest your feet on the edge of the opposite seat, which is a common position for people sitting in a cockpit especially when there is any reasonable heel on the boat. Another thing is if the cockpit is too wide and too deep, it will hold too much water in the unlikely event that you 'cop a big one', either over the bow or stern. Generally speaking, we design our cockpits to be 2ft 6in wide [760mm] and about 1ft 6in [460mm] deep. If a cockpit is too deep, it can be uncomfortable to sit in. If you build a cockpit about 1ft 6in deep [460mm], then by the time you add a teak grating or other similar arrangement, it works out just fine. As far as making a cockpit wide enough to accommodate the wheel is concerned, quite often the seats are scooped out in the area where the wheel is actually located; in that way, there is room for the wheel to be located at the correct height and still clear the cockpit seats, and the temptation of making the cockpit too wide is avoided. As far as cockpit length is concerned, the ideal is around 6ft 6in [2m] long. This allows the average person to stretch out full length on a cockpit seat, and this can have the added benefit that the seat can be used as a berth when in port in a very hot climate, thus allowing at least two of the crew to sleep comfortably on deck.

SILENT ANNIE

This Spray 36 was built by Tony Nelson, who has made a particularly fine job of the interior; so much so, in fact, that an English yachting magazine is expected to run an article on the fitting out of this boat. Some of the features of the interior include bulkhead doors fitted with stained glass panels showing east coast smacks, and a hand-carved rose on the seat end, the saloon table with 1/4in [6mm] beading and 15in [380mm] diameter compass rose inlaid in the surface. All of the galley posts and fiddle rails are hand turned, with beautiful hand-made mahogany cupboard doors and drawers. Other cupboards feature leaded doors, which gives the interior of the main saloon a beautiful hand crafted appearance. Tony says:

'What I am trying to do is to build a classic boat that will not die as so many yachts do in ten or so years, but one that will last for many, many years.

Hazebra De Lite, *another Spray 36 built by Jack Read.*

Regarding the paint job, outside I have used two coats of zinc-enriched epoxy, plus two coats of primer. Inside, one coat of winter grade epoxy, plus three coats of Admer self-healing paint, plus of course the 2in [50mm] foam insulation. All interior cladding is coated with primer on the reverse side. The two stainless steel water tanks are 68 gallons each and situated under the saloon floor. The keel is filled with steel punching, plus a welded plate over the top, and then filled with cutting oil to stop rust. The engine is an 87 hp Ford diesel with a 2:1 reduction.'

HAZEBRA PRIDE

Paul Francis first purchased *Hazebra Lady* (see p 162), a glassfibre Spray 33 built by Jack Read. After sailing this boat for some time, he decided he wanted a larger boat and commissioned Jack to build this steel Spray 36. Paul said: 'I sold *Hazebra Lady* in 1989 to Mike Ambrose, who, although having only limited experience, bought it to sail to Chesapeake Bay, Maryland, USA.' Details of Mike's trip are given under the *Hazebra Lady* heading in Chapter 9. Paul wrote:

'*Hazebra Lady* is extremely seakindly, very gentle and predictable; she allows you to get away with mistakes. We sailed her for three years with many North Sea crossings covering approximately 5000 miles without a moment's worry.

Our second Spray, *Hazebra Pride,* the 36ft [10.9m] aft cabin version that we have had since August 1989, is owned jointly by my son and myself. To date, we have covered 9000 miles [14 483 km] exploring the Ijselmeer, and Holland in general plus the Belgian and French coasts as well as the east coast of England.

Hazebra Pride is a lovely sea boat, again very safe and seakindly; it is noticeable we are one of the last to reef down. Our most noteworthy trip was the return journey to the UK from Flushing in October 1990. [Paul related in detail this trip, where the weather forecast of force 4 to 5 turned into a storm with winds in excess of force 9.] 'During the crossing in these extreme conditions, *Hazebra Pride* gave us not a moment's worry and all gear stood the strain. We have so much confidence in our Spray we would go anywhere in her.'

Paul Francis is the founding Commodore of the Slocum Spray Society, and is taking a very active part in the centenary celebrations and other activities associated with the furthering interest in the original Spray and her descendants.

Sally Belle

This steel Spray 36 was built by John Osborne, who decided to build her after he had been coerced into doing so by his friend David Sinnett-Jones. David, as you will read later, had decided to build his own Spray, so it seemed like a good idea for the two hulls to be built side by side. David Sinnett-Jones's first task was to persuade his wife to accept the idea of his building two steel hulls on the concrete yard outside their disused cowsheds, and a much easier task was to coerce his old friend John Osborne into building one of the hulls for himself while they helped each other in the construction. John Osborne completed his Spray 36 *Sally Belle,* and launched her, and she now sits snugly in Aberaeron harbour in Wales. John gets a lot of enjoyment from his boat and uses her for coastal cruising. He contacted me with the following comments:

'I enclose a photo of *Sally Belle* high and dry, but sitting nicely on her legs in the Cardigan estuary. I am very pleased with the way *Sally Belle* sails. On the way back from the Cardigan trip I sailed back with only the staysail set in a rolling sea, doing $5^1/_2$ to $6^1/_2$ knots. Smashing! On another trip last year we did it all to windward – quite a crashing sail. But I also enjoy peaceful sails and I like the way *Sally Belle* keeps going in light airs down to about 2 knots.'

Many Spray owners have remarked on their boat's ability to keep going in the lightest of airs. Not all sailing (fortunately) is done under gale conditions, so it is important to have a cruising boat that handles the light stuff as well as the roughest conditions.

Zane Spray

As mentioned above, *Zane Spray* was built in company with *Sally Belle* for it is quite common for two builders to get together and build boats side by side. In fact, we have seen several brothers build similar boats, father and son, or perhaps two friends or neighbours, or sometimes more than two people with a shared interest who want to share the companionship of undertaking a similar project at the same time.

David Sinnett-Jones had a rather special reason to want to build his boat with some help, as he writes:

'I had been diagnosed as having advanced lung cancer and had to have urgent major surgery to remove one of my lungs and part of the wall of my heart. Luckily, a few months earlier I had taken up sub-aqua diving and my doctor had spotted the problem when I went for a medical check-up and X-ray. Twenty years before that, in my motor racing days, I was blinded in the right eye on being thrown through the windscreen of a car, and now – at the age of 53 – was getting a bit stiff in the bones. Some of the worst things that have happened in my life have led the way to some of the most exciting ones. I would never have started sailing if I hadn't had cancer, nor farming if I hadn't been in and out of Sir Archibald McIndoe's guinea pig ward, having eye operations and 75 stitches in my face. McIndoe was a pioneer in skin grafting and plastic surgery during the Second World War, treating most of the Royal Air Force pilots who had severe burns; and when I was in there, the ward still had a very relaxed attitude towards the patients.'

Right from the outset of building their boats, John Osborne and David Sinnett-Jones were looking to build the boats for as little money as possible; and, with this end in mind, they used an old steel-framed harvest trailer on which to set up the frames. When the hulls were completed, they moved them down to a car park by the harbour. The idea was that they were going to have their yachts lifted into the water when the rest of the yachtsmen were having theirs lifted out at the end of the season – another example of taking

David Sinnett-Jones, owner-builder of Zane Spray *and Vice-Commodore of the Slocum Spray Society, visits the Slocum Memorial in Fairhaven USA. In addition to being an author, David has also been a singlehanded circumnavigator and Transatlantic Race competitor.*

the most economical route. Regarding the masts, John and David found some clear unknotted Douglas fir in a timber yard that was about to go bankrupt, and for £350 they bought enough timber to build the masts and the booms as well. *Zane Spray* features a centre cockpit layout with a small pilot house and is cutter rigged. The auxiliary is a Massey Ferguson 165 tractor engine that David marinised using second-hand parts. His idea of using the Massey was that he figured that wherever he might go in the world, he would be bound to find one in the corner of a field. John and David made their own sails, and in all they made three sails for each boat, but no spares. However, David was to take a roll of cloth and an electric zig-zag sewing machine with him on his round-the-world voyage. He was fortunate in that John was a good friend and actually stopped work on his own boat so that he could help David for the six months before he was due to leave on his voyage. David comments on this by saying, 'This was a great sacrifice, as he wanted to see *Sally Belle* sailing, but perhaps he knew that once I had gone, he would get a bit of peace and quiet.'

Once *Zane Spray* was complete she was taken for a trial sail, and again I quote David's words:

'Once at sea, we stopped the engine and unfurled the staysail in easy stages and half the main. She picked up speed straight away in the stiff, south-west wind. We put out more sail until we had all 1000sq ft [92.9sq m] up, and she raced along, throwing spray into the air, and the lee scuppers in foaming water. We took turns at the wheel, each one of us hogging it as long as we could. As we trimmed the sail she got up to 7 knots and then 7.5. We were overjoyed with our work. The boat was good, fast and strong – old Joshua would have been pleased with us!'

Can you imagine the joy of these two friends out for a sail on the first of the two boats they were building, and to have the boat perform as they had hoped. Both would have been equally overjoyed. David Sinnett-Jones was fortunate. His friendly open-handed manner and his life-long habit of easily making friends, including the period that he spent racing cars, came to fruition when many people offered to sponsor him and his boat. They offered various pieces of equipment that otherwise would have cost him a considerable amount of money. Not only did friends from the past act in this way, but often complete strangers would come up, introduce themselves to David, and take an interest in the project; this led to various sponsorships and donations of gear and equipment. David also had a friend called Eric Williams, who is a HAM radio operator and had also worked with him on previous voyages. He found David a very reasonably priced transceiver that would do nicely for the trip. Originally, David had not planned a singlehanded voyage; however, one by one, the people who had planned to accompany him on various stages of the cruise became unavailable for one reason or another.

Another lucky break for David was when he met Phill Davies, known locally as 'Phill Photo'; Phill takes HTV news film and stills for the newspapers. As the media had previously given David good coverage, he thought that he would ask Phill if HTV might be interested in David sending back news reports on the voyage. The idea was to bring in some money. Phill suggested that David should go and see the opera singer Sir Geraint Evans, who lives in Aberaeron and is on the board of HTV. The upshot of all this was that HTV eventually worked out an excellent sponsorship arrangement with David, whereby David was to make a film of his voyage that would be sent back and screened on HTV. All of this worked out very well. HTV got some very interesting and exciting film, and David secured very worthwhile sponsorship.

On 17 September 1985, exactly three years to the day from the time David Sinnett-Jones had arrived home in his previous boat, *Zane II,* he motored out of the harbour and set sail on his great adventure. David completed his circumnavigation, and on his return to Wales he was feted. He received a considerable amount of press coverage, not only from HTV who had in part sponsored the trip, but also from the local newspapers.

David's singlehanded voyage would have been a magnificent achievement for an able bodied person, but even more so for someone who has lost both a lung, and the sight of one eye. David has approached HTV to allow him to use the film in the form of a video, which will be available to other Spray enthusiasts. Sailing round the world singlehanded is not a first for mankind, but an amazing achievement for someone with David's disabilities.

When asked to comment on the most memorable part of his trip, David chose Percy Island off Australia, a perfect tropical island that is kept by a former triathlon Englishman for the benefit of passing sailors.

Well, one would think that was enough adventuring for one man. Not so with David Sinnett-Jones. In June 1992, at the age of 62, David took care of another ambition when he started in the singlehanded Transatlantic Race, currently known as the Europe One Star. *Zane Spray* had been given a new rig and suit of North headsails, and David was overjoyed to cross the line in Newport, Rhode Island, USA, in 40 days. This is the same time that Francis Chichester had taken to win the inaugural race in 1960. David is now living in a waterfront cottage in Aberaeron, Wales; and his book *Not All Plain Sailing* has been completed and

Zane Spray *with her skipper, David Sinnett-Jones, at the start of the Transatlantic Race in 1992.*

Moss Spray, *a steel Spray 36, was built by Mr Moss in the USA.*

published along with another book covering his voyages prior to building *Zane Spray.* According to David, his sailing days are still not yet over.

Because David Sinnett-Jones is a very friendly and generous person, he has offered to pass on advice to those interested in learning more about the Spray and her sailing qualities, and other aspects of preparing for and executing world cruises. Some of this can of course be found in his book *Not All Plain Sailing,* however, he is more than happy to talk to anybody who is interested in the subject of the Spray and cruising in general. (See Appendix)

JOHN HENRY

Mark J Tompkins of Tolono, Illinois, USA was building a steel Spray in 1991. He used the table of offsets to lay up full scale the frames for the hull, deck and cabin top. He also wanted an aft cockpit with a long and cosy cabin. He was planning to build the mast and boom from two flagpoles, one 35ft [10.6m] and one 30ft [9.1m] donated from two local McDonald's restaurants. Mark promised to take them sailing!

We know of many cases where various aluminium poles have been turned into masts. One was Tom Corkhill, who sailed his catamaran *Ninetails* around the world. *Ninetails* has covered many additional thousands of miles on trips between Australia, Indonesia and so forth. Tom built his catamaran at our Brisbane boatyard way back in 1967, and he is still sailing the same boat. He rigged his cat with a light pole mast, and to my knowledge it is still in service. People have used a complete assortment of items as masts, from cutting down a tree, through to light poles and flagpoles, and of course purchasing a complete ready-made, custom-built, aluminium spar with all the goodies.

NASCIMENTO SPRAY

In July 1991 Edison Do Nascimento wrote:

'I bought a plan of your Spray 36 in 1987 when I was living in San Jose, California. I ordered the multi-chine plywood plan, but with the full-size patterns for glassfibre because I will build the boat in round-bilge, cold-moulded construction. Today I am living in Campinas, Brazil. I built a temporary shed and bought the necessary timber to build the boat. I am now starting to build a Spray model in the same scale of drawings as the plans, $1/2$ in = 1ft [1=24].

Here in Brazil the economic situation doesn't feel nice, and the boat construction is stopped for a while. Two years ago, a very hard storm destroyed my temporary shed just when I had started to put the frames on the strong back. The frames were saved, but I had to build the shed again. This time I'm trying to sell my powerboat to get back on the Spray construction. As you know, whoever buys a Spray plan is a dreamer, and as a dreamer we will never give up.'

GYPSY LADY

In 1986 Mr E Marvin Johnson of Salem, Oregon, wrote of his Spray 36: 'With 7000lb [3175kg] of lead poured into the keel, and a Vetus P 421 engine, she is beginning to show signs of wanting to go to sea, so thought it best to keep her tied up!' The photograph reveals a mooring line from the bollards, through the fairlead, and the boat is secured to a post in the shed. 'You don't have to be crazy to start a project like this, but it helps. She is a fine retirement project and I'm having a lot of fun working on her. I'll call her *Gypsy Lady*.'

SWEET ECSTASY

Calvin Ayers of Boyne city, Michigan, USA described the building of his Roberts Spray 36 in steel:

'I've been sailing and building sailboats since I was a kid, and after going to sea in the Navy I was hooked. I conducted five years of research before choosing to build a Spray 36 in steel, with the centre cockpit layout, and decided to rig the boat as a cutter. Before I started building her I had maybe 15 minutes of welding experience. Needless to say, 125lb [57kg] of welding rod later, my welding skills have greatly improved. I used the method of building the hull upright, welding the keel to an "I" beam set in concrete. The reason for doing this is the cost of wood for framing. I am building this boat on a shoestring, so every dollar spent has to represent a tool or part of the finished boat. The only change in the design I am making is to add freshwater cooling by adding a welded-up box made from T-section about 6in [150mm] deep at its aft end, and when added to the bottom of the keel that will be used as a heat exchanger. I am having a ball putting her together!'

ALPENGLOW

Back in the late 1970s the newsletter called *The Steel Yacht* was edited and published in California by Bill Tapia. It was a three or four page photocopied publication, which after a few issues grew into something a little more substantial. Unfortunately, this could not be sustained and eventually it went out

The photograph of this beautiful glassfibre Spray was given to me by her American builder. I await his wrath for not crediting him by name.

of business. Bill Tapia had some good ideas, and there was –, and still is – a need for publications of this kind which give the builder and/or cruising yachtsman good hard information. Because of the popularity of steel Spray replicas, they were often featured in the magazine. To quote from one contribution:

'Doug Knight of South Lake Tahoe, California, chose the Spray 36 design because he was concerned with having enough living space for long distance cruising. "I never heard of that fellow called Slocum", said Doug, "until my boat was well under construction. I must have lived a hundred years ago, because when I first saw the hull lines I knew right then and there that the Spray design would be my next boat." In changing the interior layout, Doug Knight moved the cockpit aft, containing the interior to one space. "In having one main area there will be no problem in heating the cabin in the northern latitudes where my boat *Alpenglow* will spend much of her life." The freeboard on *Alpenglow* was raised 3in [75mm] above the stock plans, and Knight is still thinking about adding an additional 2in [50mm] that will give the bulwark a total height of 9in [230mm]. With the main cabin contained into one area, the bulkheads were changed to suit the rest of the interior. Doug Knight is very enthusiastic about his Spray 36: "I've always kept privacy in mind, because I could never rule out the possibility of charter service. I plan on having a solid timber mast that will support an enlarged sail plan of the gaff rig. This working sail plan is just that, a working sail plan and not a show piece. With five sails working, no type of wind conditions should cause problems."'

CHAPTER 9

Spray 33 – Eighty Per Cent Roberts Spray

The Spray 33 is one of the few Spray designs that we prepared without any firm order from a particular client. Many of the designs offered by our company are the result of custom design orders that we feel will have a wide enough appeal to be offered as stock plans. The Spray 33, though, was a design we felt would be well accepted; and plans and patterns were prepared without a firm order being to hand. As with any business activity, you win some and lose some. Fortunately the Spray 33 has turned out to be a big winner.

ROBERTS SPRAY 33

Although we feel that this size is better suited to a single mast arrangement, some builders have chosen a ketch rig.

SPRAY 33 DIMENSIONS	
LOD	32ft 11in [10.03m]
LWL	26ft 7in [8.13m]
Beam	12ft 0in [3.6m]
Draft	4ft 0in [1.2m]
Headroom	6ft 4in [1.93m]
Displacement	22 000lb [9972kg]
Ballast	Varies
Spars	Timber or aluminium
Auxiliary	30 to 50 hp
Sail area	Varies
Sail plans	Cutter, ketch or Schooner
Construction materials	Glassfibre, steel or wood/epoxy

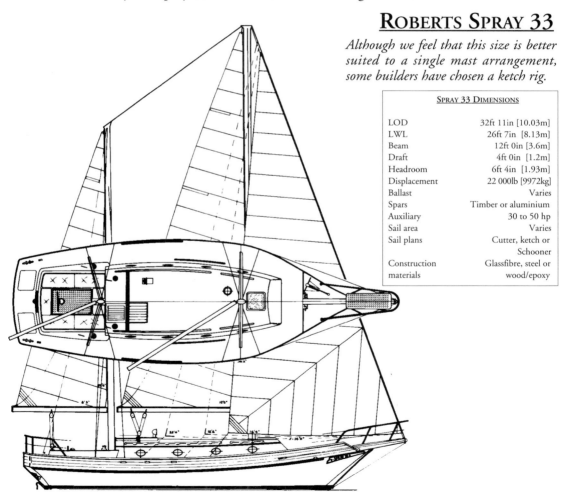

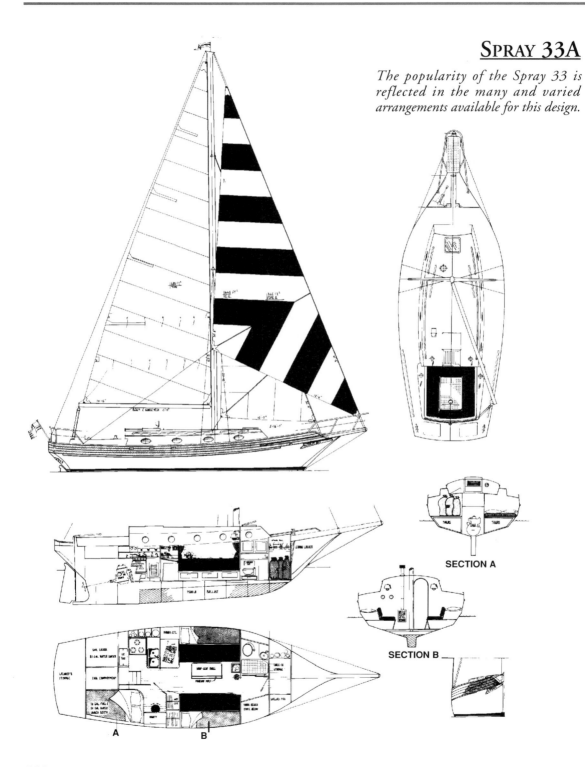

SPRAY 33A

The popularity of the Spray 33 is reflected in the many and varied arrangements available for this design.

SECTION A

SECTION B

ROYAL SPRAY

Perhaps someone will translate the inscription on this version of the Spray 33 which is reprinted below.

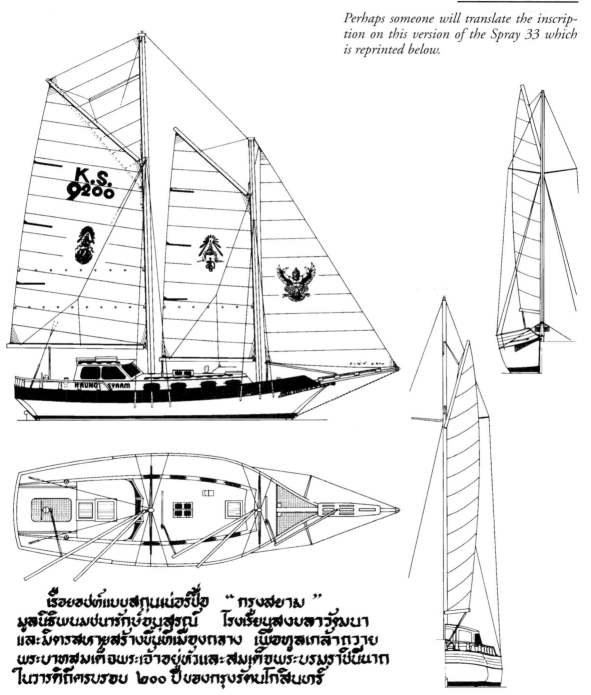

เรือยอชต์แบบสกูนเนอร์ปื้อ " กรุงสยาม "
มูลนิธิพนมปนารักษ์อนุสรณ์   โรงเรียนสงบสารวัฒนา
และมีดารสมหายสร้างขึ้นเผณฑองกลาง เพื่อทูลเกล้าถวาย
พระบาทสมเด็จพระเจ้าอยู่หัวและสมเด็จพระบรมราชินีนาถ
ในวารที่ถีศรบรอบ ๒๐๐ ปีบองกรุงรัตนโกสินทร์

ROYAL SPRAY

One of the most unusual Spray 33s we designed was one for the King of Thailand. We were approached by the Boy Scouts' Association of Thailand, who wanted to build a boat as a gift for the King to celebrate the 200th anniversary of the dynasty. As my own grandfather had been a mining engineer who spent most of his life in the Far East and often dined with the present king's father, this project was of particular interest to me. We were sent a considerable amount of material written in Thai script, including three drawings, one of which represented the crest of the King, another the crest of the Queen, and the third was the crest for the nation. This last crest took the form of a sacred bird. We faithfully copied all of the script to be included on the plans, which obviously were intended to be presented to the King along with the boat. Our associate designer Graham Williams also copied the crest of the King, Queen and the country on to the sail plan. We had a lot of communication with the people who were handling the work. We received photographs showing the hull being built and then no more was heard from the principals concerned. We understand that the boat has now been completed.

SIMPLICITY

This ferro-cement Spray was once owned by the boating journalist and publisher Pete Greenfield and here are some of Pete's comments:

'Maggie and I built a 33ft [10m] LOD version of Joshua Slocum's famous Spray. I wrote about her rather a lot, though she has now moved on to new owners. We adapted her in the building, with the permission of her designer, the late Percy Dalton. Build-it yourself plans of a version of a Spray exactly the same size as *Simplicity* are available from Bruce Roberts. The modern sailplan option clearly isn't Spray, but Bruce Roberts makes the point that the Bermudan cutter rig balances very well and drives this hull at maximum hull speed in any sort of breeze. It has been found that the Spray hull is very easily driven and the performance is creditable under actual cruising conditions. Spray can carry her full working rig longer and stand up to a

Simplicity, *a ferro-cement Spray.*

breeze when other boats are reducing sail. I can attest to the fact that under that short, tubby hull there is a long flat run aft which starts well forward, and does indeed produce a quite surprisingly slippery vessel, but though I might claim to be trying to emulate the original's famed self-steering qualities rather than admit it would be simply for the look of her, I think I would favour a lower and longer-based gaff rig like the cutter or if you can afford the marina charges, why not be really radical and go for a yawl? That's half the fun of building your own boat. As long as there's someone with real knowledge to consult like the designer, just to ensure that you don't do anything too radical.'

Pete Greenfield also sent me additional material about the building and sailing of his Spray *Simplicity*, as well as arranging the loan of an excellent photograph of Pete Culler's *Oxford Spray*.

CORA

Pelle Christoffersen built his steel Spray 33 *Cora* in Sweden, starting construction in 1988 and launching her in 1992. The recently received letter that accompanied an excellent set of photographs was written in Swedish so unfortunately I am unable to quote directly from Pelle's comments.

Fortunately the photographs speak for themselves; Pelle has made a beautiful job of not only building the hull; the quality of workmanship exhibited in the fitting out of the interior is first class. Solid mahogany timber was used extensively and the cabinet work is all of the highest professional standard.

The decks and cabin top are all sheathed with a laid teak deck and again the photographs reveal a well thought out arrangement and high standard of workmanship throughout. Pelle has fitted the Ketch rig and I notice he has chosen tan sails that always look attractive on a traditional boat like the Spray.

SOUTHERLY BUSTER

This Spray 33 was built at Ballina NSW Australia by John Page and launched in 1982. She was completed in a very creditable eight-months. This must be one of the most travelled Spray 33s ever built; John has successfully completed many singlehanded ocean voyages in *Southerly Buster* cruis-

Probably the most travelled Spray 33 ever built, Southerly Buster *has extensively cruised the Pacific and even completed a global circumnavigation. Built by John Page in under eight months, she is seen here off Tahiti.*

ing to New Guinea, the Solomon Islands, Thailand by way of Christmas Islands, the Philippines and Indonesia.

The most notable voyage, a complete circumnavigation, was undertaken with English born Carol Larkin as crew. Countries visited included South Africa, Brazil, various Caribbean Islands, Panama, and back to Australia calling at Brisbane, before completing the voyage at Darwin, Northern Territory, Australia.

The worst weather encountered was 200 miles off Townsville, Queensland, when in 1989 *Southerly Buster* rode out Cyclone Ivor. John found himself 40 miles from the centre of the storm and considered himself lucky to avoid the worst of a very serious cyclone; he only experienced 80 knots; at the centre it was reliably reported that the wind speed reached well over 100 knots.

John reported his best passage was Cocos Keeling Islands to Rodrigues, a distance of 2000 miles [5179 km] covered in 13 days. During this crossing the crew slept every night with winds of 25 to 35 knots on the quarter.

Anna Lee

Joseph W Rohloff of Nunica, Michigan, bought plans for the Spray 33 and had the hull shell built in Canada. The Spray was extended 2ft [610mm] in length. This was before we designed the Spray 36, but Rohloff also made other important changes. He used a steel bowsprit and arranged the foredeck flush all the way to the bow. The bow was closed resulting in a large foredeck. The builder also raised the gunwhale 2-8in [50-200mm], a change that some others are also making. It makes sense, because high bulwarks mean safety at sea.

In December 1993 we heard from Jo Rohloff:

'Anna Lee was launched on 4 June 1987. So far, she has been sailed on the Great Lakes in Canada. She has met or exceeded all my expectations and could certainly take me anywhere in the world.'

Joe explained that Anna Lee is fitted with 6000lb [2721kg] of lead ballast. The cutter sail package for the Spray 36 was installed to suit the longer overall length. A section of the keel was closed

Joseph Rohloff of Nunica, Michigan, wanted a bigger boat than the Spray 33, which was the largest Roberts design then available. Nothing daunted, he had Anna Lee's builder stretch her to 35 feet.

and used for a closed-system engine cooling, which worked very well. A 20 hp Humpah diesel provides adequate power through an 18in x 12in [457mm x 305mm] three-bladed prop.

ISAMBARD

This boat is jointly owned by Reverend Richard Gregory, and Mr G D Luton, both of Dorchester in Dorset, UK. Back in 1986, we heard from Reverend Gregory:

'It gives me great pleasure to write and tell you that the plans I bought for the steel Spray 33 at the latter end of 1979 have this season led to the launching of our centre-cockpit, gaff cutter, *Isambard*, which we named after the great engineer Isambard Brunel. I extended the coachroof forward about 18in [457mm], and cut it off 2ft [610mm] aft, and added an after cabin, which is really spacious with an athwartships double berth. The two cabins connect via the cockpit, and also by a passage down the starboard side under the cockpit seat. This gives excellent access to the engine, which I fitted

Reverend Richard Gregory and his co-owner Mr G D Luton derived great satisfaction from building their own Spray 33, Isambard, *even though it took them six years to complete her.*

further forward than shown in the plans. I raised the topsides by 7in [178mm] abaft the cockpit, but laid the afterdeck without the 4in [100mm] bulwarks, so I gained 11in [280mm] headroom for the after cabin and reduced the apparent height of the after coach roof. Under the stern there are four galleon windows, so that the after cabin is very light, and there is a nice view for those that occupy the after berth. Forward of the saloon, the forepeak is 5ft [1.52m] between bulkheads, and is fitted out with a workbench and a store.'

After launching in July, they managed a five-day cruise in light winds and have since done a fair amount of day sailing. Although they have yet to experience any seriously testing conditions, their verdict is that *Isambard* is a most comfortable yacht, and excellently stiff and reassuring to live aboard. They say that she sails well in light winds and has impressed some very experienced sailors.

Reverend Gregory said:

'It's been a long slog building the boat, only one day a week and no evenings from my job as a parish priest, but I have enjoyed it all – except the grinding down and wire brushing. She does not leak a drop, either from above or below, and I have not had any condensation either, even though as yet the lining has not been done. I am, as you can gather, very pleased with the design and look forward to many happy seasons of good cruising.'

He goes on to say that they have been restricted in their sailing to the English Channel and Brittany because of work commitments, but that their boat has 'dug a groove in the sea' between England and Normandy, and that they have found her very seakindly whatever the weather. Reverend Gregory plans cruising at $5^1/_2$ to 6 knots, and though with a

Rev. Richard Gregory and G D Luton's Isambard *in Dorset, England.* strong wind they have done 8 knots, $5^3/_4$ knots seems to be the hull speed. They have had a number of grounding experiences, and September gales parted the mooring chain and drove the vessel on to a rocky beach. The boat's underwater configuration, combined with the well-protected rudder and screw, and beaminess, all proved good insurance against damage, which did not take them long to repair. Reverend Gregory comments that many glassfibre boats did not survive nearly so well in these gales:

'Despite dire warnings that a boatbuilding project that becomes too protracted leads to loss of enthusiasm, I must say that for the six years we were building her, the project gave me tremendous satisfaction, and I have gained such useful skills, especially in metalworking, that I never could have imagined would be so valuable and in so many fields. At present they are being used in the sculpture class, for which the students need steel armatures. This winter my co-owner,

Mr Luton, has been building a large wood frame screen, and we are extending the Spray hood to cover the hull cockpit. It must be a sign of ageing!'

OYSTERMAN SPRAY

This steel Spray 33 was built for Mr and Mrs Giddy of St Athan, South Glamorgan, UK. Other than a photograph of the boat and a short note from Mrs Giddy, I did not know much about this particular vessel. 'Enclosed, photographs of our Spray on the day of launching. At the moment we have none of her sailing, but hope we might have some soon as we know other members of the club have taken some photographs. However, as usual this is a view that we never seem to get ourselves.' You may note that *Oysterman* is the same name as the Roberts Spray 40 which was built in glassfibre by Roger and Riva Palmer back in the late 60s. *Oysterman* is a natural name for any Spray because apparently the original Spray was used for oyster fishing before she came into Slocum's ownership. When I later spoke to Mr Giddy I learned that *Oysterman* had been sold and cruised down to Malta in 1990 by her new owners.

The subsequent history of *Oysterman* came to me via a communication entitled 'The Malta Un-connection'. Due to the death of the owner, *Oysterman* had been left in Terry Erskine's boatyard on the island of Gozo, Malta.

This Spray 33, built of steel some 12 years ago, had never been properly maintained and was left virtually abandoned for the previous four years. She was indeed a sorry sight when prospective buyer Mr Bob Stewart first saw her late in 1993. Bob was smitten with the boat and returned to the UK and negotiated the purchase and in early 1994 became the proud owner of a very tatty Spray 33.

Oysterman was sitting in a locked boat yard that had now ceased to trade and was caught up in the usual mess of third party properties. Terry Erskine, the only director of this business still remaining in Malta, was in limbo with all sorts of restraining orders forbidding him to leave the islands while at the same time not allowing him to be there. Notwithstanding all of these problems, Terry agreed to help Bob liberate his new boat and also to assist on a quick 'tart up' and re-launch of the vessel, so it could be sailed back to the UK.

After a few days of working on the boat Terry Erskine knew that the 'tart up' was in reality a major refit. Almost everything on the boat was in need of attention and Terry worked long and hard to prepare it for sea. Bob Stewart arrived for his three week vacation and worked a 14 hour day alongside Terry, virtually rebuilding his recently acquired boat. At the end of his time off, Bob returned to his oil rig job and left Terry to complete the refit and re-launch the Spray 33 by the middle of May. After a herculean last minute rush, common to all refit and building jobs, *Oysterman* was launched.

As Terry Erskine had an 'impediment of departure' placed on his person by the Maltese government, it was with some trepidation that *Oysterman* was sailed out of the harbour under the watchful eye of a Maltese gunboat. After engine trials for an hour Bob then hoisted the sails, put aside his worries about clearance and set a northerly course for Sicily.

Bob continues:

'By the next morning we were motor sailing along the Sicilian coast when we received a buzz from an Italian patrol boat asking where we were bound. We replied, "France", and they lost interest in us at that point, waving us on our way. After sailing through some thick fog, plus an encounter with a large section of hatch cover netting, we pressed on towards southern France.

Next morning, a German warship was on the RT asking for "yacht in position so and so to identify itself" and of course it was us! We were informed that we had entered a 40 mile radius, war games area, where live missiles were being fired! They ordered us to leave the area on 110 degrees which was back the way we had just come. We tried a 60 degree course, to slip out of the area without losing too much ground, but very shortly a large bow wave was sighted, belonging to the destroyer, and we were told to clear out of the area immediately. We politely explained there was no wind and we were a sailing boat with very little fuel for our 33 hp diesel engine. After a pause the warship came alongside with the crew lining the rails and we were given a jerry can of fuel and they filled our two plastic containers as well. They waited for the return of the jerry can; it was the only one they had! It seems that the whole of the North Mediterranean was closed to all shipping, except for a narrow three mile channel at the top of the French coast.

At dusk we found ourselves in the three mile channel with all of the shipping of the Med. funnelling through it and by now the winds were up to force 5 and right on the nose. It was a

Oysterman 33 *was built in the early 1980s for Mr and Mrs Giddy of Glamorgan, Wales. She eventually found her way to a boatyard in Malta where she sat for about four years, neglected and forgotten, until she was discovered by Bob Stewart. Bob, and Terry Erskine of the boatyard, managed to virtually refit the boat in three weeks, so that she could be sailed back to England in 1994.*

very uncomfortable night with winds increasing to force 6 and 7, and by morning we were off St Tropez. We finally arrived at Toulon where we tied up at the hospitable Du Port De Saint Mandrier marina. We searched out the customs and were asked why we bothered, we had no drugs did we ? We were British were we not? So all was fine, no paper stamping or form filling needed here. Next day we headed off again, finally arriving at Sete. There was no room at the marina so we anchored in the commercial dock basin. We had covered 872 nautical sea miles, 7 nights at sea and an average of 4.98 knots; not bad for a Spray 33.

The next job was to un-rig the boat and prepare for the passage through France via the Canal Du Midi and Canal Lateral, from Sete to Bordeaux. Sete is a nice holiday town totally dominated by the port docks and canals. There are lifting and swing bridges dividing the town into areas of fishing boats plus docks for commercial and tourist activity. It is possible to spend considerable time in Sete without paying mooring fees. The bridges open at set times to allow ships and yachts to negotiate the various areas and passage into the large Etang De Thau. For the next month we spent time tied up in various locations taking advantage of the free moorings and sampling the local wine.

During this time we met many passage-making yachts and boats arriving and leaving the French canals so we were able to gain valuable information that would be useful on the next stage of our trip. Several tyres were procured from local garages and carried back to the boat and strung around the sides of the hull as a canal "defence system".

Bob returned for another stint of leave so we were able to proceed through the lifting bridge that would admit us to the canal system. We tied up in the dark near the first lock, ready for an early start the next day. At 0800 the lock opened for business and we paid the keeper a fixed fee that would cover us for the whole passage through the canals. Our first day's run of 66km ended at the junction of the Canal De La Robine, and having negotiated 16 locks, we felt that our target of seven days to Bordeaux was possible.

Now we were in amongst the hire boats, nicknamed by the locals as "bumper boats". These plastic boats are crewed and skippered by people of all nationalities and levels of proficiency. An example of this experience is the memory of one skipper who, when his lady crew fell overboard, immediately proceeded to reverse over her. He said he did not know how to find neutral! The lady had a lucky escape.

After a 52km [32M], 20 lock, day's run we were greeted with the news that the lock keepers throughout France were now on STRIKE! Tied up in the middle of nowhere with 85 degree heat, there was only one thing for it, we would declare a "make and mend day", and change the engine oil etc. Terry rowed back 3km [1.8M] to the village of Trebes and secured a can of oil from the English owned hire boat company.

The strike only lasted one day and with the lock keepers back to work we were able to continue our passage along the Canal Du Midi. Our next day's run was 41km [24.4M] and 24 locks. Next day, we ran aground when the canal water dropped one foot! Within a minute of the lock keeper's start up time, a surge of lock water was released to float us off and allow us to continue on our way.

When we left the Canal Du Midi and entered the Canal Lateral we soon cleared our first automatic lock.The rest of the passage was uneventful and we arrived in Bordeaux having travelled 572km [355M] and 148 locks in the very respectable time of nine days.

The canals were a great experience and they can present some minor difficulties to yachts with masts laid on deck. They are a necessary part of moving around Europe and a boon for those of us who do not have unlimited time to sail around rather than through France. At time of writing, *Oysterman* is in Bordeaux, re-rigged and ready for the next and final stage of her return to the UK.'

DRAGON SPRAY

This steel Spray 33 was built by Dragon Marine, then located on Hayling Island near Southampton. Dave Folwell of Dragon Marine has built many Bruce Roberts-designed steel boats, and he built a Spray 33 for his own use. Often he would be out sailing and some of the so-called 'hot' keel boats would think his Spray was a pushover, and would come alongside wanting to show their superiority. However, in anything but a hard punch to windward, the Spray 33, which could carry full sail long after the other boats were reefed down, would surprise all concerned. Many of these impromptu challenges ended with the Spray 33 showing the other boats a clean pair of heels.

COLUMBINE

I saw this steel Spray 33 when I was visiting Minnesota Beach Marina in North Carolina. Dr Keith Wolfenbarger and his charming wife, Judy, carved out a 200-berth marina from swampland off the Noose River, and they had personally owned four Bruce Roberts-designed boats including Roberts 53s. There is always at least one Spray visiting the marina, including one that sailed over from South Africa. The couple that brought her over, worked in the marina for some time, hoping to remain in the USA. Columbine displayed as her home port the little town of Littleton, Colorado.

Colorado is more or less in the centre of the USA, and a very mountainous state; it is famous for its skiing rather than its boating activities. However some people prefer to register their boats in their home town, no matter whether the town is miles from the ocean. Also, in the USA it was at one time an acceptable practice to register your boat in a state that had few boating facilities, and consequently no taxes aimed directly at the sailor. By registering the vessel locally, one could thereafter escape the taxes of the state where the boat was kept. Of course, the authorities soon woke up to this ruse, and consequently any boat that appeared in a marina in their state could be slapped with a tax demand. This in turn led to unfair situations in the extreme, as one could be visiting a marina or anchorage for just a few days and have the taxman knocking on your hull.

NORTHERN SPRAY

This boat was built by John E Bushnell of St Paul, Minnesota. I remember well the day that John walked into my design office and said that while he found the Spray 33 an attractive boat, he would really prefer to build something just a little longer, and would help in designing a stretched version of the Spray 33. At that time, I considered this to be a one-off request, so I consented to assist John with some additional sheets added to the Spray 33 plans which would enable him to build a slightly longer version of this boat. John chose glassfibre as his boatbuilding material, so we set about outlining the changes that would give him the space he required. At this time, there were no plans to design the boat that is now known as the Spray 36. This was simply a one-off exercise for a client who wanted something just a little different. John subsequently went ahead and built his Spray. After a considerable amount of cruising around the Caribbean, John wrote:

'It is now four years since 4 July 1979, which was when I started constructing *Northern Spray*. Suddenly the long task had become worthwhile. I cruised the Bahamas alone for several months. Alone? Not really. At every anchorage I met other boaters. At one of them in the Berri chain, my offer of a tray of ice cubes each evening from the plenty my refrigerator turned out provided me in return with surplus fish from their snorkelling expeditions.'

John then goes on to chronicle all of the places he visited around the Caribbean and the friends he made both afloat and ashore, and the chance meeting with boats that he had met up with several times, and all in one wonderful year of cruising. After that he went back home to Minnesota to spend a winter with his family, and his letter closed by saying, 'When I resume cruising this spring, it will again be towards home, and then finally to Lake Superior to taper off with short trips on the Great Lakes for parts of the summers.' Shortly afterwards, in January 1985, I received another note from John. It read:

'I have owed you a letter for a long time to inform you how *Northern Spray* has turned out. In essence, you in design, and I in execution, have both done a fine job on her. There is no detail of design and execution that was not suitable for the requirements of a fine, comfortable cruising boat. In the year and a half since I arrived in the Gulf, after a fine trip motoring down the Mississippi, I have been fortunate enough never to have been in any long-lasting heavy gale, but on quite a few occasions I have sailed in very fresh winds. At no time have I had any green water on deck, nor has Northern Spray heeled over far enough to put the deck under water. She has stood up well in the occasional heavy gusts of winds such as those that often precede a thunder shower. I have never had any failure concerning any of the rigging or operation of any part of *Northern Spray.*'

BRASS LOON

This boat, owned by Leuder L Kerr of Comox, British Columbia, Canada, is of aluminium construction, cutter rigged, and has a Perkins 4 108 auxiliary engine. The hull was built in 1979 by a yard in

Aluminium was the material chosen by Leuder Kerr for his Spray 33, Brass Loon. *Her extremely strong hull is impervious to the floating logs which are a common sailing hazard in her local waters off British Columbia.*

Vancouver specialising in aluminium fishing vessels. It was then finished by the previous owner over a three-year period and launched in 1982. The main departure from the plans was the addition of a pilot house, which works very well, and the installation of a larger engine.

Leuder Kerr is currently living aboard and finds it very comfortable; the pilot house allows him to sail in the Pacific north-west all the year round. It is not a fast boat but he particularly likes its stability, seakindliness and the sense of security its massive strength gives him. He has run into floating logs, which are a local hazard – often at night and while at full speed – without hull damage. Another plus is the keel configuration coupled with the wide beam. It lets him run ashore on a sand or mud beach at low tide to clean the bottom, heeling only about 25 degrees. On the next tide, he simply changes sides!

HAZEBRA LADY

This fibreglass Spray 33 was the first of several Sprays built by Jack Read, and we visited this boat when it was moored on the Norfolk Broads. *Hazebra Lady* is fitted with a Vetus 33 hp diesel, and rigged as a Bermudan cutter. When Jack built this boat, he wrote the following: 'Since being launched in June we have spent a month cruising from Norfolk to Portsmouth and back, and hope to get over to Amsterdam next week. She took ten months full-time work to complete and cost £12 500. Timber is genuine teak, except for the mahogany cabin sides. I am well pleased, and she has been much admired at all ports of call.'

Jack Read eventually sold *Hazebra Lady* to Paul Francis, who owned her for three years and cruised for 5000 miles. Paul Francis has a most complimentary opinion of this boat, and only sold her to order a larger Spray 36, named *Hazebra Pride*.

Hazebra Lady was sold to the present owner, Mike Ambrose, and he has since crossed the Atlantic in this Spray 33. The route was Walton-on-the-Naze, Ramsgate, Southampton, Falmouth, Lisbon, Gibraltar, Canary Islands, Barbados, Trinidad, Honduras and Guatemala. Last report was that Mike was sailing *Hazebra Lady* north to Mexico and then on to the USA.

Hazebra Lady *was the first Spray 33 to be built by Jack Read and is now owned by Mike Ambrose, who has crossed the Atlantic in her.*

MOULDED SPRAY

Some years ago we received a call from Florida from someone who suggested he was going to build a mould for the Spray 33; his company would produce glassfibre hulls. We were pleasantly surprised when we received photographs of a beautiful moulded Spray 33. Also enclosed with the photographs was a picture of a well-built mould. Some time later I was in touch with the company, who informed me that so far they had only built the one hull, for pressure of other business had caused them to put the project to one side. The photographs reveal a hull that is incredibly fair, but I wonder where it is now?

PLUCKY LADY

This boat was built by Mr and Mrs Depreitere in France, and I first became aware of this particular Spray when I received the following communication headed 'In the Wake of an Obsession':

'It all began in 1987 when my husband fell in love: he saw the first picture of the Spray. After owning three other boats he had finally found his dream boat, so we bought the plans. The hull and deck were to be built by a professional, but two months before it was finished the company went bankrupt and we lost everything. In 1989 we decided to buy another boat. After visiting quite a few sailboats, my husband said that if we couldn't have a Spray to sail in, then he didin't want to sail. In August 1989 we rented a broken-down farmhouse with lots of land space. We did not have a lot of money, but the courage was there. My husband did not have any experience in welding, but that did not stop him. With the help of some friends, it was OK after a few weeks. It is now 1994 and we will be launching in the summer of 1995. My husband's dreams, which also became mine, were not lost. It was a beautiful dream come true. She is a real plucky lady, which of course is the name of our boat.'

SCESNEY SPRAY

This Spray 33 will soon be launched by George A Scesney of Atlanta, Georgia, USA. George has written to inform us about his boat and to request information about the use of a solid spar for his mast. One of the few designs in which we would recommend the use of a solid spar is the Spray series. The Spray is so inherently stiff that the solid spar with its additional weight may even be of some advantage over an aluminium mast of similar strength.

HAMBLIN SPRAY

In 1982 Doug Hamblin was already well advanced in the building of his steel Spray 33, and as Doug had a few ideas of his own, it is worth quoting him here:

'It has been necessary to deviate from the suggested building plan in several cases. I have chosen the upside down building method on a steel jig. The steel jig costs about the same as a wooden one, and I feel the steel is sturdier, longer lasting and does not change shape with the weather. I set the frames up on the jig with a transit to level the head stocks. I built a complete framework for the transom. I decided to use a hydraulic drive system; instead of putting in an angled propeller shaft, I have mounted the sterntube horizontally 16in [406mm] above the keel. The hydraulic motor is to be mounted deep in the keel. I plan to use a Mazda RX7 rotary engine because of its smoothness. It will drive a Rex-Roth variable displacement hydraulic pump. This unit should put about 50 hp at 3000 engine rpm and 900 propeller rpm.

Even with limited space available, this boat is still easy to build. Thanks to the multi-chine design, the skin plates are kept to a reasonable size. I have had no problem whatsoever building this boat alone.'

CALIFORNIA SPRAY

This glassfibre Spray 33 was built in California. As our office at that time was located nearby in Newport Beach, we had quite a lot of contact with the builder of this boat. When the time came for launching, which was to take place near San Diego, I and another member of my design team were invited to the big event. Accompanied by my long-term Australian friend and associate designer, Graham Williams, we proceeded to San Diego in time to see the boat being trailed down to the marina. As is typical in California, the launching was undertaken using a travel lift, so there was none of the panic that is sometimes associated with these events. There was plenty

This glassfibre Spray 33, California Spray, *was apparently subjected to piracy on her launch day, when she was stolen by her builder! See (below) her beautifully laid teak deck.*

of time for us to inspect the boat, which was beautifully built and finished – both inside and out. The boat was rigged as a gaff cutter, and all of the masts and equipment had been custom made. This was really a beautiful boat, and one that I would be proud to own.

After this very joyous occasion, it was surprising and somewhat disillusioning to receive a phone call a few months later from a doctor who lived in the area. The conversation went something like this.

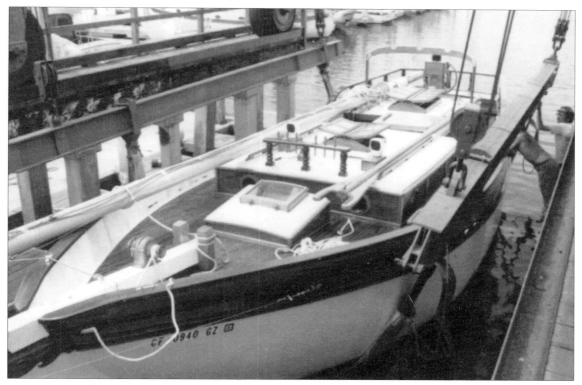

Can you blame the builder for not wanting to part with beautifully finished California Spray?

'Have you read about my boat......?' 'No,' I admitted, I had not heard anything. 'Well, the fellow who built it absconded with the boat.' The doctor explained that the person who had built the boat, and who had been officiating at the launching, was only the builder and not the owner. This was certainly a very different impression from that obtained by all who were present at the launching party. It seems that the launching was held while the doctor, self-declared owner, was away. On his return, he found his boat missing; the person who built the boat had sailed off into the unknown. The doctor alerted the authorities and a full-blown helicopter and aircraft search was made for the vessel. However they did not find the Spray 33. A few days later though she was sailed back into port voluntarily and the builder was arrested. The doctor now wanted to sell the boat, and unfortunately at the time I did not have the sense to buy it myself. I have to assume that the story told by the doctor was correct; the facts would have been easy to check.

PILOT HOUSE SPRAY 33
This steel Spray was built by Terry Erskine when he was operating his boatyard in the UK. Terry later moved his operation to Malta to take advantage of the low taxes and other incentives being offered by that country. However, he found Malta too far removed from the marketplace, so we hope to see him back in the UK and again building boats for those lucky few who are able to obtain his services.

BELLAVIA

This steel Spray 33 was built in England for an American client who took delivery of her and sailed down through the Mediterranean, and subsequently the boat was sailed across the Atlantic and now is in the United States. I did have the opportunity to see her being built and also be present at the launching and trials. This Spray 33 certainly sails well and she was beautifully built and fitted out by Wistocks of Woodbridge, Suffolk.

LUCIA

This Spray 33 was built by Paul Fay, who also built a Spray 36 called *Faizark,* details of which appear in Chapter 8. Paul is now a full-time professional boatbuilder and has made a wonderful job of building *Lucia* for Maureen Dawson of Westward Ho, Devon, UK. Maureen intends to sail this boat singlehanded across the Atlantic, and will be sponsored by the Variety Club of Great Britain. Her purpose in making this singlehanded transatlantic crossing is to raise funds for her favourite charity. She is hoping to leave England in April of 1995, to

Built in England by Wistocks of Woodbridge, Bellavia, *a steel Spray 33, has crossed the Atlantic and is now in American waters.*

coincide with the date on which Slocum left the USA on his singlehanded round-the-world voyage. Several other Spray owners are planning similar trips and hoping to leave on the same date.

RAHMANI

This boat was built by Major Pat Garnett MBE, who is attached to the Sultanate of Oman Ministry of Defence. There are a few British military officers who serve in the Sultan of Oman's Army, and Pat Garnett has served in this capacity for several years. During his stay in Oman, Pat built the Spray 33 called *Rahmani,* as well as the Roberts 434 radius chine steel *Omani,* which he sailed singlehanded around the world in 218 days – a record in itself for the 27 000 mile [43 451km] voyage. Pat has also been involved in the construction of a Roberts Waverunner 44, which was built for the Fisheries Inspectorate in Oman. Pat is also planning to build a Roberts New York 65, which he will be sailing singlehanded around the world and trying to establish a record. But here is Pat's Spray story:

'In November 1986 I sailed my Spray 33 *Rahmani* singlehanded from Muscat to Bombay. During the voyage I suffered from increasingly severe pain in the left buttock. By the time I reached Bombay, I was barely able to walk. The Breach Kandy Hospital diagnosed a prolapsed disc and recommended that I be admitted and put in traction.

This posed a number of problems, so I repaired to the five star Oberoi Towers Hotel to consider the options. Should I leave the boat and fly home? (Unthinkable.) Should I accept the treatment? (Not attractive – it could be an indefinite period.) Could I find a crew, at least two, and pay the return fares? (Probably difficult, expensive, and what about visas?) Time was short, with only 14 days' leave remaining. Perhaps the pain would go away, but when?

In a blinding flash of foolhardy inspiration, I resolved to let *Rahmani* take me home. When I informed the hotel doctor that I was going home, he said he would make the necessary arrangements with the airline. I told him I was going by sea. In that case, I must give the following instructions to my cabin steward. I explained as gently as I could what I had in mind. His manner changed rapidly from incredulity to alarm, and he insisted that I sign a note exonerating him from all responsibility. Doubtless, he still has it.

The tindal (headboatman) of the Royal Bombay Yacht Club rowed me out to where *Rahmani* was anchored off the Gateway of India. It took some time to persuade him to hoist the mainsail and the No.2 jib and to crank in the anchor. He was standing in the tender as I motored away in a flat calm, and the expression on his face was memorable.

The sea breeze came up around noon and *Rahmani* put her shoulder into it and began that gentle pitching motion that is so characteristic of the Spray 33. In order to avoid the fickle winds of the Gulf Oman, I set a course for Oman's southern port of Salalah, a distance of about 1100 sea miles [1770km]; but I hoped to be able to go the whole way on an easy reach in the north east monsoon wind. I set up the Aries and lay down flat on the cockpit seat. Except for easing the sheets for the land breeze, I remained there all night.

The pain was worse by the next day, but we were starting to feel the northerly wind so I extended the Aries control lines to run below, prepared a stock of food and water close at hand, and assumed a prone position on the lee berth. I was not to set foot in the cockpit again until we reached Salalah.

A cunningly placed shaving mirror reflected the compass, and I checked the general heading by the position of the sun and the constellations sweeping past the open hatch. Each night I took the altitude of Polaris. No fancy corrections, altitude Polaris – latitude is good enough for government work. This was much less painful than hanging around waiting for a meridian passage.

I was in excruciating pain and great distress. The pills were gobbled up too quickly and I resorted to whisky. I read the Walker log with the camera telephoto lens and, when I felt able to do so, I took a morning sight draped on the ladder with elbows on the bridgedeck. A position line worked up by the Haversine method gave me a pretty good check on longitude.

These navigational excursions presented an opportunity to dump my urine bottles and plastic-bag bedpans overboard. No navigation lights. The battery was flat and I was in no state to hand crank the engine. No lookout of any kind. It was a disgracefully unseamanlike performance, but we reached Salalah in eight days; 130 miles [209km] a day virtually without touching a rope.

I anchored at about 2 knots in some disarray and then spent three months in traction in various hospitals – ample time to reflect on the remarkable qualities of the Spray.'

It is typical of the Spray's forgiving, seakindly qualities that Rahmani *could be sailed safely from Bombay to Salalah, Oman with her skipper, Major Pat Garnett, disabled with a prolapsed disc.*

Major Garnett's friend Sarah Wright enjoying the helm on passage from Oman to India on Rahmani.

Not long after I had received the story from Pat about their experiences I heard from Sarah Wright, Pat's long-time friend and associate, who has made several cruises with him on his various boats. One trip was from Oman to Goa, India, and Sarah sent me the log of this trip; it runs to 40 pages, so could not be reproduced here. The sail from Oman to Goa takes about ten days and Sarah's log reveals a relatively uneventful sail. Sarah, who at this stage was a relatively inexperienced yachtswoman, found handling the Spray quite easy, and managed to carry out her watches without any problems. As *Rahmani* has the characteristics common to all Sprays – that is, she will steer herself for long periods – the log of the voyage to India has many passages that tell of nice easy cruising. No big crises, and good daily runs with the Spray looking after herself much of the time.

After a few days of rest and relaxation Sarah and Peter sailed the Spray back to Oman. Again it was a pleasant easy sail without any drama.

Pat went on to build his Roberts 434 *Omani,* which he sailed singlehanded around the world in only 218 days, and now he is planning to build the Roberts *Omani 65* for another attempt at the round the world record.

Bruce Schrader built this sloop-rigged steel Spray 33 Handmaiden *(left) in the USA.*

Turkish Spray 33 (below) with a modified bow, was built in characteristic Turkish fashion using the wood and epoxy technique favoured by boatbuilders in that country.

CHAPTER 10
The Popular Smaller Sprays 28, 27 and 22

The Spray 28 design was drawn when a client wanted to build a Spray, but found the Spray 33 too large for his needs. This a common story where prospective builders and/or owners want a boat, but the size available just doesn't suit them for one reason or another. Either it is too big, too small, too wide, too deep, too expensive, or too something. Consequently, we have tried to oblige by redesigning the Spray to various sizes and materials. In the case of the Spray 28, we originally designed this for steel construction and that has proved quite popular. However, the boat has now been built in glassfibre, as well as by using wood/epoxy construction technique. The wood/epoxy plans feature multi-chine hull, and virtually the same plans as for the steel or aluminium version. These same plans and patterns were used to build an inexpensive masonite mould in which several glassfibre hulls have been constructed.

ROBERTS SPRAY 28

Several examples of Spray 28 have been built in chine glassfibre as well as in steel and aluminium.

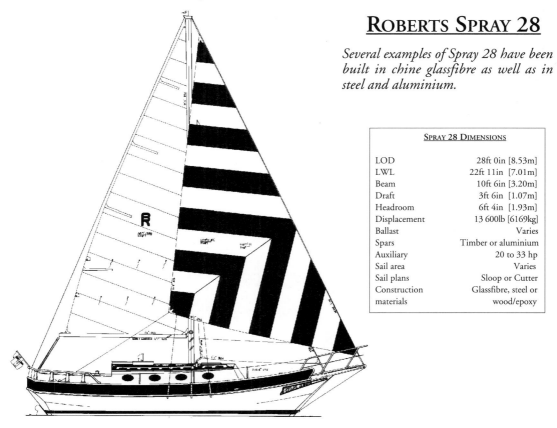

SPRAY 28 DIMENSIONS	
LOD	28ft 0in [8.53m]
LWL	22ft 11in [7.01m]
Beam	10ft 6in [3.20m]
Draft	3ft 6in [1.07m]
Headroom	6ft 4in [1.93m]
Displacement	13 600lb [6169kg]
Ballast	Varies
Spars	Timber or aluminium
Auxiliary	20 to 33 hp
Sail area	Varies
Sail plans	Sloop or Cutter
Construction materials	Glassfibre, steel or wood/epoxy

Roberts Spray 28

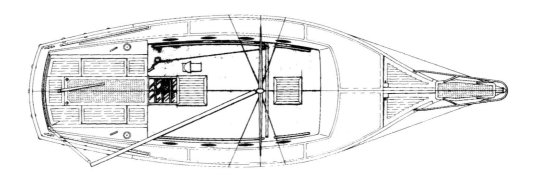

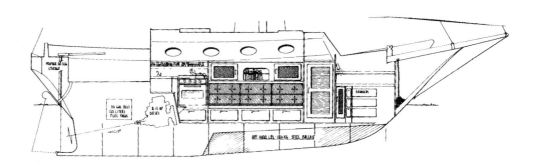

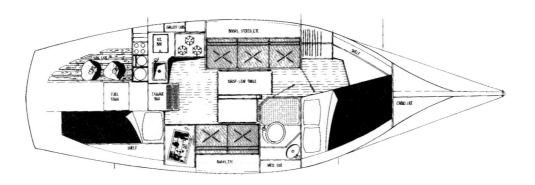

K*I*S*S

This Spray 28 is fitted with an attractive pilot house, adapted by the original owner from another Roberts design. This vessel was built by Roger Apperley of Watercraft in Diglis Woodchester, England. Roger has built several steel Sprays, including many Spray 28s, 38s, 33s and 40s. *K*I*S*S* was built for Hal and Dorothy Stufft of Imler, Pennsylvania, USA. They purchased their plans from our US office and then, having heard of Roger Apperley's building skills, decided to have the boat built in the UK.

The hull was completed in 1987 by Watercraft, then the owner finished the interior and launched the boat in June 1989. This is a rugged go-anywhere vessel and, according to her owner, has been much complimented wherever she has been. When we saw her she was in Holland, having already

One of the best Spray 28s afloat, K*I*S*S *was built by Watercraft UK with a raised fishing boat style pilot house, which can seat four or five people. The picture below shows her moored for an overnight stay at Weesp in Holland. Her shallow draft and generous accommodation make her an ideal boat for cruising inland waterways.*

cruised the River Seine and the canal system in France, as well as offshore trips to Ireland, Scotland, the Mediterranean and Scandinavia. When we discovered K*I*S*S was for sale we couldn't resist buying her for ourselves.

Although K*I*S*S has covered a wide area and visited many countries, much of her cruising has been on the inland waterways. The Spray is an ideal vessel for cruising the canals of Holland, France and Germany, as well as the

Kilifi, built by Watercraft UK and owned by Jenny and Ian Gorham (seen at the helm, on opposite page). This Spray was based on the 28, but stretched to 31ft, retaining the same beam.

canal that transits Sweden. Her shallow draft and generous accommodation make living aboard and cruising these areas a pleasure, and by the time this book is published we hope to have transited the Dutch, Belgian and French canals in her, ready for Mediterranean cruising. K*I*S*S is well fitted out and mahogany timber is featured in much of the joinery. The head is formica lined with a custom glassfibre floor moulding and a shower, with additional storage behind the head. The pilot house seats four to five people and converts to a single or double berth. To sum up K*I*S*S's qualities, she is a rugged, go-anywhere boat.

KILIFI

This is another Roger Apperley-built steel Spray 28. However, Roger stretched this boat to 31ft [9.45m]. Ian and Jenny Gorham wanted a boat a little bigger than the Spray 28, but not as big as the Spray 33. Often the beam is a governing factor. Some people may want a boat that is a little longer, but want to retain the same beam for a variety of reasons; that was exactly the case with the Gorhams.

Kilifi is currently in Spain, having been cruised from the UK to the Mediterranean and the Gorhams have had many pleasant months cruising around that area.

SPRAY

This particular Spray 28 was photographed at Britton Ferry in South Wales, UK. The boat was built by Roger Apperley of Watercraft, and is fitted with bilge keels. The fitting of bilge keels is quite popular in the UK, as the tidal nature of many of the rivers and estuaries means that many vessels dry out in various harbours. The rise and fall of the tide is usually such that it is necessary to have some method of keeping the boat upright. Some boats bury themselves in the mud, and for a boat with a deep keel this can become quite a problem. Although the basic part of the canoe body will make itself a nice easy impression, the keel tends to get sucked down in the mud – and this can be a nuisance if you are trying to get in or out of your berth at half tide. The Spray with her shoal draft makes an ideal boat for these conditions. However, some owners still

find it advantageous to fit small bilge keels, which are usually just plates that keep the boat totally upright under all circumstances. Several owners have found the bilge plates unnecessary and, after removing these appendages, their boat speed has increased by $1^1/_2$ knots.

HARCLA

This is a multi chine fibreglass Spray 28 that was moulded by Humber Boats in England. Sir Christopher Musgrave wrote to us as follows:

'My own boat, *Harcla*, was built by Ron Atherton of the Humber Boat Company...I was originally looking for a boat to live on and cruise blue water with, around 30-35ft [9.1-10.6m]. When I saw Ron's advertisement...I went to see the yard to discuss my requirements with him. He had at that time just completed a Spray 28 that stood outside. I had a look around the hull and deck mouldings and took some measurements and photographs. I went home to dream.

About four months later I took delivery, and started to fit out in Scunthorpe at Ron's yard. I had designed a gaff rig for her for several reasons. It looks more appropriate for the hull and I prefer to sail with it; and, most importantly for some of the places I intend to cruise in, in the years ahead it can be modified or repaired with low-tech resources. I redesigned the interior, apart from the forward cabin, and I find it very spacious and workable. I checked the Bermudan mast position in the sail plan and your centre of effort, which I find to be correct. It was quite interesting to compare how she sails with the more modern boats of equivalent size. In heavy

Another Spray 28 built by Watercraft UK. Her bilge keel makes her a very suitable craft for drying moorings.

weather, as one would expect, she has an easy, soft motion at sea, and stands up well to sail. Discounting the topsail, which I have yet to rig, the first reef goes in at the top of force 5. In a force 6, the second reef goes in and the jib comes off, leaving her with a slight weather helm, up to the point where the helm is totally neutral and can be left for ages. As yet, the strongest she has sailed in is a force 7 from the Humber to Wales, which was done with two reefs and staysail all the way,

averaging just over 5 knots, but reaching 6 knots at times. A few anxious moments, but they soon passed when we realised she wasn't going to do anything daft.'

Sir Christopher wrote that the real surprise to him is in the light air with calmer seas, where the vessel just sails along at 2-3 knots with no apparent wind. He comments that it is quite amusing in these circumstances to see the others twitching with their sheets while *Harcla* glides majestically past them. He continued:

'I once took her out in the Humber in a force 6 with all plain sail up to see how she performed. Usually, the vessel tacks safely and predictably, but this day she was tacking like a dinghy with weather helm, so obviously that tends to increase in line with the wind, which is a good safety feature. *Harcla* has pitch pine laid decks with oak rubbing strips, and with the Douglas fir spars and cream sails, she looks very traditional. With her brown hull, she often confuses people as to her age, which causes me great amusement. Although she is rather overweight at 7½ tons [6804kg], she imbibes a great feeling of solidarity and confidence in everyone who comes aboard. Overall, I am well pleased with the design. Given my time again, I would do everything the same – maybe one or two alterations in constructional methods with the benefit of hindsight, but the boat rig and accommodation are basically too good to change. I sometimes wonder if I should have built a larger version, particularly when I am trying to figure out where to stow something, but I know I can handle *Harcla* on my own at sea with ease, and having a proper cutter rig means I run my bowsprit in – in other words, a housing bowsprit, so marinas only charge me for the 28ft [8.5m], much to their disgust!

Harcla, the name of Sir Christopher's boat, is a family name. It is the name of a castle that still exists, built by one of Sir Christopher's ancestors when he came to England with William the Conqueror.'

Longshot's name stemmed from doubts by friends of 66-year-old Bob Phillips that he would ever finish building her. Not only was this Spray 28 completed by Bob without any outside assistance, but he now spends his summers cruising her on his local waters of Narragansett and Buzzard's Bay.

LONGSHOT

This boat was built by Bob Phillips of Milbury, Massachusetts, who commented:

'The name *Longshot* is the result of many remarks of friends, who said I would never finish it. I not only finished it, but I built every inch of it alone. It sails brilliantly, and I didn't have one drop of leakage in all those welds. I am a retired 66-year-old and enjoying my summers on Narragansett and Buzzard's Bay areas. The boat never fails to turn heads and draw favourable comments.'

WEBBER SPRAY

This steel Spray 28 was built by Jacques R Webber of Cudahy, Wisconsin, USA. Many enjoyable family hours have been spent on her creation. She has taken on a life of her own and we look forward to giving her a rich and colourful history. She is the topic of the neighbourhood, friends and the local newspaper. Because of the low budget available, every component and fitting has a story of its own.

Mr Webber has put his budget to good use as there are some very attractive interior shots of the boat, and one can see by the general construction and the quality of the fitting out that he intends her to be a credit to both himself and to the design.

SPRAY

This particular boat is another of the mouldings from the Humber Boat Company, and is owned by Philip and Cynthia Sheaf of Easton, Suffolk. At present this Spray is located in a Woodbridge boatyard where Phil and Cynthia are completing the fitting out. The boat is fitted

One of the many glassfibre Spray 28s under construction by the Humber Boat Company UK.

with a Lister 27/30 hp 3 cylinder diesel, with a Hurth gearbox, installed on flexible mounts and coupled to an Aquadrive self-aligning thrust-bearing. Phil paid particular attention when this boat was being moulded and below the waterline she has some epoxy sheathing and a few other extra features. Phil and Cynthia Sheath have owned several boats and enjoy building and fitting out, so they may sell this boat on to finance the next.

HUMBER SPRAYS

Ron Atherton of the Humber Boat Company, which is in Scunthorpe, Humberside, UK sent me a folio which contained photographs of several of the Spray 28s that he has moulded in glassfibre. There are too many to include here; however, I will mention a couple. One is Ron's own boat, which is a blue hulled Spray 28, and another, a pilot house version where Ron has built a mould to create a small pilot house. This no doubt will be quite popular for the northern latitudes.

CARTER SPRAY

This beautiful Spray was built by Mr B W Carter. The boat is multi-chine, and Mr Carter has built the boat of plywood, and then heavily covered the exterior with glassfibre. The finish is magnificent – Mr Carter and his sons have certainly produced a most attractive vessel.

The finish on Carter Spray, *a Spray 28, is a credit to her builders, Mr B W Carter and his sons.*

Hazebra Too *is another Spray 28 built and sailed by British boatbuilder Jack Read.*

HAZEBRA TOO

This Spray 28 motor sailer is another of the Sprays built by Jack Read. As mentioned elsewhere, he has built several Sprays, some in round bilge glassfibre, some in multi-chine glassfibre and others in steel. I know that he did cruise in this boat and sold her on before building his next Spray.

Renalee II, *built by Mr J Kowalski of Rockhampton, Queensland is currently cruising in the Pacific.*

SPRAY 27

The Spray 27 is, as the modern saying goes, the result of 'consumer driven' requirements. Several customers stretched the Spray 22 plans to various lengths between 22ft [6.7m] and 27ft [8.2m], so we decided to make the design available as a stock plan that could be built in glassfibre, steel or plywood. This boat can be legally trailed in most countries.

ROBERTS SPRAY 27

Although designed to be trailerable, several boats built to this design are kept in the water for the whole sailing season.

SPRAY 27 DIMENSIONS	
LOD	27ft 0in [8.23m]
LWL	21ft 6in [6.55m]
Beam	8ft 6in [2.59m]
Draft	2ft 9in [0.84m]
Headroom	6ft 0in [1.83m]
Displacement	4885lb [2216kg]
Ballast	1425lb [646kg]
Spars	Timber or aluminium
Auxiliary	10 hp
Sail area	Varies
Sail plans	Sloop or Cutter
Construction materials	Glassfibre, steel or wood/epoxy

ROBERTS SPRAY 27

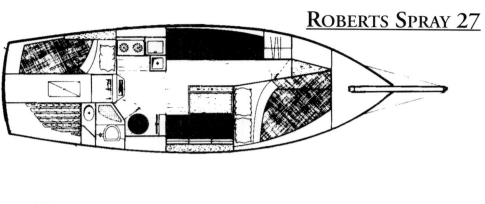

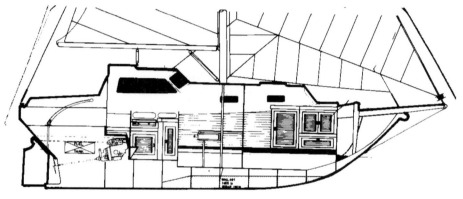

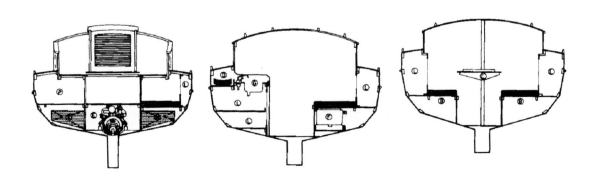

ROBERTS SPRAY 27C

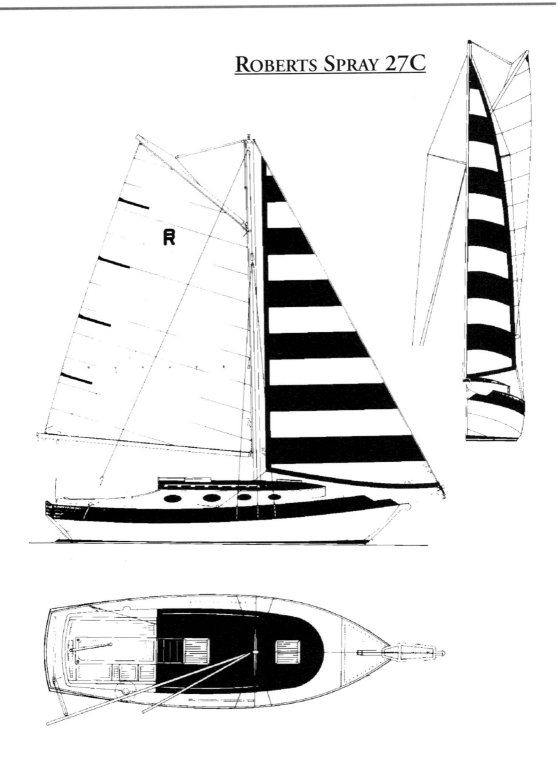

A four-year backyard project came to fruition when 65-year-old Mr A J Culp of Santa Maria, California, launched his schooner-rigged Spray 27, MS Voncille, *in 1989.*

MS VONCILLE

Mr A J Culp of Santa Maria, California, provided the following information:

'I received my Spray 27 plans at Christmas 1985 and immediately went to work building her in the backyard. Her name is *MS Voncille* and I launched her on my 65th birthday, 12 January 1989. Her construction is all steel and I eliminated the cockpit and enlarged the pilot house and put two fishing chairs on the poop deck. I rigged her as a two-masted schooner to keep the mast short, so I can go under all bridges in Seattle without waiting for them to open. With hot and cold water, refrigeration, Loran, autopilot, inside and outside steering, electric anchor windlass, etc, she is the best-equipped boat I have ever owned. *MS Voncille* has cruised the west coast from Los Angeles to Friday Harbour in the San Juan Islands of Washington State. I usually sail singlehanded, since my wife's eye doctor told her to stay away from the ocean. I do a lot of powering up and down the coast, so the 20 hp Vetus diesel was really a wise investment. I enjoyed building the boat and have enjoyed sailing her.'

Mathematically minded readers will easily work out that by now Mr Culp is 71 years of age, so one is never too old to take up cruising providing you have 'the right boat' and enjoy good health.

COPELAND SPRAY

Jack C Copeland of Defiance, Ohio, USA has almost completed his Spray 27. He wrote:

'I am building the decks, cabin and cockpit from aluminium which is 3/16/5086 marine grade. The superstructure inside is 6061-T6 1in x 2in x $^{1}/_{8}$in [25mm x 50mm x 3mm] channel. The engine is a 20 hp Perkins diesel. I have built all the railings and fittings from 316 stainless steel; also, the rudder is made from stainless, with Teflon bearings to insulate it from the steel. The connection between deck and hull will have a gasket with neoprene sleeves to insulate it from the hull.'

Pizza Spray. *A Spray used as a working boat – with a difference! Sam Tasto converted his Spray into a floating pizza kitchen!*

PIZZA SPRAY

Sam Tasto, an American of Italian descent who is really something of a character, built this boat. He brought a photo to my office and explained that he had fitted her out as a mobile pizza parlour, because he was making pizzas on the boat and delivering them to all the yachts in his area. It seems that he had built up a good business, for he was considering building a larger boat. Quite a character, and quite a boat!

MALWINE

This boat was built for Volker Wesenverg in Germany, and I quote from his letter:

'In 1990 I ordered from you plans for the Spray 27 in wood epoxy. Due to lack of time and building site I contracted out the hull and rig to a small East German shipyard. Fittings and equipment were built by myself. The rig was transformed into a gaff cutter and glued at the shipyard. The gaff remains underneath the spreader. Both port berth and starboard seating bench in the saloon were increased in the width at expense of the foot space. The saloon table has been altered and transformed into a card table, with the large compartment within, and an additional lengthwise bulkhead has been added to separate the interior more conveniently. In a few days I am going to put the sailing characteristics to the test.'

Although many other Spray 27s have been built – for example, by Land and Sea in Maryland – for some reason, we have not received the same response from builders of these boats as from Sprays in the other size ranges.

SPRAY 22

During the late 1970s a customer approached our design office wanting to build a miniature version of the Spray, and asking if we felt the boat could be built while still retaining most of the Spray's favourable characteristics. He wanted to build the boat in a garage, and had a limited period in which to build it. He made a deal with his wife: if he could build the hull during the summer and get it out of the garage before the first snow fall, he could use that space. She wanted her garage back come the winter, so he had to be sure that not only would the boat fit, but also that it would be built quickly enough to get it out in time!

ROBERTS SPRAY 22

An ideal compromise for those who enjoy the romance of the Spray, but require a smaller boat, or wish to trail.

SPRAY 22 DIMENSIONS	
LOA	21ft 4in [6.50m]
LWL	16ft 11in [5.18m]
Beam	8ft 0in [2.44m]
Draft	2ft 6n [0.76m]
Headroom	5ft 0in [1.52m]
Displacement	2935lb [1331kg]
Weight on Trailer	2219lb [1006kg]
Ballast	700lb [317kg]
Auxiliary	5 to 10 hp
Sail area	310ft^2[28.80m^2]
Sail plans	Gaff or Berm. sloop
Construction	Glassfibre, steel or
materials	wood/epoxy

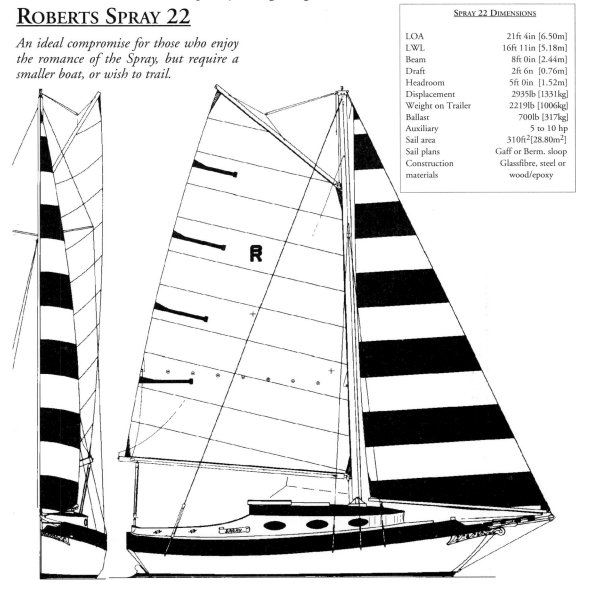

ROBERTS SPRAY 22

Generous sitting headroom is a feature of this miniature Spray.

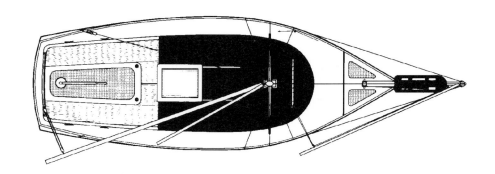

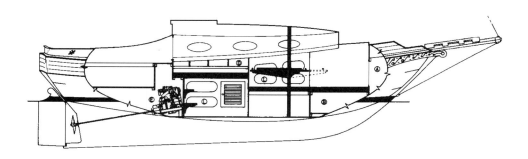

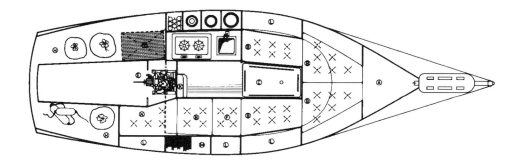

Initially, plans were drawn up for glassfibre construction. However, some additional calculations revealed that provided the decks and superstructure were kept light, it would be possible to build the hull from steel. It was decided to include a steel version with the plans. Since that time, many Spray 22s have been built. This boat is easily trailerable and numerous examples have been cruised extensively around the coastal waters of various countries.

A female mould was built for the Spray 22 in Brisbane, Australia, and hulls are available from the Marine Park, 189 Molle Rd, Ransome, Queensland, 4154 Australia.

PILLSBURY SPRAY

Harold Pillsbury of North Ridge, California, has built his Spray using the wood epoxy technique, and is planning to trail his boat across the USA from California to the east coast, and commence his cruising where there are cruising grounds ideally suited to the Spray 22. There are plenty of sheltered anchorages and islands to explore.

IVEY SPRAY

Some time ago, we heard from James Ivey of Oakley, Michigan, USA who said:

'I would like to be able to discuss the sailing ability of my Spray 24, but unfortunately the boat is still not finished. I built my Spray from your 22ft [6.7m] plans, which I stretched to 24ft [7.3m] LOD, by increasing the station spacing as you suggested, altering the bow a little, and adding 3in [75mm] to the freeboard. I added about 200lb [91kg] to the ballast, which consists of scrap lead, steel and steel punchings, solidified with polyester resin "bog". I also made some interior changes, including adding a head. I kept the mast support in the position on the 22ft [6.7m] plan, my reasoning being that I thought it might work well for a cutter rig. Maybe I should have consulted you on this. I feel it came together nicely. The mould was not difficult to construct, and the sheathing went better than I had anticipated. To cut the metal, I found – after trying a disc saw and an acetylene torch – that I could simply take the templates to a local metal fabricating shop where I was purchasing the steel, trace the template on the sheet, and have it cut out on large nibbler shears. If I was careful to trace with the template the proper side up, the slight stretch the nibbler produced would work to my favour, causing the panel almost to follow the contours of the hull. After tacking the hull together at 3in [75mm] intervals, I opted to weld it with MIG welder to keep the heat to a minimum, resulting in what I feel is a very fair hull without the need for fillers. After grinding the weld smooth, I had the hull blasted to white metal and primed with Pettits Rustlok. I think if I were doing it again, I might opt to right the hull and then complete the welding inside before blasting and priming the outside, as the inside welding tended to affect the outside priming. I have enjoyed working on the project and have received many favourable comments from people who have seen it.'

JOSHUA SLOCUM

Joshua Slocum is one of the moulded Spray 22 hulls that were produced at Marine Park, Gumdale, Brisbane. This was in fact the first, so we were most interested to see how the boat would perform. Fortunately, Andrew Slorach took the boat out and gave it a good trial then sent us this report:

Spray in miniature – Joshua Slocum, *one of the moulded Spray 22s produced at Marine Park, Gumdale, Brisbane, Australia. The advantage of these scaled-down Sprays is that they can be easily trailed.*

'It has been a long time coming! I am sure every builder knows the feeling. After months of slaving away on my Roberts Spray 22 glassfibre boat, the day had finally arrived; it was time for the sea trials.

My project started when I asked Bruce Roberts to prepare plans for a glassfibre version of the Spray 22. I was already familiar with the basic design as I had some experience with the steel and plywood versions of the same boat. I wanted a round-bilge version, and the best way to go was to build in glassfibre.

After careful consideration of all the available glassfibre building methods, I decided to build a foam sandwich hull with the hope of using this as a plug to build a female mould. Further conversation with Bruce Roberts seemed to suggest that there would be a market for this boat in Australia.

The building of the sandwich hull proceeded without any unforeseen hitches, and the plywood plug for the deck and cabin structure was built using the details from the plywood plan as a guide. Some minor changes were necessary in the area of the deck and cabin, for this was to be a plug and the mould would later have to release smoothly from the structure. No room for reverse outward leaning shapes here. A little extra time spent in planning the deck plug paid off handsomely when the mould later released without a hitch.

The moulding of the first hull and deck went smoothly, the fitting out of the interior was

Andrew's trial of the gaff-rigged Spray 22 impressed him with its easy handling and typical Spray seakindliness.

accomplished quickly with the help of Peter McCoy, my long-time boatbuilding friend. Now here I was just a step away from the launching and sailing trials, but no, not so fast. Bruce Roberts suggested that I show the boat at the Brisbane Boat Show. Indeed, why not?'

The boat show exhibit went well. The comments on the boat, its overall finish and the roominess of the interior all combined to give Andrew a most successful boat show, resulting in two firm orders and many serious prospects.

A few days after the show finished Andrew was able to get the time to schedule the sailing trials. The season had now started of the strong south-easters, which start at 15 knots and quickly go through the 25 knot range, so that Andrew's chances of getting a medium day of say 12 to 15 knots seemed unlikely. He prefers to give boats their first trials in medium wind strengths, for there are always some things, no matter how small, that will go wrong. It is much better to have the time to deal with these small problems without half a gale of wind. No matter, it was time to get on with the trials.

Andrew was anxious to see how the Roberts Spray 22 would handle as a singlehanded boat. Most of his sailing is done either alone or with his wife as crew, and generally he likes to handle the boat on his own. He invited Peter McCoy along to do the actual sailing, for that would give him the opportunity to study objectively the boat's handling in the conditions they expected to experience during this first sail.

Andrew wrote:

'Well, we got our 25 knots all right, and then some. The day started off with the southeaster blowing at a steady 10 knots. At this wind speed, the Spray 22 carried her full gaff mainsail with ease – a great feeling as she sliced through the short chop.

Soon the wind piped up to 15 knots. We put the Spray through her paces, full sail was still carried and we tacked, and brought her hard on the wind. She sailed closer to the breeze than I had hoped. I guess the proportionally deeper keel was doing its job. OK, so far so good. The boat was most satisfactory upwind, and as I had some experience with the Roberts Spray 33 this did not come as a total surprise. I expected at least creditable upwind performance.

By now, the wind had increased to 25 knots and it was time to take in a reef. With the jiffy reefing set-up we have, reefing the gaff mainsail could be handled by one person, again a nice thought for my singlehanding in the future. Sailing downwind and reaching were something of an anticlimax. Almost anything will perform well on these points of sailing. The Spray scooted along, feeling comfortable and secure at all times.

It is certainly a boat for the whole family to enjoy and a boat I will be most happy to single-hand at any time. For those who prefer it, a Bermudan sail plan is now available, which will appeal to those who want the simplest of rigs.'

CHAPTER 11

Designer's Comments

TRADITIONAL REPLICA OR A SPRAY SERIES COPY?

If you are planning to build or purchase a Spray for yourself, then the choice between a replica, copy or near-copy may be one of your first decisions. A full replica, to be considered as such, must be built of timber. However, even the most ardent Spray enthusiast will have to admit that timber involves considerable maintenance which is not normally associated with owning a steel or glassfibre boat. Despite these drawbacks, we have decided to offer plans and full-size patterns for building an exact replica of the original Spray in timber.

If you can get to boatbuilding timber at a reasonable price, or if, like some of the early builders of Spray replicas, you have suitable timber growing on your own land, then by all means consider a timber replica. If you are fortunate enough not to have to worry about costs at all, and if you have proven timber boatbuilding skills, then a traditional replica may well be for you. However, if these conditions don't apply to you, then perhaps steel or glassfibre would be better material with which to build your Spray.

ROUND BILGE OR DOUBLE-CHINE CONFIGURATION?

Generally speaking most of the round-bilge Spray hulls are built of glassfibre, and the majority of double-chine hulls are built using steel as the basic material. However there are exceptions: there are in existence several glassfibre chine Spray 28s and many plywood wood/epoxy-chine Spray hulls of various sizes built to our plans.

The original reason for designing multi-chine Spray hulls was to make it relatively easy for a home builder or small yard (which may not have elaborate bending and plate rolling equipment) to build these boats in steel – and the enormous popularity of the steel Sprays has convinced us that our decision was correct.

In the past we were often asked, 'How does the double-chine hull perform compared to the round-bilge configuration?' The answer is that there is no apparent difference in performance either under sail or power between the two hull types. Whether round-bilge or double-chine configuration, the Spray is a fine cruising boat.

PILOT HOUSE

Many builders have elected to incorporate pilot houses into their Spray building programme. On one occasion when I commented to a builder about the less than beautiful pilot house that he had added to his boat, he responded, 'Bruce, I will remove that pilot house when you take your drawing board outside'! We now provide, as an option, detailed drawings of pilot houses for all sizes of boats in the Spray series.

About five years ago, Hall Stufft had a Spray 28 built in the UK. He decided to take the pilot house design from our Roberts 281 and to graft it on to the steel Spray 28. This pilot house features reverse forward facing windows. Some thirty years ago, I remember discussing the merits of aft sloping (attractive) and forward sloping (practical, preventing light reflection) pilot house windows with a very experienced trawler operator, for whom we were building one of the first glassfibre trawlers. This customer would have none of those aft-sloping, modern-looking windows. I was to recall all of this quite recently when cruising in my steel Spray 28 K*I*S*S. Provided you do not object to the appearance of the forward-leaning pilot house windows, there are none better – you get a superior view, and the pilot house seems much roomier and spacious, even on a 28 footer [8.5m].

SAIL PLANS

In all the years that we have been associated with designing Sprays, not once have we been asked to prepare a copy of the yawl sail plan as used on the original Spray, although reporting this, no doubt, will bring forth demands for just such a rig!

You cannot fail to notice the variety of sail plans employed not only by builders of Spray series boats, but also by many people who have built true copies of the original Spray. In fact just about every small-boat rig ever heard of has been tried. This is another reason why people love the Spray – you can be individualistic when it comes to the sail plan.

My own choice of rig for the larger Sprays would depend on where I intended to use the boat. For instance if my cruising was of a local nature, for example UK coastal waters, then I might let my heart overrule my head and go for a full gaff rig with all the trimmings. The gaff rig allows for a wonderful set of 'extras', including a infinite number of flying jibs, and additional sails set off the main including a water-sail. Square-sails of all sizes and cuts look right on a gaff rigged boat.

If I was planning to undertake serious offshore world cruising, then the 30 years of personal boating experience combined with the experiences of many others would dictate that I choose a Bermudan rig. This opinion regards the Bermudan rig is not shared by many who have contributed to this book; you have noticed the large number of serious cruising people who have chosen and are happy with their gaff rigged Sprays.

For one of the smaller Sprays, I would choose the sliding gunter rig; relatively short mast with the gaff snugged up along the top third of the spar combines many of the advantages of the Bermudan and gaff sail plans into the one rig. As it turned out, my recently acquired Spray 28 K*I*S*S has a regular Bermudan cutter sail plan that works well; and for reasons of economy I will be keeping this rig for the foreseeable future.

When it comes down to it, the choice of rig is a personal matter and one of many decisions you must make for yourself. Listen to all the advice available, consider your future cruising plans and finally leave the choice of rig until the stage of construction dictates that you must make your decision.

MAST MATERIALS

Over time builders have used a variety of mast-building materials, these days aluminium is the obvious choice especially for a Bermudan rig. Many builders have successfully converted street lighting poles, flag poles and similar aluminium tubes into durable and long-lasting masts, and

I see no problem with this providing you research the origin and type of material used in the manufacture of the chosen tube. If possible, do some tests as to its suitability for the intended use. At least one builder has successfully used a steel tube for the mast on his cutter-rigged Spray 40. I have not previously recommended steel as a mast-building material, but if you are convinced that the weight and strength factors are comparable to, say, solid timber, then you may wish to explore the use of steel for a mast; however I would not recommend steel for the gaff or boom as it would be preferable to use suitable timber for these spars.

For a gaff-rigged boat, timber is a good choice for the mast, gaff and boom. Smaller gaff-rigged Sprays under 35ft [10.6m] may use aluminium spars, but the problems of rigging a gaff to a large aluminium mast are probably not worth the effort when one can achieve the same results more easily and cheaply by using timber for all the spars. Many builders have been able to obtain suitable growing timber from which to make their masts; so if you have access to trees of suitable species, then this would be a better choice.

KEELS AND DRAFT

The main variations between the keels on the versions of the Spray are the relative differences in the draft. The original Spray had a draft of around 4ft 3in [1.3m]. I say 'around', because as Slocum took on stores, carried cargo etc, the draft would have varied from time to time by an inch or two; thus making a big issue about the exact draft of the original Spray is something of a nonsense.

Several builders have added to the draft of some of the early replicas by deepening the keel. We found that with the Spray 40, our first Spray replica, the addition of one foot [304mm] of extra depth to the keel greatly improved the windward performance, while not adversely affecting the handling or other sailing characteristics.

With the experience gained from the Spray 40, along with the feedback we were receiving from the owners of various other Sprays, we made the decision to proportionally increase the draft on the other sizes in the Spray Series range. We have never regretted this decision; the Spray sails just that much better with a little extra draft.

Some builders, especially in the UK where harbours and marinas dry out at low tide, have chosen to fit bilge plates to their Spray hulls. However most Sprays, even with increased draft, will settle into the mud and stand relatively upright without the addition of bilge plates, support legs or other similar arrangements. The Spray is so 'flat floored' that the hull does not heel over excessively when the boat is left to dry out. Also Sprays do not suffer from the problem experienced by some deep-draft less beamy hulls which will fill with water before they rise on the incoming tide.

Although we have on request designed bilge plates to suit some of the versions in the Spray Series, I would not fit them to my own Spray hull. One of the main reasons for my objections to these appendages is that it has been proved by adding and then removing bilge plates from various Spray hulls that these keels do slow the boat down by one or two knots.

In some of the early versions of the Spray 40 we designed a centreboard into the hull but when we found that the boats sailed just as well on all points of sail with the board up as with it lowered, the centreboard option was dropped.

DISPLACEMENT

There is considerable variation between Sprays of the same length built and fitted out by various builders. The Spray is a great load carrier, and it seems impossible to spoil her inherent good manners and good all-round performance by loading her up with stores and equipment.

If you are building a Spray, I would advise you to keep the building weights within reasonable limits and only to install 70 per cent of the recommended ballast. After the boat is launched, trialled, and stores and all extra equipment are aboard, you will probably find that additional trim ballast is not required. Slocum's Spray carried no permanent ballast, so by comparison modern replicas are well served with a modest ballast ratio.

In our own Spray Series designs, we have used similar displacement-length ratios to those used in the original boat. Also the use of modern building materials such as glassfibre and wood/epoxy and employing up-to-date steel boatbuilding techniques have allowed us to provide for a generous ballast ratio.

HANDLING CHARACTERISTICS

Having read this far you will know that the Spray handles impeccably under all types of wind and sea conditions; and there is a mountain of evidence to support the superb behaviour of this design, especially when the going gets tough.

Sprays are well adapted for heavy-weather sailing. Although few of us go out looking for adverse conditions, sooner or later we will all encounter what we believe to be the ultimate storm. At this point, it is very comforting to know that others have found the Spray to be extremely reliable under extreme conditions.

Slocum wrote about his original vessel: 'While the sloop was reaching under short sail, a tremendous wave – the culmination, it seemed, of many waves – rolled down upon her in a storm, roaring as it came. I had only a moment to get all sail down and myself up on the peak halyards and out of danger, when I saw a mighty crest towering mast high above me. The mountain of water submerged my vessel. She shook in every timber and reeled under the weight of the sea, but rose quickly out of it and rode grandly over the rollers that followed.' There have been many similar (if not quite so dramatic) experiences related by owners of Spray replicas, all testament to the boat's resilience in the worst conditions at sea.

Because much cruising time is spent under power, it is appropriate to make some comment on this subject. Often when I have listened to cruising experiences recounted by owners of boats built to my design, I have wondered (silently) why the person bothered to have a sail boat in the first place. Well now I have my answer. The Spray is an ideal compromise for those who expect to, and will anyway, undertake a considerable amount of their cruising employing the 'iron topsail'.

Les Pearson, owner of the Spray replica *Thane,* told me in great detail about the superb handling of his Spray under both sail and power. On the subject of power Len says, 'Right angle 180 degree turns and single boat length 360 degree circles in both directions are certainly desirable features of my boat.'

Other owners when questioned on the subject of handling all without exception were favourably impressed by the ability of the Spray to negotiate tight situations under power as well as under sail.

As recently as the past few weeks my own Spray *K*I*S*S* has been used to cruise the beautiful canals of Holland. As it is some time since I had the opportunity of enjoying this relaxed style of cruising, I was greatly impressed with the handling and manoeuvrability of the Spray. Despite the busy canal traffic *K*I*S*S* negotiated the locks, the many line-ups for opening bridges, and other tight situations in such a way as to make me feel proud of her. On one occasion, a not so attentive bridge keeper allowed me to follow closely behind a very large commercial barge and then at the last minute changed the light from green to red. I had no option but to hurriedly engage reverse; even more urgent action was called for when the bridge keeper allowed a large barge straight through from the opposite direction. The sight of this very large vessel bearing down on my boat, was enough for me to put *K*I*S*S* through her reversing tests without delay. I am pleased to report that she passed with flying colours.

The ultimate cruising boat? So is the case proven? Is Spray the ideal cruising boat and if so, which Spray? The Spray has many descendants and like all offspring they are not all exactly the same. If human families share the same genes, does the Spray family share the same genes? In my opinion, the answer is without doubt a resounding yes!

After being associated with the original Spray design and the Spray series that followed for over 25 years, I have often wondered if the various Spray derivatives have maintained the favourable performance and handling characteristics of the original. I give my answer here. Each Spray has told its own story in the reports contributed by the builders, owners and the many cruising families who are out there using their boats.

This is the end of my collection of Spray reports, but it may be the beginning of your experience with the Spray. If you are serious about wanting a good cruising boat, how could you possibly look elsewhere?

Appendix: Useful Names & Addresses

Some useful names and addresses for anyone wishing to extend their knowledge of the Spray.

Roger Apperley
(Spray owner, custom builder of all sizes of steel Sprays)
Watercraft, Basin Road, Diglis, Worchester, Worcs WR5 3DA UK

Andrew Bishop
(Spray owner, Secretary of Slocum Spray Society and organiser of Spray rallies)
24 Kingsley Road, Wimbledon, London, SW19 8HF, UK

Blue Jacket Shipscrafters
(Spray model kits)
PO Box 425, Stockton Springs, ME 04981, USA

Peter Cartwright
(Spray builder and director Great Circle Yachts Ltd)
Harfield Farm House, Curdridge, Hampshire, SO3 2DU

Custom Yachts
(Spray Builders)
PO Box 1086, Severna Park, Maryland, 21146, USA

Bob and Betty Dack
(Spray Cruises on *St Kilda Spray*)
PO Box 83, Metung, Victoria, 3904, Australia

Terry Erskine
(Marine consultant and master steel boatbuilder)
1 Glendower, Gonvena Hill, Wadebridge, Cornwall, PL27 6DQ, UK

Mr Flowers
(Custom builder of steel Sprays)
PO Box 148, 102 Yacht Dr, Merritt, NC 28556, USA

Paul Francis
(Spray owner and Commodore of the Slocum Spray Society), 79 Dumont Avenue, St Osyth, Essex, CO16 8JB, UK

Bruce Roberts-Goodson AM SNAME
(Spray owner, author and yacht designer)
13 Preston Grove, Faversham, Kent ME13 8JZ, UK

Pete Greenfield
(Former Spray owner/builder, marine journalist and publisher) *The Boatman*, PO Box 1992, Falmouth, Cornwall TR11 3RU, UK

Philip Grosvenor
(Master steel boatbuilder)
Sirius Yachts, Redstone Wharf, Sandy Lane, Stourport-on-Severn DY13 9PN, UK

Bill Ingram
(Spray builder and director of Bruce Roberts International), 19 Vera St, Redland Bay, Queensland, Australia

Ulrich Kronberg
(Spray owner, editor German boating magazine *Der Palstek*) Der Palstek, Verlag GmbH, Bismarckstr 84, 20253, Hamburg, Germany

Keith Lawrence
(Editor of *Boatbuilder* Magazine)
PO Box 540638, Merritt Island, Florida, 32954, USA

Len Pearson
(Charter operator of Spray *Thane*)
PO Box, 8206, Victoria, BC,
V8W 3R8, Canada

Sven Pettersen
(Custom builder of Sprays in steel)
Tekno Material, PO Box 120, 64522, Strangnas, Sweden

Philip Sheaf
(Spray owner and UK agent for Spray plans)
'Orchids', Schoolhouse lane, Easton, Suffolk, IP13 OES, UK

David Sinnett-Jones
(Vice Commodore of the Slocum Spray Society, Spray circumnavigator, author)
Seaway, Harbour Lane, Aberaeron, Dyfed, SA46 0BA, Wales, UK
Telephone: (0545) 570 711

Colonel Donn C Slocum
(Contact for the US based Slocum Society)
12 Par Del Rio, Clifton Park, New York, 12065, USA

Jenny Williams
(Source for Spray plans and director of Bruce Roberts, USA)
PO Box 1086, Severna Park,
Maryland, 21146, USA

Index